Helen Perry Curtis and

The European Trip
of a Lifetime

Helen Perry Curtis, by Clara Sipprell.
Clara E. Sipprell Papers, Special Collections Research Center, Syracuse University Libraries.

Helen Perry Curtis and

The European Trip of a Lifetime

To Fritz,
With warm wishes,
and the hope that
you enjoy Helen's
story, with its
many connections
to Kent Place
School and
its proud
traditions.
Laura Gellott
October, 2021

Laura Gellott

First Edition 2020
ISBN: 978-1-950843-27-5

Parafine Press
3143 West 33rd Street, Cleveland, Ohio 44109
www.parafinepress.com
Cover and book design by Meredith Pangrace

To the memory of my mother

Table of Contents

PROLOGUE 9

CHAPTER 1: A Prairie Childhood 17

CHAPTER 2: Going East 39

CHAPTER 3: Transitions..................................... 63

CHAPTER 4: Europe, and a World at War..................... 83

CHAPTER 5: Homelands 106

CHAPTER 6: "The Touch of a Woman's Hand" 127

CHAPTER 7: Marriage and Motherhood 154

CHAPTER 8: "... under eighty cents a day
per person" 182

CHAPTER 9: Mapping *Jean & Company,
Unlimited* 208

CHAPTER 10: European Coda 235

CHAPTER 11: After Europe................................. 246

EPILOGUE 273

ACKNOWLEDGEMENTS 281

Prologue

I was not yet ten years old when, standing beside my mother in front of one of the floor-to-ceiling bookshelves that lined the walls at my grandfather's house, my mother pulled a book from the shelf, and, handing it to me, said: "Here, you'll like this. It's about a girl who goes to Europe."

I didn't just like this book. I fell in love with it. *Jean & Company, Unlimited*, by Helen Perry Curtis, published in 1937, was just what my mother said: the story of a teenaged girl who, with her mother, sails to Europe aboard a glamorous ocean liner. While Jean's mother travels the Continent collecting material on folk costumes for a book she is writing, Jean spends a year at a boarding school run by Dominican nuns in Provence. There she meets girls from across Europe: Jeanette from France, Giovanna from Italy, Hannah from Austria, Jenny from Norway, Janesika from Czechoslovakia—all Jeans. The girls form a club with the businesslike name "Jean & Company." Jean spends the summer vacation and a second year traveling with her mother, visiting these new friends in their own countries. Jean's father, we are told, is working in Russia as an engineering adviser, close enough that he could occasionally join his wife and daughter (Christmas in Switzerland, Budapest, a cruise up the Adriatic Coast) but far enough removed so as not to intrude on the mother-daughter adventure.

Jean & Company sent me on my own journey. The interest in Europe it inspired led me to a PhD in European history, followed by a thirty-year college teaching career. And with that came my own trips to Europe—to many of the places visited by Jean. The book became, as I often said only half-facetiously, "the only guidebook I ever needed." "It's just like *Jean*," I found myself saying, dodging the pigeons in St. Mark's Square in Venice, slipping into the cathedral in Salzburg, or running through the water spouts in the Hellbrunn Gardens. It was with Jean in mind that I gazed across the Danube in Budapest and over the rooftops of Prague. Topics on which I would hold forth at length in the classroom: the Salzburg Festival, the Thirty Years War, the "Marseillaise," all these and more I first encountered in the pages of *Jean & Company, Unlimited*.

My greatest pleasure as a child was reading. My mother taught all seven of her children to read before we started kindergarten. I have a clear memory of the day my mother taught me to read the first pages of the primary reader that had once been hers. Mom took us to the public library, housed in a stately old mansion overlooking the river, every Saturday. The children's room was on the second floor, and one climbed the curving staircase to be greeted by the sight of a stained-glass window behind the librarian's desk at the top of the stairs. Going to the library carried with it the solemnity of going to church.

There were other influential books in my childhood, again thanks to my mother and her firm good judgment. One day, she came home from Grandpa's house with an armload of books. "Read these," she said. "These" turned out to be four romanticized biographies of Austria's Habsburg dynasty, written in the 1930s by Bertita Harding. The teen-aged Marie Antoinette on her fateful journey to France, Maximilian and Carlota in Mexico, Franz Joseph and Elisabeth, Karl and Zita. I was captivated by these people as well, and fascinated to find an overlap with what I had read in *Jean & Company*. In Yugoslavia, Jean and her mother "came to Sarajevo. . .the city where the Austrian prince was assassinated, and the firebrand kindled that started the World War." At Buda Castle Jean and her friend Jovanka toured the royal palace and the private apartments of Empress Elisabeth while Jean's mother "told them. . .of this beautiful and tragic woman, who had hated the pomp and ceremony of being an empress. . . . They stood on Elisabeth's balcony and looked down over the garden she had planned, where she had been happier than anywhere else in her great kingdom."

On my own I discovered the Betsy-Tacy series, the thinly fictionalized account of author Maud Hart Lovelace's Midwestern childhood and young adulthood in Mankato, Minnesota. My favorite was *Betsy and the Great World*, wherein Betsy spends the year 1914 in Europe, a trip cut short by the outbreak of the First World War. My devotion to the Betsy-Tacy books led to rare disagreements between Mom and me over reading. "Those again?" Mom would say when I came downstairs to meet her in the adult room. "You should be reading different books."

Maureen Corrigan, bibliophile *par excellence*, writes in *Leave Me Alone, I'm Reading* that "you find the books you need when you need them." From the reading of *Jean & Company* and the dreams of going to Europe it inspired, through graduate school and the rigors of an academic career, *Jean & Company* was the book I regularly pulled off the shelf to re-read, rediscovering therein the love of European history it first inspired.

Always in my mind there was the question: "How much of this is true?" Helen Perry Curtis tells us in the Preface:

> This book was never really written. It wrote itself. Jean made a journey, and for her Europe suddenly came to life. Together she and her mother visited every country mentioned in this book, with the exception of Iceland. Only Jean's father saw that, but by the time he had finished the telling, the others felt that they had been there, too.

There is here already some acknowledgement of literary license. But really, who *were* these people who could spend two years traveling in Europe? What happened afterwards? Did Jean's friendships with the girls in the Jean Club survive the destruction that came upon the Continent with the Second World War?

From time to time in that now-remote pre-internet world I would interrupt some serious research to look up Helen's name in sources such as *The Readers' Guide to Periodical Literature*, with little luck. There were a few reviews of *Jean & Company* from 1937 and 1938. I found listings of articles in women's magazines written by Helen about gardening or sewing, but nothing that I could connect to *my* special book. Come the age of Google I made further attempts at a search, turning up only the occasional used copy of *Jean* on Amazon or eBay.

But then in January, 2015, I came across a copy of M.F.K. Fisher's *Two Towns in Provence* at a Little Free Library, one of those "take a book / leave a book" stands that spring up in front yards in neighborhoods of a certain sort. I had somehow gotten this far in life without encountering Fisher, a noted midcentury food and travel writer, but *Jean & Company*'s two chapters set in Provence was endorsement enough for me. Reading Fisher late one night, I came across a mention of enrolling her daughters in a boarding school run by Dominican nuns in Aix-en-Provence while she traveled and wrote. "Just like *Jean*!" I thought. And then: "There *has* to be a way to find that boarding school! There *has* to be a way to find Helen!" Setting aside Fisher, I Googled Helen's name and came up with a hit: a Helen Perry Curtis Room in the student center at Doane College in Crete, Nebraska.

This struck me as unlikely. *My* Helen Perry Curtis was a sophisticated New Yorker who took her daughter on a dazzling trip. . . . Nevertheless, I drilled down into the Doane College website and sent off an inquiry to the college library.

I was rewarded next morning with the first of a flurry of emails exchanged with Janet Jeffries. Yes, she wrote, this was the person I was looking for. Helen's father was president of Doane College for forty years; Helen was born and raised in Crete. More details emerged from Janet's emails, reinforcing aspects of *Jean & Company*. "My strong bonding with Helen," wrote Janet, "has to do with her European travels and the collection of folk costumes and then her career as a museum curator." Crete, Janet informed me, "is the heart of Nebraska's Czech country." Helen's exposure to European folk culture would thus have been an early one.

But the most important piece of information in Janet's emails was that at a Doane family reunion on Cape Cod:

> I met the granddaughters! . . . Susie and Pat were excited that
> I was so into the Czech culture since their grandma liked
> the Eastern European culture so much. They sent me a skirt
> and apron that Helen had collected in South Moravia. I have
> correspondence from Susie at home and actually you and
> Susie should connect. I think the granddaughters would be so
> excited that someone else is interested in Helen.

I wrote to Susie, and several days later received an enthusiastic reply:

> I was so pleased to receive your letter today! How well I
> know how books, at any time in one's life, but especially
> when we're young, and so open to all things, can be
> a tremendous influence on our lives. How wonderful
> that *Jean & Company* did that for you. I have so many,
> many things that I could tell you about my grandmother. . . .
>   As soon as I finished reading your letter this morning,
> I called my cousins Martha and Pat and read it to them.
> [They] immediately asked me to send a copy of your letter,
> and asked that I give you their email address.

Over the course of the next weeks our correspondence deepened. The most startling discovery was that Jean was actually a composite of two girls: Helen's daughters Jeanne and Polly. Susie was Jeanne's daughter, and Martha and Pat were Polly's. Susie sent me an unpublished family history, recounting Jeanne and Polly's first trip to Europe with their mother in 1932-1933. The basic ingredients of *Jean & Company* were there, including the convent school, but Jeanne and Polly were twelve and eleven years old, not the teenaged Jean of the book.

Further discoveries revealed additional license Helen took in writing *Jean & Company*. I followed up on a clue I had shamefully neglected from the Preface: "With grateful acknowledgment to the *American Girl* magazine, in whose pages most of these chapters were first published." *American Girl* was, from 1920 to 1979, the magazine of the Girl Scouts. The Milwaukee Public Library, a short distance from where I live, has a superb archive of magazines, so there I went and asked for all the issues of *American Girl* from the 1930s. Going issue by issue (*American Girl* was never indexed in the *Readers' Guide*) I found eleven of the sixteen chapters of *Jean & Company* in nascent form. What was most surprising was that the girl is named Sue, and there is no mention of the girls from the boarding school forming a club, which in the book provides the narrative framework. One of the most appealing aspects of *Jean & Company*—the "Company"—turned out to be an invention.

The dismay of this discovery, however, was soon countered by a message that popped up in my inbox: "Please Come Visit Us!" Martha and Pat wrote that Susie was coming for her annual summer visit to New Jersey. The invitation promised "lots of family photos, letters, genealogy, diaries, etc.," as well as day trips to Newark and Trenton where Helen had worked in museums. Who could resist?

What follows is a biography of Helen Perry Curtis, a woman very much of her times. She was shaped by the Progressive Era in which she came of age, participating in its currents of social reform: higher education for women, the settlement house, and women's suffrage. She was acquainted, either directly or at one degree of remove, with significant figures in the reform milieu: Jane Addams, Carrie Chapman Catt, John Cotton Dana, John Dewey, Frederic Howe. She lived in a time of dramatic, disruptive change, and experienced tragedy. Her life intersected both World Wars; twice she volunteered in support of war-relief work, including going to France in 1918 to work in a YMCA canteen. She was an advocate for progressive childrearing. Her interest in the arts drew her into the orbit of avant-garde figures and movements of the time. Helen excelled in the art of befriending influential people, not in a cynical or self-serving way, valuable though these connections proved to be, but because she found such people to be accomplished and interesting. She enjoyed advantages of birth and education—especially education—but it was the ends to which she turned those advantages that make her life so compelling.

But Helen's story is equally that of a woman *ahead* of her times. Decades before the terms "gig economy" and "networking" entered the lexicon, she repeatedly adapted, reinvented, and reasserted herself. She began her museum career as a contract worker. She worked in turn as a curator and museum director, an interior decorator, a freelance writer, tour guide, director of non-profit organizations, and owner of a small business. The backstory of *Jean & Company, Unlimited* is that of a woman writing her way, story by story, chapter by chapter, across Europe, supporting her family while so doing.

While she embraced challenge and change, Helen exhibited stability and strength of character. In times of profound change, she recognized when it was time to let go. She had the sense of an ending: when her time of European travel was over, or when a long marriage had reached its end. Helen adopted the wisdom of her friend, the writer and activist Sidonie Gruenberg: "Women have to choose not once, but many times, and at each stage of life, with the same degree of uncertainty."

Helen's story offers timeless lessons about community and service thereto. A spirit of volunteerism was a through-line in her life. She inherited from her parents and grandparents a dedication to the work of building community, whether that took the form of participating in civic organizations, of serving the needs of immigrants, or inventing an organization to address the needs of refugees. In the words of Helen's fictionalized character, Jean, she sought "to reach into the unknown for knowledge, and then give it as a gift to the world."

This account of Helen's life is told through the prism of her love of Europe and European travel. It is also, in part, the story of my search for the origins of a beloved childhood book. That search reveals the ways in which Helen drew on the experiences of a lifetime to craft the story of an American girl's first encounter with Europe.

This book is titled *Helen Perry Curtis and the European Trip of a Lifetime*. Helen's trip of a lifetime spanned three decades, bookended by the last weeks of peace before the First World War and the penultimate summer before the Second. My own *Jean & Company*-inspired European trip now spans five decades of travel to and teaching about Europe.

This book is dedicated to the memory of my mother. Unlike Helen and her daughters, my mother and I were together in Europe only once: when my parents came to visit me during a summer when I was doing research in Vienna. There I was able to show Mom the places connected with the Habsburgs, whose biographies she first gave me, and to recall together the book that started it all, *Jean & Company, Unlimited.*

Chapter 1
A Prairie Childhood

The railroad built the town.

In 1870, the Burlington and Missouri River Railroad pushed westward from Plattsmouth, Nebraska, laying 240 miles of track as far as Kearney. There it joined the Union Pacific Railroad, linking southern Nebraska with the rest of the continent. Chief engineer for the project was Thomas Doane. Along the route, the railroad platted towns to which Doane, in alphabetic order, assigned names from his native New England: Asylum, Berks, Dorchester, Exeter, Fairmont, Grafton, Harvard, Inland, Juniata, Kenesaw, and Lowell. A homestead claim on the banks of the Big Blue River in Saline County had been established as early as 1863 by Jesse and Elizabeth Bickle, and anticipating the land rush accompanying the arrival of the railroad, Bickle had platted a town site on his homestead, giving it the name Blue River City. Thomas Doane needed a "C" name at that locale, to fit the string of "alphabet towns." In March, 1871, the Bickles agreed to the name "Crete," after the town in Illinois from whence they came.

Thomas Doane was Helen Perry Curtis's grandfather. Crete was where Helen was born in 1888, where she attended school and graduated from a college named for her grandfather, where her father was president. The town and college shaped her. The founders intended Crete and Doane College as reproductions of New England. Years later, paying tribute to her grandfather and parents, Helen wrote that they created an "environment of eastern background combined with frontier living and missionary zeal . . . a little bit of New England . . . transplanted to the Nebraska prairie." The eastern influence shaped Helen's aspirations, directing her to a career as an artist, museum curator, and writer. But a Nebraska-born thriftiness, practicality, and egalitarianism were ever the hallmarks of her character. Doane College, from its origins, admitted women on an equal footing with men, and women made up a significant portion of the faculty. That Helen throughout her life surrounded herself with well-educated, independent-minded women was no accident. Long before she made European folk culture a focus of her professional life,

Helen was exposed to immigrant culture in Nebraska, where one-fifth of the population of Saline County was foreign born. And the railroad which built the town served as the perfect metaphor for the woman who became a world traveler.

Helen's grandfather Thomas Doane was born in 1821 in Orleans, Massachusetts, from the hardiest of old New England stock. The Doanes traced their arrival in America to 1630, when Deacon John Doane served on Plymouth Colony's governing council. Thomas Doane's father, another John Doane, went by the honorific "Squire," reflecting his standing as a landowner, lawyer, Massachusetts state senator, and esteemed member of the Cape Cod community of Orleans. Thomas Doane was the oldest of the eight children of Squire and Polly Eldridge Doane. Squire Doane was a founder of Orleans Academy, where his children were educated. Thomas went on to attend Phillips Academy at Andover. At age nineteen he began an apprenticeship in the office of a civil engineer in the Charlestown section of Boston. From there, and with increasing levels of responsibility, Doane worked railroad construction in Massachusetts, New Hampshire, and Vermont.

In Brattleboro, Thomas Doane in 1850 met and married Sophia Dennison Clark. Between 1853 and 1863 the couple had five children: Helen, John, Caroline, Frances, and Thomas, though baby Thomas died in infancy. The family resided in Charlestown at 8 Pearl Street. The house was once home to Oliver Holden, Revolutionary War veteran, pastor, poet, and noted composer of religious hymns.

In 1863 Doane moved his family temporarily to North Adams, Massachusetts, where he was chief engineer of the Hoosac Tunnel, a five-mile-long project through the Berkshire Mountains. Working from both ends of the tunnel, Doane carried out rigorous surveying, and employed a technique he developed using nitroglycerin and electric charges, along with compressed air and pneumatic drills. So exacting was his work that, when the tunnel met in the middle of the mountain, it was less than one inch out of alignment.

Doane's work took him away from his family for stretches of time, even from their temporary residence. In September, 1863, Doane wrote a letter to ten-year-old Helen from his work site twenty miles from North Adams. The letter is equal parts lesson for his daughter and insight into its author.

> While riding up from Springfield I noticed some cows in a
> field near the Rail Road, and a little girl not so large as you,

I think, watching them. It rained very hard, and the ground seemed almost covered with water . . . and the little girl had an old umbrella over her. It seemed very hard that so little a child should be so exposed, and I could not but think, how should I feel if my little ones had to suffer such hardship. How thankful we ought to be for God's goodness to us, in providing us good homes, and friends to take us in, and all we need. We do not prize our blessings as we ought. And when we have so much, let us not forget those who are in want all about us, but let us be thoughtful of them, and do what we can for those who . . . suffer.

The birth and death of her youngest child left Sophia an invalid. She contracted tuberculosis, and died on December 1, 1868, leaving four children motherless.

Three weeks later, Thomas Doane wrote to Sophia's mother in Brattleboro. "I have just been reading and praying with the children, saying the Commandments, etc., duties which Sophie used to perform, and they have sung their evening hymn and all gone upstairs to bed." The children were keenly feeling their mother's absence; he was acutely sensing the loss as well.

Whether, had I not encroached upon your household some 20 years ago, she would have been spared longer to you, we cannot tell, nor is there now any remedy. . . . Whether a different manner of life, or a residence in a different climate, or less of the perils, pains, and anxiety of child bearing and rearing would have prolonged her life we do not know. . . . She has given me some beautiful children, who are . . . everything I could wish. . . . Sophie promised me, if it could be so, to be our guardian angel . . . and to intercede with Him for blessings upon our heads.

In 1869 Thomas Doane went to Nebraska—a state which entered the union two years earlier—as chief engineer with the Burlington and Missouri Railroad project. He took Helen with him to his headquarters at Plattsmouth. They returned to Charlestown several months later for a visit, during which time Thomas went to Vermont to see Sophia's relatives. There he again met Louisa Barber, a friend of Sophia's and headmistress of a boarding and day school for girls.

On November 19, 1870, Thomas and Louisa were married. Thomas wrote Sophia's mother, explaining that the visit to Brattleboro had "very materially changed the relation in which Louisa and I then stood to each other." This outcome, he continued, was not anticipated, especially so soon after Sophia's death and so close to the anniversary thereof. "I hope our marriage may never make me less a son to you, my dear Mother. . . . Do not hesitate to make any demands on me you choose at any time." The children embraced their stepmother. All four called Louisa "mother."

Two months later Thomas Doane brought his wife to Nebraska, leaving the children in Charlestown with relatives for the remainder of the school year. The children joined their parents that summer, living in a small farmhouse in Crete. The dwelling was roughly finished: unpainted boards, low ceilings, lacking carpets and curtains. But in an example of New England refinement on the Nebraska plains, Louisa entertained an inspection team from the railroad. Helen, then eighteen years old, recalled that her stepmother, dressed in black satin, welcomed the visitors to a table set with linen, silver, and china. "Those men took some time to reconcile house, table, and people."

The farmhouse was a temporary residence. Thomas Doane had taken a liking to the town on the Big Blue River, and was building a home, The Grange, on a hilltop a mile from Crete. The family moved into The Grange in early 1872. Doane installed a telegraph apparatus, and from there directed railroad operations. He became a gentleman farmer. On sixty acres contiguous to The Grange he kept horses, a cow, pigs, chickens, and a pony, Proxy, for the children. Helen recalled her sister Frances, "a picture in her plaid dress, tearing over the prairie" on Proxy.

It was not only a house and home that Thomas Doane established in Crete. He collaborated with Reverend Frederick Alley and the American Home Missionary Society to establish the First Congregational Church in Crete. In Charlestown the Doanes had worshiped at the historic Winthrop Congregational Church, where Thomas was a deacon. Louisa was Episcopalian, and it is a measure of the respect the couple had for each other that Louisa supported Thomas in founding a Congregational church in Crete while she attended the town's Episcopal church. Thomas Doane served as Sunday school superintendent and taught classes for the congregation.

Of equal importance for Thomas Doane was the establishment of a school. He loaned $2,000 towards its construction, in recognition of which the new institution bore the name Doane Academy. His actions recalled Squire John Doane's founding of the academy at Orleans. Doane Academy opened in the fall of 1871, with forty-five students.

Church services were held in the school until the dedication of the frame church in 1877. All four Doane children attended the academy.

Thomas Doane then made the case to the Nebraska Congregational Association for approval of a college in Crete. He convinced the railroad to donate 600 acres, thus securing the approval, in the face of competition, for siting the college in Crete. Thomas Doane never attended college himself, something he always regretted.[1] He now founded one instead. The college admitted its first students in the fall of 1872.

The college, which bore his name, remained a lifelong commitment for Thomas Doane, even after he completed his work and returned to Charlestown. Doane served on the board of trustees, attending its annual meeting, often remaining in Crete for months at a time. He never missed a Commencement. From his home in Charlestown he continued to fundraise and recruit faculty, drawing on a network of social connections. He set up his younger brother Charles as a sheep farmer on a portion of the acreage next to The Grange, and kept up a correspondence with nurseryman E.F. Stephens concerning the transplanting of trees native to New England to the prairie. He maintained his interest in the State Bank of Nebraska, of which he was founder, first president, and majority shareholder.

Through the establishment of the academy and the college, through the founding of civic institutions, and through his interest in farming and forestation, Thomas Doane—literally—transplanted a slice of New England to the Nebraska prairie. One of his associates, describing Doane at work, captured the figure of the New England gentleman engaged in the task of building the frontier. The man recalled coming upon Doane standing in a frame box, partially submerged in the Big Blue River. Doane, dressed in his customary "broadcloth suit, light felt hat and polished shoes," was "vigorously stabbing the earth under the water, making a personal examination of the character of the foundation on which to build this important masonry pier."[2]

In forging the New England-Nebraska nexus, Thomas Doane established a pattern that would be followed in the lives of his children,

---

[1] In 1907, on the occasion of the dedication of the Lee Chapel on the campus, Doane's son, Reverend John Doane, stated that his father always "profoundly regretted this lack of what he called a liberal education." Thomas Doane once told his son that "a college training would have made me more useful as a citizen, given me a greater power of discernment, and of influencing my fellow man." "Thomas Doane, One of the Founders of Doane College," cited in Don Ziegler, *A College on a Hill and Beyond* (Crete, NE: Doane College, 2007), 418, n. 17.

[2] I.S.P. Weeks, "Thomas Doane as a Business Man," *Nebraska Congregational News*, vol. 23 (1902), cited in Janet Jeffries, "Gentility on the Prairie: Urbanization and Refinement in Crete, Nebraska, 1871-1891" (master's thesis, University of Nebraska, 1966), 56.

notably his daughter Helen, her husband Brainerd Perry, and their daughter, Helen Perry Curtis.

David Brainerd Perry arrived in Nebraska in April, 1872. Brainerd, as he was called, came from the same deeply rooted New England stock as the Doanes. The Perrys were farmers and weavers in England, occupations their descendants continued after settling in Massachusetts Colony in 1666. In 1751, Josiah Perry, Brainerd's great-great-grandfather, bought property in Worcester, where seven generations of the family continued to weave and farm and raise large families. Brainerd, born in 1839, was the seventh of the ten children of Samuel and Mary Harrington Perry. The family was described as thrifty and industrious, loving and happy. Of his siblings, Brainerd was the only one to leave Worcester, but he "never lost the distinctive accent and demeanor of his proper Puritan upbringing." [3]

Brainerd Perry earned three degrees from Yale College: a bachelor's in 1863, master's in 1866, and bachelor of divinity in 1867. During the Civil War Brainerd, under the auspices of the YMCA, spent two months as a chaplain in military hospitals and battlefields in Virginia. Following completion of the divinity degree he went to Europe, traveling through Italy and attending the University of Heidelberg. Returning home, he became a tutor at Yale.

The relentless intellectual work led to a breakdown of Brainerd's health. Seeking a change, he went to Nebraska under the sponsorship of the Connecticut Missionary Society, charged with establishing Congregational churches and living the life of a circuit-riding preacher. Crossing the Missouri River, his first glimpse of the state that was to be home for the rest of his life was from "that lofty outlook, well called the High School of Omaha, so that my entrance to Nebraska was in some sense educational both as regards my point of observation and my guide." A day later, Perry reached Lincoln, on his way to his assignment in Hamilton County. "On my way . . . I passed through Crete, with its new academy building and few houses, little thinking I should ever make my home there." [4] In short order, he founded churches in Aurora, Harvard, and Sutton. Walking, or riding his pony, Kate, he traversed prairies, waded streams, and took refuge in dripping sod dugouts. If what he sought was "an abundance of work" in an "invigorating setting," he certainly got his wish.

[3] Ziegler, 3.
[4] David Brainerd Perry, "The Evolution of Educational Work in Our State," May 12, 1896, Doane Archives, 5/1, Box 3.

It was for the purpose of securing approval for two new churches that Brainerd Perry attended the meeting of the Congregational Association in Omaha in June, 1872, when the siting of a college in Crete was approved. There he met Thomas Doane and Reverend Alley, both of whom were impressed by the young man's Yale credentials. On July 11, 1872, Brainerd was ordained to the ministry at a service held at Doane Academy. At his ordination, Brainerd learned that "the trustees were thinking of asking me to take charge of the infant College." [5]

The beginnings of the college could not have been humbler. Brainerd was the only employee. He taught preparatory courses to thirteen students in the academy building, living in one room, simultaneously serving as teacher, treasurer, and janitor: chopping wood to keep the building's stoves fired. For the first two years he drew no salary; in the next two years he was paid in promissory notes. Brainerd also turned over to the college the annual salary of $400 he received from the Connecticut Missionary Society for his duties as circuit preacher. His tasks included soliciting churches for support of the college. Thomas Doane pledged $10,000, contingent on raising $5,000 in Nebraska and $10,000 out of state. In the first year Brainerd, working with another pastor, met the goal.

Thomas Doane and Brainerd Perry shared a vision for the college. "We are trying to reproduce New England in Nebraska," Brainerd told an eastern audience during an 1875 fundraising tour.[6] He meant that literally. From its simple origins in the academy building, the college grew to a campus shaded with transplanted New England trees. The college's motto, "We Build on Christ," was echoed in Brainerd's personal creed, "This one thing I do."

David Brainerd Perry.
Doane University Archives.

Helen Doane Perry.
Doane University Archives.

---

[5] Brainerd Perry diary, quoted in Ziegler, 5.
[6] Ziegler, 62.

The alliance between Thomas Doane and Brainerd Perry was solemnized when Brainerd married Helen Doane, Thomas's daughter, in 1876. But first Helen spent the summer of 1873 in Vermont, with the families of her mother Sophia and stepmother Louisa. There, she wrote, "I had my first taste of society and my first love affair." The latter experience was soon eclipsed. Brainerd, returning from a fundraising trip in the east, accompanied Helen back to Nebraska. "Breakfast at Syracuse for Miss Helen and myself, 75 cents," he recorded in his diary on September 3, adding: "beautiful day, pleasant company." At the college, Brainerd was Helen's classics tutor. "I read Virgil with Mr. Perry and was the only student," Helen wrote in her memoir. "'Nuf said.'" The two began courting. "October 6th: Moonlight ride with Miss H," Brainerd wrote in his diary. "November 27th: Thanksgiving! Supper and oysters for Miss Helen." "March 1st: Miss H. never looked sweeter than when after the Sabbath service she greeted me." In the spring of 1874, Brainerd asked Thomas Doane for his daughter's hand in marriage.

Doane was taken aback. Brainerd was thirty-five, fifteen years Helen's senior. Even Helen "was quite undecided. He was older, very serious, 'life was real, life was earnest' to him; and I was full of fun, and ready for all sorts of good times, quite popular, and only twenty!" In the end it was a long talk between Brainerd and Louisa Doane that moved matters forward. After a three-month delay, Helen accepted Brainerd's proposal and Thomas Doane gave his blessing. [7]

Nevertheless, the couple waited another two years before marrying. Thomas Doane finished his work with the railroad and returned to Charlestown, taking his family, including Helen, home to 8 Pearl Street. Brainerd came east during the summer of 1874 and brought his fiancée to Worcester to meet sixty assembled relatives. When Brainerd returned to Crete Helen remained in Charlestown, "trying to fit myself to be the wife of a college professor. I studied German. . .[and] the science of housekeeping and planned for marriage."

Brainerd and Helen were married on July 3, 1876, at Winthrop Church; Helen in a gown of embroidered muslin, Caroline and Frances as bridesmaids. Flowers brought that morning from Orleans decorated the church. "I did make a lovely bride," Helen recalled, nearly sixty years later in her memoir. "Nobody left to say that now,

---

[7] Ziegler, 381-384; Helen Doane Perry, "Memories of Me and Mine," 1933.

but myself." Brainerd's diary put it simply: "Helen looked like Venus rising from the sea."

One hundred guests attended the reception at 8 Pearl Street: lobster salad, sandwiches, cake, and—given the "fearfully hot day"—lemonade and ice cream. The couple went to Orleans for their wedding trip. A honeymoon on Cape Cod was not all it would appear. "Let me warn those who can still profit by it," Helen's memoir states, "never go among relatives for a honeymoon!" The newlyweds spent the remainder of the summer in the east, attending the Philadelphia Centennial Exposition in August before returning to Crete. They took up residence in The Grange, which Thomas Doane deeded to his daughter as a wedding gift.

Helen went back to Charlestown in March. She was pregnant, and wanted to have the baby at home, with her stepmother Louisa in attendance. Thomas Doane Perry was born on May 27, 1877. Brainerd first saw Tom when he came east following Commencement; walking in, Helen recalled, on "his son and heir in a bath, with the poor young mother struggling with the first care of baby." In giving their eldest child his grandfather's full name, Helen and Brainerd continued a tradition of using surnames as middle names. Mary Thornton, a friend who eleven months earlier served at the wedding reception, wrote to Helen: "Uncle Wingate writes, 'Mr. Doane is a grandfather!' Now, who but a man would say so much and no more? Not how *you* are, or what the baby's name is! We can't call the little thing anything but 'it' and all we can say about you is, 'I wonder. . .!'"

In August 1879, Helen gave birth to Brainerd Clark Perry, the middle name a tribute to her mother, Sophia Dennison Clark. The infant, called Ned, lived less than a year. In January 1884, Charles Boswell Perry, known as Carl, was born. Carl was named after a generous Connecticut benefactor of Doane College. Boswell Observatory, the second building erected on campus, was a gift from Boswell; Boswell Avenue skirted the college's western boundary.[8]

On February 17, 1888, Helen Clark Perry, Brainerd and Helen's only daughter, was born. Little Helen's arrival was greeted joyously. "My dear daughter Helen," Louisa Doane wrote. "I have not been able to settle at any work since this morning's mail brought Brainerd's letter. I can't realize I have a grand-daughter yet. . . . I took the letter to the office at once. Papa's face beamed on me when he read it. We have been

---

[8] Charles Boswell gave the college $19,000, an amount equivalent to nearly $540,000 in 2020.

thinking of you most of the time since Her arrival." Brainerd's sister Julia wrote: "So glad God has given you a daughter. I want to know what Tom and especially Carl say about a little sister." "I congratulate you," a Doane cousin wrote, "upon the safe arrival of little Miss Perry. I hope the beauty and graces of her Mother and Doane Aunts will be developed in her." John Doane, Helen's brother, wrote a letter, which arrived with a charming pre-script from his wife, Alice:

> My dear little niece: Your Uncle John wrote you a long letter this morning but was so particular to having every phrase just right that he only made the first draft of it. . . . He didn't even take that much pains when he wrote to ask me if I would be his wife! But . . . I forgave him and knowing he was very tired, and really hated to copy things, I offered to do it for him. So here you have his welcoming letter in my handwriting, and so of course, it is partly mine too.

John Doane's letter was equally charming.

> Although you are young in days, you have already a warm place in my heart, where the seed of love for you has been planted and will grow. Your relatives have been longing for you for many months, but were in doubt whether you would really come after all, or send one of your brothers instead, as you have already done three times. But now that you are really here yourself, rejoicing knows no bounds, and I have no doubt that the entire Perry tribe is a veritable Perry-grin-nation, going about to tell its glory with a smiling face.

In the tones of the ordained minister that he was, John concluded with words of benediction, ordaining Helen's future. "I . . . wish for your very great happiness in life, and you can only be happy yourself by making others happy. . . . Be lady-like . . . and begin cultivating at once a modest ease in the presence of strangers. . . . Our family rejoice that you have come to such a lovely home, and with your Mama and Papa and brothers, that they have you among them."

The fact that mother and daughter now shared a name was a potential source of confusion. The family took to referring to Helen Doane Perry as "Big Helen," a name which remained for the rest of her life.

Helen's birth was followed little more than a year later, in October, 1889, by that of Henry Eldridge Perry; Eldridge the maiden name of Thomas Doane's mother Polly. Of all the children, Helen and Henry were the closest in age. In her childish prattle, Helen referred to herself and her brother as if they were a single person: "Me and Henry," a reference picked up and embraced by the rest of the family.

"Me and Henry" with Grandfather Thomas Doane.

The Grange was the center of life not only for the growing Perry family but for the college as well. In her role as first lady, Helen established traditions which endured for decades: lawn parties welcoming students in the fall, teas for women faculty, receptions for graduates and their parents at Commencement, a dinner for returning alumni.

The Grange hosted numerous Doane relatives. Thomas Doane, often accompanied by Louisa, stayed in his former home whenever he returned to Crete. His brother Charles and wife Mary Doane, whose foray into sheep farming Thomas sponsored, lived with Brainerd and Helen at The Grange while building their own house. Howard Doane, a distant cousin, was a classics professor at the college; he and his wife Addie, a music instructor, lived nearby. Big Helen's siblings visited The Grange; they had, after all, spent a period of their childhood there. Big Helen's brother John attended Harvard (where Teddy Roosevelt was a classmate), and then worked a year with a railroad crew in the Dakotas before enrolling at Oberlin. John was ordained from Andover Theological Seminary in Massachusetts. By 1893 John and his wife Alice, who met while both were students at Oberlin, were in Lincoln, where John was pastor of Plymouth Congregational Church. Helen and John's families alternated Thanksgiving and Christmas at each other's homes. Helen's sisters Caroline and Frances were regular visitors. "My sisters spent much time with us and the place was full of fun when they were there," Helen recalled. "They both had very active love affairs which kept them occupied while there. I well remember the early morning tennis games, when I would give breakfast to four very jolly youngsters." Caroline married William O. Weeden, also a Congregational minister, in 1888. William pastored a church in Beatrice, Nebraska, thirty miles away. Frances married Henry Twombly, a lawyer, in 1889. Harry, as he was known, was the son of Reverend Alexander Twombly, pastor of Charlestown's Winthrop Church, and the presider at Helen and

The Grange.
Doane University Archives.

Brainerd's wedding. Frances and Harry were to become two of the most important people in the lives of the Perrys, particularly young Helen.

In October 1883, one of Brainerd's sisters, Mary Stone Perry, came to Crete. She arrived unexpectedly, a letter having gone astray—and stayed for the next two years. While this visit occurred before little Helen's birth, her diary offers a glimpse into the world in which Helen was born: life at The Grange, the college, and the town on the Nebraska prairie.

From The Grange, Mary could look north to "the so-called city of Crete. . . . Its classification as a city is inappropriate. But this is the name it bears." The work of Thomas Doane and E.F. Stephens was much in evidence. "If ever a town was abundantly, superfluously planted with trees, it is Crete." She could also see the college's buildings, three in number, "which, as they are located on a hill, can be seen from afar." Beyond was a view of the Academy, reminding her of "Worcester . . . as seen from the old Homestead when I was a child."

If Mary Stone Perry was underwhelmed by Crete, the immensity of the landscape made a deep impression.

> I like this country more and more. . . . Far away from my
> home, I am sitting in a grove of evergreen trees in the heart
> of the Continent. In the far west, it seems to the people of
> Massachusetts, but only about midway between the Atlantic
> and the Pacific. We have fine sunsets—or perhaps I should
> say twilights. It is not so much the tinting of the clouds at
> the sunset as the splendid afterglow of colored light. . . .
> Last night the western sky was brilliant with a peculiar light
> and the phenomena was tonight repeated. The beauty is
> indescribable. . . . Rich crimson and saffron shade off into the
> most delicate tints and the windows look straight out onto glory.

With sisterly concern, Mary called Brainerd "the busiest of busy men. . . . Will he *never rest?* . . . Yesterday he was busy all day. Next Sabbath he preaches. Next week he expects to start for the East, to solicit for the college." Brainerd undertook these fundraising trips—five, six, eight weeks in duration—at least twice a year. In addition, there were meetings in Lincoln with church and education leaders from around the state, and trips accompanying students to scholarly and athletic competitions. Brainerd preached at Crete's First Congregational Church, and served as a visiting pastor at various churches. He continued to teach at the college. A representative semester included courses in Old Testament, Psychology, and Constitutional Heritage of the United States. At least Brainerd was no longer shouldering the burden of the college alone. Mary Merrill, a German and French teacher at Crete's public high school, was hired in 1873 as preceptress and principal of the Preparatory Department. Arthur Fairchild, destined to be Brainerd's closest friend and colleague, was hired in 1874 as mathematics professor. Fairchild gradually assumed the roles of college librarian and treasurer. In 1883, the year of Mary Stone Perry's arrival in Crete, the college had fourteen faculty and staff; and enrollment topped 120 students. In 1881, Brainerd was officially named president of the college, replacing the simple designation of "head."

Life at The Grange was busy as well. Mary described mornings assisting her sister-in-law in washing and wiping dishes, making beds, sweeping and dusting, laundering clothes, mending stockings, paring potatoes for the noon and evening meals. Summertime meant canning fruits and vegetables and putting up preserves. Helen sold eggs gathered from the chickens, seven cents a dozen (a job her son Carl took over as he got older, charging double the money). A series of German immigrant domestics were part of the household. During Mary Stone Perry's two years in Crete first Marie, then Caroline, Lizzie, and Lena worked for the Perrys, each leaving employment as they married. Every year there was a "chore boy" who earned room and board while attending the college and living at The Grange. The chore boy chopped wood, cared for the animals (cow, pigs, chickens, dog, cats), and served as a male presence during Brainerd's frequent absences. A task that regularly fell to the chore boy involved Brainerd's horse, Pete. Brainerd, preoccupied with his thoughts, frequently walked home, forgetting his horse and buggy tethered to the hitching post outside Merrill Hall. The chore boy had to go retrieve these.

Big Helen's household responsibilities were compounded by her duties as first lady of the college. Mary Stone Perry described teas for faculty women, an evening reception for college trustees, a party for the football team, the President's Reception held on the eve of Thanksgiving. "There were about seventy of us in all. Helen made . . . 20 loaves of bread of different kinds. Apples, nuts . . . and raisins were also provided." All this was carried out without modern conveniences. The Grange lacked gas, electricity, and central heating. It did not even have proper fireplaces; wood stoves in the kitchen and several of the rooms served for cooking and heating, even in the bitterest of Nebraska winters. During Mary's stay, Brainerd installed a funnel to her room from the one below. "It does not heat the room as much as Brainerd expected...but it takes off the chill." Helen wrote in her memoir that she brought the children up with "baths in a teacup," and carried out her duties as first lady of the college by candlelight and kerosene.

Apart from her official duties, Helen belonged to the Ladies of the Congregational Church, the Missionary Society, the Sewing Circle, and the Round Table, a literary club. Mary Stone Perry contrasted social life in Crete with that of New England. "There is not the stiffness in these social gathering, with which one is so familiar in the East— partly because people are more on a level." Mrs. James Dawes, wife of Nebraska's governor, "a very estimable woman," was Helen's closest friend. The governor practiced law in Crete prior to his election in 1882; his wife returned often for a visit, staying at The Grange. Helen in turn visited Mrs. Dawes at the governor's mansion. Mary commented, not always kindly, on Helen's independence. "Business calls Helen away a great deal of the time...in the last twenty days she has left the house perhaps a dozen times...I wish Helen could realize how much more she is able to leave home than most mothers who have babies."

Mary Stone Perry observed Tom and Carl (the only Perry children during her stay). Tom she found to be a bright little boy. He was "very fond of a good time—unlike his father—very demonstrative, and very easily made happy." Tom "reads a little...but has a greater taste for figures." It was a prescient observation, inasmuch as Tom, like his grandfather, would become an engineer. Marie, the Perry's domestic, was teaching Tom German, which he was learning "with great facility ...he and Marie communicate with ease." Tom was a big help in the kitchen, "running with the clean dishes from the kitchen sink to the sitting room table, and going down cellar for apples and potatoes." Tom even helped with college tasks. The six-year-old and his mother folded two hundred and fifty printed circulars to be mailed out to prospective donors. Tom's sense of responsibility, evident as a child, foreshadowed the role he would shoulder as an adult: the person to whom his family turned in times of crisis.

Mary was in Crete when Carl was born, and she became very attached to him. Carl as an infant was high-strung, crying frequently, demanding attention. Mary took it upon herself to write Carl's "autobiography," making handwritten copies to send to relatives back east. As with Tom, she revealed more than she realized at the time. "I give people a great deal of trouble," Mary has the infant say, "but I do not mind much about that. . . . What am I here for, if not to be taken care of?" [9]

A feature of life in Crete that appealed to Mary Stone Perry was the town's connection to the Chautauqua movement. Chautauqua was founded in 1874 in upstate New York to provide summer training for Sunday school teachers. Four years later it broadened its purpose, offering a four-year correspondence course of readings, essays, and examinations, providing participants "the essential knowledge of a College education." At the time of her stay in Crete, Mary was completing the course. The original Chautauqua gave rise to "Daughter Chautauquas" throughout the country. In 1882, the Nebraska Sunday School Association reconstituted itself as a Chautauqua. Meetings were held at Crete's First Congregational Church until 1884, when a permanent site, Chautauqua Park, was built on the banks of the Big Blue River. By 1888, the year of young Helen's birth, Crete's Chautauqua was second in size only to that of New York. It annually drew thousands of visitors to hear nationally known speakers, including Nebraska's own William Jennings Bryan and Willa Cather.[10] Representing the college, Brainerd and Helen entertained speakers who came to Crete for the annual event. Mary Merrill, instructor and preceptress at Doane College ("one of the best educated ladies in the city," Mary Stone Perry wrote admiringly), was president of the local Chautauqua Circle. Mary's diary records a reception hosted by Helen and Louisa Doane, who was spending part of the summer of 1884 in Crete. Mary listed names of the women present, representing Crete's most distinguished families. Ministers' wives, club women, college instructors, Chautauquans, "Mrs. Thomas Doane and Helen congratulated themselves on having as guests, women of uncommon intelligence." It was another illustration of the culture of strong, accomplished, well-educated women into which young Helen Perry was born. [11]

---

[9] Carl's upbringing was another source of discord between Helen and her sister-in-law, an unmarried woman thirty years Helen's senior. There is an edge to this "autobiography," apart from the presumption involved in representing someone else's child to the extended family. Through Mary's words, Baby Carl complains that he does not get enough to eat, his Aunt Mary tries to feed him, only to be reprimanded by his mother. Carl cries, and Aunt Mary—or his father—soothes him; his mother thinks he ought not to be rocked or picked up. Carl's mama spends a lot of time away from him, visiting friends, leaving him in Aunt Mary's care. It is revealing that Helen, in her memoir, never mentions this two-year long visit from her sister-in-law.

[10] https://chq.org/about-us/history [accessed 5-13-2020]; Janet Jeffries, *Images of America: Crete* (Charleston, SC: Arcadia, 2012), 97.

[11] Years later, Helen Perry Curtis's daughter Jeanne, listing her mother's accomplishments, told an interviewer: "I didn't really understand women's liberation because I didn't know anything else." *Far Brook Bulletin* (1998): 13-14.

"You children had a very happy childhood," Helen Doane Perry recalled in her memoir, "and you will all remember the Sunday afternoon walks with your father, and the knowledge you got of birds. . . . He had very little time for play . . . but he loved his children, and when he did play, there were great doings." Brainerd's letters bear this out, as he uses young Helen's own phrase for herself and her brother: "This afternoon 'Me and Henry' and I have been strolling about in orchards, ravines, and fields, hoping to see a robin or blue bird. . . . Little Helen has been hanging round my neck, inviting me to her little party where the doll dishes will be brought out. Henry has come with his comic pictures for me to laugh at." Brainerd described "the fun of putting [them] to bed—despotically controlled by the affectionate imps insisting that I must tell them stories, multiplying prayers to detain me, calling for water when I have gone that they may again delight themselves with sight of me—to say nothing about the difficulty with which they restrain laughter while saying these prayers." Brainerd wrote to "My dear Helen and Henry," from the train on one of his fundraising trips. "As I look out the window, sometimes I see a light in some home and of course I wonder whether there are as nice girls and boys there as I know in Crete. . . . The car in which I am riding is very bright. . . . You would think it great fun to see the porter make up 12 beds, each of them about as wide as your beds."

Big Helen wrote to her sisters that Helen "finds it a great cross to be a girl. I discovered her hanging by the knees from a trapeze the other day, her clothes over her head, she doesn't see why she can't do those things as well as Henry." As the only girl, Helen grew up a tomboy. "You would have laughed this afternoon to see Helen out in the snow," her mother wrote on another occasion. "I put a pair of Carl's trousers on her and she looked and acted the boy to perfection." Helen rode horseback and played football with her brothers. Saturday afternoons in autumn the family went to college football games, where first Tom, then Carl, played for the Doane Tigers. Tom was a steady player, his mother recalled; Carl quick and erratic.

Helen and Henry attended Crete's public elementary school together, and were often in a shared classroom. "I feel that we have no babies left. They are away from home nearly all day, and the house seems quiet and lonely," their mother wrote. Big Helen strove to turn her daughter into a little lady. "Have made Helen a very pretty wrapper from one of

Caroline's, and a handsome dress from one of Frances'. Contributions for such a cause thankfully received." Letters between young Helen and her Doane grandparents show that Big Helen was successful in getting her daughter to take up needlework, and that Helen, perhaps endowed with some innate talent derived from generations of weavers on the Perry side, enjoyed the work. Thomas Doane wrote to Helen in November of 1894, when she was six years old, thanking her for the

> little five-leaved doily, which I am very glad to have, especially
> as it is in the work of your own eyes and little fingers, and
> thumbs. It must have required no little industry too, to take
> so many stiches. Your real Grandma and your stead Grandma
> both could do very nice sewing—perhaps you will be like them.

Helen's early efforts at artwork also met with the same encouragement from an indulgent grandparent. Thomas Doane wrote that the little drawing sent to Grandma was "quite successful . . . one can easily see that it is not a house, nor a horse, nor a mouse, but a real plant, which grows. . . . Keep on trying to do better each time, and by and by you may draw as well as your Aunts Caroline and Frances and Great-Aunt Mary . . . and perhaps a great deal better, if you try hard enough and long enough."

In the summer of 1895, when Helen was seven, the entire Doane clan gathered at the homestead on Cape Cod. Thomas Doane bought all the railway tickets, and hired two domestics to keep house for the summer. The gathering brought together the six Perrys; Big Helen's brother John, wife Alice, and their three children; and Caroline and William Weeden, now living in Cleveland. Frances and Henry Twombly and four-year-old Edward came from Summit, New Jersey. The men came and went as business called, but the women and children spent the entire summer on the Cape. "It was a beautiful summer," Big Helen recalled. The only rule laid down by Thomas Doane was that each night someone take a turn at writing up the day's activities and events. Some did so in the form of poems, others in humorous style, often with illustrations. The keeping of a written record inspired the family, once the summer came to an end, to start a circular letter, "The Whirl." Many years later, Helen Perry Curtis used The Whirl as the inspiration for the "Round Robin" in *Jean & Company*. "'It's a fat letter that goes from one to the other, and keeps going all the time,'" Jean explains to her puzzled schoolmates. "'When it comes back to me again, I take out my old one and put in a new one. Each of you does the same, so that each time the letter comes, we all hear from everybody else.'"

The Doane clan kept The Whirl going for several years after the reunion on the Cape. No contribution was too small. Henry Perry wrote: "Dear Friends I think I am the youngest Whirl writer. We have a mourning dove nest in the study with one egg in it. Helen and I and Kenneth went down in the ravine and took off our shoes and stockings and had a dandy time and I went to the bridge with Kenneth when he went home. Good bye. Henry." Helen's contribution was a bit more substantive. "Dear Friends: I have been making May Baskets. I wish you were near enough so I could hang you some. I have got candy, violets, and cherry blossoms to fill them with. This year I am going to try to get a collection of leaves and flowers and I hope Grandma will teach me about them when she comes down. Good bye, Helen."

The summer on the Cape forged a friendship between "Me and Henry" and cousin Edward Twombly. The three exchanged letters, apart from The Whirl. "My dear Helen," Edward wrote:

I forgot to write you at Christmas. Have you had good coasting?... We spent Christmas at grandpa Twombly's house, I got on Christmas a game of bagatelle, a game of parcheesi, and a game of parlor croquet, games of flags, birds, robbing the miller, tiddlywinks, two puzzles, ten books, a penknife, a pencle, handkerchefs (sic), stamps, one dollar, and Youth's Companion.

Two years later, and with somewhat improved spelling, Edward wrote about a trip into New York City with his mother to see "Rip Van Wynkle," outlining the plot and adding, "Tell Henry that I didn't write to him because he didn't write me." Still, the two boys, two years apart in age, formed a special friendship. "Henry cried when Helen had a letter from Edward and he didn't, but when his came he was radically happy," Big Helen wrote to Frances. "How I do wish those two boys could grow up together." Big Helen got her wish. When Henry was eleven years old, he spent a year in Summit with the Twomblys. Mary Stone Perry's earlier observation proved an apt metaphor: "When the plants are large enough they are sent East where they are set out and budded, and in due time are returned to the West; the eastern soil being more favorable to the early growth of the tree after the budding."

If the gathering on Cape Cod marked the start of friendships among the youngest members of the family, it was the end of an era for their parents. On October 12, 1897, Thomas Doane suffered a heart attack, ironically, running to catch a train while he and Louisa were en route to Vermont to visit relatives. The attack was judged to be a mild one, and doctors treating him were optimistic. But on October 20 Big Helen received a telegram urging her to come at once to Vermont. She and her brother John traveled together from Lincoln, but upon reaching Boston they received the news that their father was dead. Thomas Doane's body was brought back to Charlestown, where he was laid out in the parlor of his beloved home on Pearl Street. Tributes poured in from colleagues, letters of sympathy and flowers from friends. Doane had dedicated the last years of his life to community service. He was the first president of the Charlestown branch of the YMCA, vice president of Hunt Asylum for Destitute Children, and on the board of directors of Associated Charities of Boston. He served for a decade, upon his return from Nebraska, as president of the Boston Society of Civil Engineers. In 1895, shortly before gathering his family one last time on Cape Cod, Thomas Doane fulfilled a lifelong wish: earning a college degree. Doane College intended to confer an honorary master of science degree, but Doane insisted on writing a thesis and defending it before a panel of faculty members. The Class of 1895 photo shows Doane, snowy beard contrasting with the black cap and gown, seated in the midst of students fifty years his junior.

Thomas Doane was buried in the cemetery at Orleans. Uncle Harry Twombly presided at the reading of the will. After providing annuities for each of his children and bequests for his grandchildren, the remainder of Thomas Doane's estate went to the college in Nebraska that bore his name.

Thomas Doane's death had a dramatic impact on the life of his grandson and namesake, Thomas Doane Perry. Tom graduated from Doane College in the spring of 1897, and was working in a railroad camp in the Black Hills at the time of his grandfather's death. "This is an entirely new experience. I think this outdoor work will be good for me," Tom wrote earlier that fall in The Whirl. "I am getting along finely, but am afraid I shall lose all my nice manners." The family made other plans for him. Tom would go to Boston, fulfilling sooner rather than later the hope of attending the Massachusetts Institute of Technology. He would live at 8 Pearl Street, caring for his widowed step-grandmother Louisa and Aunt Jane, the blind sister of his natural grandmother, Sophia Clark. Jane had been living with Thomas and Louisa, thus fulfilling the pledge Thomas Doane long ago made to his first mother-in-law: "Do not hesitate to make any demands on me you choose at any time." Tom Perry now inherited that promise. "It was a responsibility and care for a twenty-year-old lad," Big Helen wrote in her memoir, "but he rose to it as his father or grandfather would have done, and for five years he stood by the helm and made those two women happy." Tom completed an engineering degree at MIT. In Boston he met Ethel Goodenough Britten, a distant relative from Springfield, Vermont. Ethel was a graduate of Boston University and taught Latin and German. Tom and Ethel were married in October of 1903, three weeks before Louisa Doane passed away. Blind Aunt Jane preceded Louisa in death.

The remaining Perry children were growing up and moving on as well. Carl, described by his mother as "brilliant, good looking, a fine conversationalist . . . and determined to see the world," graduated from Doane in 1906, and entered the diplomatic service. His first assignment was in Turkey, still part of the Ottoman Empire, as secretary to the American consul at Trebizond. Helen graduated from Crete High School in 1906, the same year Carl finished college. She then enrolled at Doane College, following in the footsteps of her brothers.

Helen Perry, 1904.

High school and college brought Helen into closer contact with the ethnic and religious diversity of the town. Crete's population in 1900 was less than 4,000, but the town boasted eighty-three commercial, industrial, and professional businesses. The major industry was a grist mill, processing grain from the Nebraska plains, shipping as far away as Scotland. Twenty percent of Crete's population was foreign born.

The town's churches reflected this diversity. Catholic and Lutheran churches were the site of worship and community gatherings for the German population. Czechs attended the Czech Methodist Church or St. Ludmilla's Catholic Church, and socialized at Sokol Hall. Helen's father was eager to draw students from the Czech community to the college. He taught himself Czech, and recruited Czech-speaking faculty. By 1900 the Perrys employed the daughter of Czech immigrants, Mary Machacek, as a domestic.

When Helen was in college, Brainerd wrote her an affectionate letter.

> How the years skip along and the children grow up. A little while ago it was 'Me and Henry,' and the little girl was the very thoughtful guardian of the little boy. Now both are of more than usual size and insight.. . . I suppose every Father wants his daughter to be sheltered from hard knocks, live in comfort and luxury. I suppose no one could safely plan what the future should bring, even if our wishes could be realized. I have faith that you will bravely meet the future, whatever it may bring. God will make your life a blessing to many.

In 1908, following Helen's sophomore year at Doane College, Brainerd and Big Helen made the decision to send their daughter east to Summit for a year, as Henry had done before her. The ostensible reason was to be a companion to Aunt Frances, whose health was reportedly frail. The year in Summit would balance Helen's Nebraska childhood with a first-hand experience of the New England of her ancestors. Summit's proximity to New York would expose her to a social and cultural world far beyond that of the town on the Nebraska prairie.

On an afternoon in September, 1908, Helen boarded the train, heading East.

Chapter 2
Going East

H elen left Crete on Friday, September 17, 1908, and made her way across the Midwest. The train from Lincoln brought her, via Omaha and an overnight sleeper car, to Chicago. Her intermediate destination was Holland, Michigan, where she was met by her brother Tom, now living in Grand Rapids, where he worked as a materials expert in the city's furniture industry. They took a trolley to the recreation area of Lake Macatawa, where Tom, Ethel, and baby Frances were spending time at a cottage, escaping the heat in town. Tom and Helen swam in a lake so cold that a smoky fog hung low over the water, a foghorn providing its low but reassuring sound as a constant backdrop.

Helen was enamored of her six-week-old niece. "She is really pretty and cunning and sweet and everything else that Tom and Ethel said about her. . . . I suppose I'd spoil her terribly if I stayed here very long."

Helen resumed her trip, arriving in New York City on the evening of September 24. Uncle Harry met her, wearing a flower in his lapel. "I recognized Uncle Harry right off, without even looking for the rose geranium. He's just as jolly and good-looking as ever. I know we'll have lots of fun together." Uncle Harry guided Helen "through a series of tunnels and . . . elevated tracks . . . and trains on the level. It was like a maze, and I was glad I was not doing it all alone." The trip took them through the Hudson Tunnels under the river, transferring at Hoboken for the train to Summit, where Pierre, the Twomblys' coachman, met and drove them home. It was "lovely and cool, but too dark to see much." Helen was aware only of a winding street bordered on one side by a stone wall, and the sight of her aunt waiting on the porch. It would not be until the next morning that Helen would get a good look at the house where she would spend the coming year.

"I'm here," Helen wrote to her mother, "and it's perfectly lovely." The Twombly home on Hobart Avenue was one of a number of elegant mansions in an area recently developed northeast of downtown. The houses stood on a series of bluffs, the Watchung Mountain Ridge, which commanded a view stretching from Staten Island to Newark

Bay. During the Revolutionary War the area served as a vantage point from which British troop movements could be detected. "Old Sow," an eighteen-pounder alarm gun atop Step Hill, once called the Minutemen to arms. In 1896 Summit erected a monument, a three-ton boulder and plaque, commemorating the location. It was on this site that the Twomblys chose, a decade later, to build their new home. A local history of Summit recounts what happened next:

> In the course of negotiations for purchase of the property
> in 1907, Mrs. Henry B. Twombly wrote a letter to the [Sons
> of the American Revolution]: 'Probably no one in Summit
> has more interest in historic things than Mr. Twombly
> and I have. We are, both of us, in direct and side lines,
> descendants from the *Mayflower*, and should be Sons of
> the Revolution and Colonial Dames, and all the rest of the
> series. However, if we purchase the above lot, the stone
> would be in the dining room of the new house, or on the
> front porch. . . . We are willing, and glad, to put the stone in
> the retaining wall on the street front, at our own expense.[1]

Permission was granted, and the boulder, reduced in size, was built into the stone wall on the property. Helen noted on more than one occasion "all the people going past on their Sunday afternoon walks and drives. Stacks of people stop to look at the 'Old Sow' rock and read the inscription . . . and take pictures of it."

But it was the house itself that delighted Helen, and which she described in glowing terms. "I ran out of adjectives before I'd been through two rooms and all I can do now is just gaze with my mouth open." To one side of an entry hall and reception room stretched a large living room, the exposed beams of the low ceiling stained the same dark color as the woodwork. A "silky-looking kind of burlap" covered the walls of the living room, as well as the dining room across the hallway. A fieldstone fireplace was at the far end of the living room. A broad window seat looked out over the lawn, and French doors opened onto a side porch. At the back of the house, behind the living and dining room, were a kitchen, large pantry, hallway, and a parlor for the maids. Upstairs were several bedrooms, including a suite of two bedrooms,

---

[1] Twombly file, Summit Historical Society; Edmund B. Raftis, *Summit, New Jersey: From Poverty Hill to the Hill City* (Seattle: Great Swamp Press, 1996), 2-3; 28-32.

a bathroom, and access to a screened porch, all for Uncle Harry and Aunt Patty (as Frances was familiarly known). Helen's room was furnished with an enormous four-poster bed, raised high off the floor ("it's a good thing that I'm tall or I'd need a step-ladder to clamber in"), a washstand, bureau, table, and two comfortable armchairs. A window seat ran the length of the front of the room, overlooking the sloping lawn and garden. Helen, who would one day run an antiques and decorating business, wrote that "everything in [my room] is old. I'm going to find out the history of all the separate pieces of furniture."

The Twombly home on Hobart Avenue, Summit.
The Revolutionary War memorial boulder and plaque are visible.

The grounds of the Twombly home rivaled the beauty of the house. Flowers planted that spring by Aunt Patty now found their rival in the changing colors of autumn leaves. Dogwood and sumac bordered the rear of the property. Directly across the road was the ten-acre estate of John and Isabelle Wisner. The Wisners hired Calvert Vaux, a partner of Frederick Law Olmsted, to lay out the grounds of the estate. Vaux took advantage of the natural contours of the grounds, preserving or replanting wooded areas. Helen described "a regular young forest with all kinds of colors beginning to show. . . . I'll see a real . . . New England autumn." She could not know, as she admired the estate and befriended the Wisners' daughter Ellie, that some sixty years hence she would redecorate the house for its new owners.

In the absence of cousin Edward, who had already left for his freshman year at Yale, the remainder of the household consisted of three servants, all immigrants. In addition to the French-born coachman and handyman Pierre Trousset, the Twomblys employed two Irish maids, Nellie and Mary. The presence of Irish domestic help was a commonplace in Summit. A contemporary description labeled Summit a town of two societies, a "two-way population": the owners of large properties on the one hand and the workers they employed—nearly all Irish—on the other.[2] Helen wrote that Irish girls were drawn to working for the Twomblys. "[Mary] never had a beau and Aunt Patty had married off six or seven of her servants, so she thought this would be a good place to come." The strategy appeared to be working. "Fussy coachmen in fussy carriages come to see the girls and they have a nice little parlor off the kitchen to receive them in. Nellie appears to be a very popular young lady."

The Twomblys illustrate the changing nature of class and status in America. Helen's year in Summit unfolded against the backdrop of a larger story, that of Gilded Age America, an era marked by extremes of wealth and poverty, deepening class distinctions, and unprecedented waves of immigration. By the turn of the century, the markers of status were shifting from the once highly regarded professions of ministry and law to those of science and engineering, industry and finance. Helen's father, like Uncle Harry's a generation earlier, followed the path of ordained ministry and a career in academe. Although highly respected, these professions did not bring wealth. Indeed, Helen witnessed her father's financial struggles with the college and the sacrifices her family made to support the college. Uncle Harry Twombly was a transitional figure: a lawyer, with a practice in corporate law. But even this rung of status and wealth was eclipsed by the fortunes accumulated by the bankers and industrialists, displayed in another branch of the Twombly family.

To chart this evolution, one must go back to Uncle Harry's grandfather, Alexander Hamilton Twombly. Alexander married twice: first Mary Perley and then, following her death, Caroline McKown. One of the two sons born to the first marriage was Uncle Harry's father, Alexander Stevenson Twombly. A.S., as he was known, graduated

---

[2] *Summit Herald*, April 23, 1940.

from Yale and, following study in Heidelberg (the exact path followed by Helen's father), was ordained from Andover Theological Seminary. Reverend Twombly was a teacher, prolific author, and longtime pastor at Charlestown's historic Winthrop Church, serving in that capacity from 1872-1891. Harry and Frances (Patty) met at Winthrop Church, and were married there in 1889, the groom's father witnessing the ceremony.

Uncle Harry was the second of five sons born to Reverend A.S. Twombly and Abigail Quincy Bancroft (also the descendant of a prominent Boston family). Harry and his brother Edward followed in their father's footsteps, attending Yale. Harry would be remembered for his career there as a football player in the three winning seasons, 1881-1883 (21-0-1), the first two seasons played alongside Walter Camp, future storied Yale coach and "Father of American Football." Harry is credited by some with inventing quarterback signals. The two Twombly brothers went on to Harvard: Edward to medical school and Henry to law school.

The other branch of the family took a different course. One child was born of grandfather Alexander Hamilton Twombly's second marriage, Hamilton McKown Twombly. Hamilton graduated from Harvard in 1871, and went to work for William Henry Vanderbilt, son of Commodore Cornelius Vanderbilt, and thus heir to the family fortune. Hamilton rose rapidly in the esteem of his employer, and was appointed to boards of directors of railroad, banking, and industrial concerns. In 1877 Hamilton married his employer's daughter, Florence Vanderbilt. Florence and Hamilton were numbered among "The Four Hundred," New York society's elite. Hamilton and Florence began acquiring property, consisting eventually of 1,200 acres, in Morris County, New Jersey. There they built an estate which they named Florham, combining the first syllables of their names. Designed by the firm of McKim, Mead and White, at 110 rooms the house remains to this day one of the ten largest private residences ever built in the United States. The family divided its time between several residences, spending spring and autumn at Florham, winter in their Fifth Avenue townhouse, and summering at Vinland, their estate in Newport.

There is no evidence of a close relationship between Uncle Harry and his half-uncle Hamilton, but Helen was certainly aware of the connection. That autumn, while en route to Clinton, New Jersey, in the company of a Doane cousin, they stopped for petrol outside Madison when another traveler approached and asked for directions to the Twombly estate. "Of course, he meant Uncle Ham Twombly's, but it seemed so funny that he should pick on us for said information." Helen added that Aunt Patty often said that she "[shines] in reflected light of said wealthy relative, and it's always wisest to pay for things before she gives her name." On another occasion, Helen went for a drive with a Summit neighbor. "Coming back, we drove around by Uncle Ham Twombly's big place. The house itself is a perfect monster, more like an institution of some sort than anything else." Helen's remark was prescient. In 1957 the house and 178 acres of land were purchased by Fairleigh Dickinson University to serve as the Morris County campus of the university. Helen reported that Florham had thirty-five rooms just for the servants. "Wouldn't that make a nice suite for the only poor lone servant they'd be able to get if they lived in Nebraska? Imagine Minnie in them!"

Helen quickly became familiar with Summit, regularly driving Uncle Harry (by horse and surrey) to the station for his daily commute to Manhattan. The town Helen encountered was a relatively new one, despite the fact that European settlement dated to the 1730s. Summit was incorporated in 1899, raised from township status. The population grew rapidly, from 5,300 in 1900 to 7,500 a decade later. Summit was still small enough, however, that mail addressed to "Helen Perry, Summit, New Jersey," reached her, evidence also that the post office knew of the presence of Henry and Patty Twombly's niece in Summit.

Henry B. Twombly, "Uncle Harry."   Frances Doane Twombly, "Aunt Patty."

A building boom preceded Summit's incorporation. Executed for the most part in either the elegant Beaux-Arts or Richardsonian Romanesque styles, Summit during the 1890s acquired a town hall, post office, public library, YMCA, and opera house. The Atheneum, with its regular lecture program, was founded in 1908 by a group led by Hamilton Wright Mabie, essayist and editor of *Outlook* magazine, a leading publication of the day. Taken together, these institutions were "indications of the intellectual aspirations of the community." [3]

Summit's geography presented a challenge to the newcomer. Streets and roads were laid out in serpentine curves and intersected, when they did, on nothing resembling a grid pattern. One day, attempting a different route home from the station, Helen got so turned around that she ended up on the opposite side of town, at the home of Alexander and Sophie Twombly, Uncle Harry's younger brother and his wife. It was a happy error, however, in that the couple, along with eighteen-year-old son Alexander and nine-year-old daughter Ellen, were fast becoming close friends. The route to their home would become a familiar one. Helen took to referring to every member of this family as "cousin."

Helen's circle of friends grew rapidly as well. In addition to Ellie Wisner across the road, she met another Hobart Avenue neighbor, Hilda Osborn ("a jolly girl"). Both Ellie and Hilda had graduated the previous spring from Kent Place School. Helen had been in Summit only a few days when Hilda invited her to an after-school tea party with five or six girls from Kent Place. "Very jolly, most of them a little younger, tho." This was hardly surprising, as Helen had completed two years of college while the Kent Place girls were still in high school.

Kent Place School was founded in 1894 by a group of Summit men who wanted their daughters to have educational opportunities equal to those available to their sons in the several all-boys private schools in town. The second woman to serve as Head of School at Kent Place was Sarah Woodman Paul, who held that post from 1896 until 1924. Widowed at a young age, Mrs. Paul made Kent Place her life's work. A graduate of Wellesley, she taught at the college and served there in an administrative post prior to coming to Kent Place. There Sarah Woodman Paul introduced many of the customs and rituals of the Seven Sisters colleges. She turned Kent Place into a feeder school for those elite colleges, sending numbers of graduates to the Seven Sisters. Over the course of the year Helen joined Kent Place students at a

[3] Raftis, 124.

performance of a Wellesley school play and at the Wellesley Fête Day in New York. Helen and Mrs. Paul became friends. Helen was invited to dinner, and asked to referee basketball games and serve as a judge at public speaking competitions at the school. In a future she could not yet glimpse, Helen's daughter Polly would one day graduate from Kent Place and go on to Vassar.

Life in Summit assumed a comfortable routine. Any thought that Helen was there to actually take care of Aunt Patty was quickly dispelled. She was treated, as she noted on numerous occasions, as the daughter Uncle Harry and Aunt Patty never had. In Edward's absence, Helen brought a whirl of youthful activity into the house. Two weeks after arriving in Summit, she wrote that she needed to "sport up in my best bib and tucker and return the eight calls I've had" from Kent Place friends. Helen regularly played golf with Uncle Harry, his brother Alex or young Alexander—sometimes all three—with Ellen as caddy. And Aunt Patty, Helen discovered, shared her love for clothes. The two pulled from Aunt Patty's closets numerous gowns: pale grey chiffon, black lace, a silk waist, all in need of fixing. "I'm not the only one who is persnickety about my clothes, and it suits me exactly to have a lot of pretty duds to sew on and make over." Helen took over the task of arranging flowers from the garden ("that's to be my permanent job"), filling sixteen vases at a time. Evenings, joined by Uncle Harry and often cousins Alex and Sophie Twombly as well, they read aloud to each other or looked through Uncle Harry's scrapbooks. Uncle Harry taught Helen to play bezique, coached on by Aunt Patty, and they took turns playing cribbage, a game at which Helen eventually bested her uncle. Aunt Patty played the pianola while Helen and Uncle Harry danced. Young Alexander introduced them to a novelty: jigsaw puzzles, which he made and cut.

> Have they gotten the puzzle craze in Nebraska yet? They're pictures pasted on wood, and cut in tiny pieces with a jig-saw. . . . I wish you could see my intellectual aunt slaving for hours over one of those things, pretending she hates them, and not able to keep her hands off of them when they're in the house. We'll all be driveling idiots soon, if the puzzle fad doesn't let up.

Sundays took on a tempo of their own. Helen went to church with Uncle Harry (Aunt Patty for the most part stayed home, citing frail health). The special atmosphere of Sundays carried into the evenings, when the maids had the night off. Uncle Harry and Helen took over the kitchen to prepare supper, with ensuing hilarity. On at least one occasion Aunt Patty intervened, fearing that otherwise the two of them would eat the whole supper before it made it to the table.

There was a serious side to Sundays as well, and one that showed the other side of Gilded Age Summit. Harry and Helen spent the afternoons at Neighborhood House, the settlement house located in Summit's industrial north end. Established in 1900 by Pastor Theodore White of Central Presbyterian Church (where the Twomblys worshipped), and modeled on Chicago's Hull House (founded by Jane Addams), Neighborhood House served the Armenian immigrants employed in Summit's silk mills. The lot of domestic servants was enviable compared with that of the mill workers. Men and women stirred vats of toxic dyes and carried the wet fabric with their bare hands to the dying rooms. Miserable as the mills were in the heat of summer, they were worse in winter. Drippings from the dyed fabrics formed treacherous sheets of ice on the floors, and workers' clothes froze to their bodies while walking home at the end of a shift.

The settlement house brought a benevolent approach to the problems of immigrant labor; at the same time, it sought to be a moderating influence in what might otherwise be fertile ground for radicalism. Summit's silk mills experienced labor unrest a decade earlier when mill workers went on strike, and owners' attempts to bring in replacement workers resulted in a riot. Programs at the settlement house included a kindergarten, evening classes in English for adults, and a variety of clubs for women and girls which combined the teaching of skills useful for future employment with instruction in child rearing and housekeeping. Critics charged that settlement workers were imposing middle-class standards of parenting and hygiene on families whose low wages, housing conditions, and need for outside employment of women rendered those standards unachievable. Longtime head resident at Neighborhood House, Grace Paine, acknowledged this tension when she recalled that initial efforts were met with hostility: "[S]tones were thrown at the workers by way of saying they didn't want to be done good to. And who could blame them? They don't want missionaries. They wanted opportunities like most of us human creatures." [4]

---

[4] Grace E. Paine, "Early Memories of the Neighborhood House," *Summit Herald*, November 12, 1935, cited in Raftis, 172.

Uncle Harry was involved with Neighborhood House from its origins until 1946, when its doors closed. Grace Paine was a frequent guest at the Twombly home, and Helen soon counted Miss Paine among her friends. Uncle Harry was superintendent of the Sunday school at Neighborhood House (Harry's brother Alex was its secretary) and taught a class there every week. Helen began helping with the classes. Neighborhood House's 1908 annual report lists Miss Helen Perry as one of the teachers. She assisted with other activities at the settlement as well. [5] Helen's contact with immigrants in Summit built on her familiarity with Germans and Czechs in Crete, and provided a basis for work she would one day do at the Newark Museum, showcasing immigrant culture.

Aunt Patty also involved Helen in civic volunteerism. Patty was active in the Central Presbyterian Church, and was a founder of Neighborhood House. She was a charter member of the Fortnightly Club, an organization dedicated to community service. As was the case throughout American towns and cities, Summit's women's organizations took the lead in establishing a public library. The Fortnightly Club gave birth to Summit's Town Improvement Association, of which Aunt Patty served as president for a total of seventeen years. This was an example of the kind of benevolent reform carried out by middle class women which historians have labeled "social housekeeping." The Town Improvement Association initiated and supervised programs for the removal of snow, ashes, and garbage. Aunt Patty—driven by the faithful Pierre—made inspection tours in winter to see that walkways were cleared of snow so children could walk safely to school. Patty served on Summit's Playground Commission, a forerunner of the Board of Recreation Commission. She earned the title "Mother of Recreation" for the role she played in the creation of Soldiers' Memorial Field in Summit. The Fortnightly Club also hosted a regular program of speakers on cultural and civic topics, and Helen on occasion attended meetings with her aunt.

Evenings at the Twombly home were an education in social and civic awareness. In addition to Neighborhood House's Grace Paine, another frequent guest was Mary White. A contemporary of Uncle Harry and Aunt Patty, Miss White was the daughter of Reverend Theodore White. For all his progressive views when it came to immigrants, Reverend White refused to allow Mary to attend college, believing that her role

---

[5] "Annual Statement of the Work of the Neighborhood House for 1908," 6, Summit Historical Society.

was to stay home and assist her mother at the parsonage. Despite her lack of a college education, or perhaps because of her father's intransigence in that regard, Mary became a passionate advocate of women's rights. She was a friend of suffrage leader Carrie Chapman Catt. By 1915 Mary White was working full-time for the cause of women's suffrage. She served, along with Uncle Harry, on the executive board of Neighborhood House, was president of the Fortnightly Club, and an advocate for expansion of the town's public library.[6]

Having mastered Summit's serpentine streets, to the point of finding her way home one autumn night from cousins Alex and Sophie's house in a thick fog ("I can easily imagine the blood and thundering stunts that are performed in Dickens novels on foggy nights now"), Helen was ready to take on New York City. Since that evening in September when Uncle Harry met her train, Helen had been to the city—which she dubbed "the Great and Wicked"—three times. In mid-October Uncle Harry took her to a spectacle at the new Hippodrome.[7] Helen returned a few days later with cousin Sophie. "I'm getting so I can say 'the city' in a nonchalant and careless manner, just as if I had lived next to the 'G.+W.' all my life." The two went to all the "fussy stores," McCleary's, Best's, Stears, and Lord and Taylor. Helen described the "walking fashion plates" encountered in the stores and on the sidewalks. On a final New York trip before going solo, Helen accompanied cousin Sophie, and then met her cousin Everett Perry (Everett and Helen's fathers were brothers) and his wife Lilla. Everett was a librarian, and private secretary to the director of the Astor Library, an institution later absorbed into the New York Public Library. Helen described the Perrys' "tiny little flat" on Amsterdam Avenue as "very modern and pretty," with "furniture, pictures, and baby grand piano [that] just seem to fit it." Lilla took Helen to a matinee performance by the German pianist Emil Sauer. Sauer, a student of Rubenstein and Liszt, and considered

[6] Raftis, 173.
[7] Reputed to be the largest theater in the world, and a relatively new attraction in New York, the Hippodrome was billed as a venue that "democratizes theater-going in the same way that department stores had democratized shopping." This did not prevent the builders from indulging in luxury. The Beaux-Arts building boasted an interior of deep reds with accents of gold, silver, and ivory. The performance Helen witnessed consisted of a comedic play, a boat race, a baseball game, a horse race, and a circus with a dozen trained polar bears. She described a futuristic "Battle of the Skies" set in 1950, where "the fighting was all done with airships and radium guns." Helen could not know, on that October day in 1908, how sinister a portent of her own future, a decade hence, was this supposed fantasy battle.

one of the premier artists of the time, was in the midst of an American tour. Helen and Lilla shopped at a local market on their way home, and prepared a small dinner party that evening, with Helen staying to help with the dishes afterwards. Lilla played the baby grand piano after dinner for her guests. "We had a hilarious time. Everett and she are both awfully jolly, and seem very happy together."

In mid-November, Helen ventured solo into New York, taking the train from Summit. "Aunt Patty has just been drawing me a map of the great and wicked city, which I am to inhabit tomorrow, *all alone!* In other words, your young and innocent daughter is going on a sightseeing lark without a guardian. Won't that be fun!"

The Hudson Tubes station brought Helen directly to the shopping district known as the Ladies' Mile. Centered on Sixth Avenue between West 14th and 23rd Streets, and catering to the so-called carriage trade, the Ladies Mile was home to Altman, Bergdorf Goodman, Lord and Taylor, and Tiffany's. Helen wandered the stores, getting Christmas ideas. She went to Forsyth's, where she selected items to be sent to Summit on approval for Aunt Patty. From there to Wanamaker's, "a perfect whopper of a place, with a big new addition. It nearly took my breath away to be casually referred to the seventh or seventeenth floor as nonchalantly as if it were 'next aisle over' when I asked where such and such things were."

While captivated, Helen's Nebraska-bred thriftiness was affronted. "I've never seen so much condensed cash in the shape of clothes and carriages and livery in my life before. Your country daughter stood with open mouth and gazed, I'm afraid." She was amused by the sight of the well-to-do clientele on the Ladies Mile.

> I saw a trim footman in green livery standing very solemnly
> and stiffly opposite from the doors of one of the big stores,
> holding an extremely diminutive and homely pup by a
> tether until his fussy mistress returned, I suppose. He (the
> footman, not the pup) was as solemn and stately as if he
> were lord of all he surveyed, and the pup looked dejected in
> the extreme.

Helen might, on shopping trips to New York, order quantities of hats, "waists," and accessories to be sent to Summit for Aunt Patty's inspection and approval, but for herself she shopped for fabric and trimmings and made (or re-made) her own clothes and hats. She was dismayed by the prices in the stores. Visiting a hat shop in New York City she told the clerk that she wanted a perfectly simple and very inexpensive hat

> and when the girl said "I suppose you mean about twenty-five dollars. We keep nothing under that," you should have seen your crushed and sat-on daughter beat it out the door. These patronizing shop girls, who deign to wait on poor poverty-stricken mortals like me, make you feel as if you were the scum of the earth and nothing more.

Twenty-five dollars was the sum total of the check that Helen brought with her to Summit from Nebraska.

New York did, over the course of the year, become for Helen not only "the city" of nonchalant reference but another portent of her future. One trip made a strong impression. She wrote to her mother about a visit to the Museum of Natural History. "Someday I am going to camp out in there until I've absorbed it all." She described bird specimens displayed in natural-looking settings, tree branches and flowers blending with painted backgrounds. Invisible wires held the birds suspended so that they appeared to be in mid-flight. "I still have visions of snakes and whales and diamonds and chrysanthemums all spinning around in my head at once. I was fairly dizzy when I got out." Eight years later, as director of the State Museum in Trenton, Helen would mount a bird exhibit identical to that which she described at the Museum of Natural History.

Almost as memorable was a trip to the Metropolitan Museum of Art in early December. Helen had already visited the museum; this time she was the guest of one of the curators, Fanny Morris. Helen joined female staff members in the little basement lunchroom the women ran co-operatively, taking turns providing lunch, and employing a domestic to do the clean-up afterwards. Miss Morris invited Helen to return anytime she wished. "It's fun to get on the inside track of things like that."

The cozy lunchroom was a metaphor for the largely female society Helen inhabited during her year in Summit. Aunt Patty early on, and teasingly, made Helen promise not to marry any of the men she met while in Summit, a request to which Helen could readily accede. In addition to Uncle Harry and his brother Alex, Helen's male companions during that year were cousins Edward and Alexander, and Helen's brother Carl.

Helen had not seen Edward since the family reunion in 1895, when Edward was four years old. The young man who arrived home from Yale one weekend in October, as a surprise for his mother, was equally a surprise to Helen. "He is big and tall and fine-looking, and straight as an arrow. I don't wonder his mother is proud of him." In Edward's presence, Helen reverted to her self-described "harum-scarum" tomboy self. The two went boating in a clothes basket on the highly polished wood floors only to capsize, and, upon "hearing my stern aunt approaching, we beat it." In more serious moments, Helen and Edward shared long conversations about Yale. Edward confided to Helen that he had always hoped that Henry would someday go to Yale with him. "I wish he and Henry might know each other better," Helen wrote wistfully.

Cousin Edward Twombly.

Brother Carl's arrival was more problematic. Helen cautiously discussed the circumstances surrounding it in her letters. Carl had been in Turkey for two years, serving at the American consulate. In Paris, already en route home, he lost a significant sum of money gambling. "Poor boy! His home-coming won't be near as much fun for him, but we'll be all the gladder to see him, won't we? I'm thankful that he's all right physically as he might not have been if he'd taken a drink with those old fellows and been drugged." Once Carl had safely arrived, Helen wrote to her mother that "we haven't said anything about Carl's fix at this end of the line, and I don't believe it will get out. It would be too bad for him if it did."

"This end of the line" apparently referred to those outside the Twombly household, because Uncle Harry clearly was in charge of the situation. He and Helen met Carl's boat when it docked at Hoboken. After dinner, the two men retreated behind the doors of Uncle Harry's study. Details of what transpired emerged from Helen's letters. Uncle Harry gave Carl two hundred dollars outright, and loaned him another two hundred.[8] Carl was to study for the civil service exam, with the goal of advancing in the diplomatic service. A neighbor of the Twomblys', a professor at Columbia University, secured library privileges for Carl; cousin Everett Perry provided entrée to the Astor Library. Uncle Harry kept Carl on a short leash. Carl attended Republican Party meetings with Uncle Harry in the evenings, as the fall presidential election neared (despite the fact that the Perrys were Democrats). "Carl wants to get next to the political questions as much as possible," Helen wrote. Carl went into New York every morning with Uncle Harry, and on weekends accompanied him to Sunday school at Neighborhood House.

Big Helen once described her son with startling honesty as a young man who graduated from college with honors in oratory, and "might have had them in scholarship if he had worked." Validation of this maternal judgment comes from the fact that, while Helen wrote lengthy letters to her mother twice weekly, keeping her abreast of Carl's studies and relaying requests ("he wants his calling cards sent out *at once* as he may need them"), Carl's only communication to his mother came in the form of a hastily scrawled post-script to one of Helen's letters:

Dear Mimsie: Going in on the train and haven't time for much. Things are moving nicely and I'm digging in. Have seen Everett at Astor Library and he has put me on to the ropes there. Then [I have] a card to the Columbia Library and I have found some fine reference books at both places. I have two sets of old examination questions which I'm working over to get at the general idea and am picking up lots of useful knowledge. . . . And so it goes. Am a little worried because of the number—60 to 70—to be examined, for there are few vacancies at present. However, we'll see. Love, Carl.

Over the course of the next few months Carl succeeded in passing the exam and returning to diplomatic service. In the meantime, his presence in Summit was a source of male companionship as well as fun at the expense of Helen's friends. "I had some of the Kent Place girls

---

[8] Uncle Harry's financial settlement with Carl was substantial, inasmuch as the average annual income in 1908 was between two and four hundred dollars.

quite excited about the fussy man who went to church with me but they were rather less awed when I informed them that it was my brother!"

Helen's Summit men, and then some, came together for the weekend of the Harvard-Yale football game in New Haven on November 21. Helen had been writing about the tantalizing possibility of that game almost from the time she arrived in Summit, when Uncle Harry dangled the prospect that they might attend the game. Early in November Helen reported that she and Carl had an invitation from Fred and Henry Fairchild and Cheney Jones to come to the game and to spend a day or two before or after. "Won't that be jolly?"

Harvard-Yale Football Game, November 1908. Fred Fairchild, Helen Perry, Molly Townsend, Hal Fairchild.

Fred and Henry (Hal) were the sons of Brainerd Perry's Doane College colleague, Professor Arthur Fairchild. Fred graduated from Doane in 1898, Hal in 1900. Both went on to Yale for graduate work in economics. In 1908 they were on the first rung of academic careers, as instructors at Yale. Fred would enjoy a long tenure there, retiring in 1946 as professor emeritus; Hal would join the faculty of New York University.

Cheney Jones was a former chore boy at The Grange, a job that enabled him to attend Doane College. Cheney, whose mother died when he was young, found in Big Helen a surrogate mother. "She stayed awake at night, until Carl and I returned from affairs, called downstairs, 'Is that you, boys? Wait, I am coming down,' and in slippers and dressing gown she sat at the foot of the stairs with us gathering all the details of the evening." Big Helen gave parties in Cheney and Carl's names. When Cheney graduated from Doane, Brainerd arranged with the dean of the Yale Law School to give Cheney a job in the library in exchange for tuition. If Kent Place functioned as a pipeline to the Seven Sisters, Brainerd Perry was initiating something of the same between Doane and Yale. [9]

Helen's letter describing the football weekend overflows with superlatives. "Well, to begin with, I've had the dandiest time that ever happened!! More fun than I've ever had before, or ever expect to again, because there can be only one *first* Yale-Harvard game." Helen and Carl left Summit early on Saturday morning for New York City. (Uncle Harry had gone up to New Haven the day before to attend a meeting of alumni of Skull and Bones, Yale's pre-eminent senior society.) At Grand Central Station Helen and Carl boarded one of six special trains, each consisting of twenty cars, bound for New Haven. The station in New Haven, upon their arrival, was a sea of red roses and blue violets; men bringing flowers for sweethearts and sisters according to Harvard Crimson or Yale Blue affiliation. Hal and Cheney met the train, presenting Helen with a huge bunch of violets. The group went first to the home of Molly Townsend, a New Haven girl who was Hal's fiancée. "Molly is fine!" Helen wrote to her mother. "Carl and I immediately followed Hal's example and fell in love with her too."

From there the group adjourned to Yale's Dining Commons. The weekend of the Harvard-Yale game was the one occasion when women were allowed to eat there. Afterwards, they made their way through the crowd of some 35,000 spectators, to the stadium. "The streets were jammed, traffic was blocked ... the [street]cars were full to overflowing and mobs more waiting to get on and all you could see were pennants and violets and red roses. Finally, we got standing room on the back platform of a car, and nearly had our eyes jabbed out with 'merry widows' [hats] and stiff feathers."

Helen described the back and forth of play, concluding that "everybody agreed that Harvard earned her victory." The band played "The Battle Hymn of the Republic" as the Harvard bleachers emptied onto the field. The procession wound its way under the winning team's goalpost, the men throwing their hats into the air over the bar, "regardless of whether he or somebody else got it. . . . One of Edward's friends threw up a two-dollar Derby and caught a five-dollar one that fitted, which was a good investment."

[9] Thomas Doane Perry, ed., *History of Doane College 1872-1912* (Crete, NE: Doane College, 1957), 219-221.

Helen went to the boarding house where Fred and Hal roomed, and where Helen had a "little room off the kitchen that was very comfortable and oodles nicer than being stuck off somewhere in a hotel." Mrs. Doty, the landlady, was "perfectly lovely," and Helen was entertained by the resident Angora kitten. Afterwards the men rejoined them and everyone went to Molly's home for the evening. The return to town was boisterous. "You should have seen us coming home . . . at twelve o'clock, with the boys singing Yale songs at the top of their voices. We ought to have been arrested, but luckily we happened to be very quiet and sedate the only time we met a policeman."

The New Haven weekend was rounded out with Sunday church services and a visit to Edward's rooms. On Monday, after breakfast with Mrs. Doty, Helen said goodbye "to the whole bunch, including the kitten which I wanted to swipe," and Hal and Carl took her to the train. Carl remained in New Haven until Wednesday, when he and Edward would travel home together for Thanksgiving. "I certainly had a peach of a time, and was mighty proud of the bunch of Nebraska boys. They're just about right, every one of them, and Molly's a peach. . . . I had the time of my life."

Thanksgiving launched the holiday season, which dominated the ensuing weeks. Edward and Carl arrived in Summit, and the indulgent Aunt Patty's patience was tried when the three cousins carried on a pillow and wet sponge fight, dodging each other in the upstairs hallway, ducking in and out of their bedrooms for safety. More decorously, Helen shopped for chrysanthemums for centerpieces for the table, and made place cards with illustrations and clever rhymes. On Thanksgiving morning Helen joined Uncle Harry, Edward, and Carl for a round of golf ("I played terribly, but it was lots of fun just the same"). Dinner brought together a number of Twombly and Doane relatives, including cousins Alex and Sophie and their children.

The approaching Christmas holidays meant shopping trips to New York, with Helen planning a variety of homemade gifts—bookmarks, letter openers, calendars—for family and friends at home as well as in Summit. She made calendars for the YMCA Bazaar. Volunteers dressed fifty-eight dolls for the Neighborhood House Christmas party.

Helen's letters regularly ended with a plea to her mother to "come East" for Christmas. Big Helen did just that, arriving on New Year's Day, having spent Christmas with Tom and Ethel and baby Frances in Grand Rapids. Carl, still awaiting news from Washington about an assignment, met her train in New York. It was the first time mother and son had seen each other since Carl went to Turkey two years earlier. Brainerd arrived late in January, staying into February before making the rounds of potential donors to the college. Helen had on several occasions broached just this subject.

> A New York friend of Uncle Harry's . . . suggested that
> dad should write to John S. Kennedy, 10 West 57th, New
> York City, about money. He's a Presbyterian, so dad had
> better not say too much about the college denomination,
> but he has given a little to Congregationalists, and is
> giving an extra amount to everything now because of some
> anniversary or other that he's celebrating.

Elsewhere she wrote: "I'd like to throttle some portly millionaire around here and make him hand over a little cash, which is not a ladylike idea at all, but would serve a purpose."

Given her mother's presence in Summit, there is a gap in Helen's letters, from mid-December until April 4, 1909. The only source for those four months is Big Helen's "Line a Day" diary, which she began keeping, fortuitously, on January 1, 1909, continuing it to the last days of her life.

Big Helen spent January in Summit with Helen, Carl, and the Twomblys, quickly fitting into the routine of lunches and dinners with cousins Sophie and Alex, meetings at the Fortnightly Club with her sister Patty, and shopping trips to New York with her daughter. Early February brought good news for Carl: an assignment to the American consulate in Halifax, Nova Scotia. He was to sail from Boston. This coincided with Big Helen's plans to go to Boston in February with her daughter to visit Doane and Perry relations there. Brainerd joined them, and all three of them saw Carl off. The two Helens stayed in the Boston area until early March, when they returned to New Jersey by way of New Haven. There they saw Edward, and Big Helen enjoyed an affectionate reunion with Cheney Jones. Fred and Hal Fairchild and Molly joined them as well. It was an opportunity for Big Helen to meet Hal's fiancée, so as to be able to report to the Fairchilds, who had not yet met their future daughter-in-law. Sunday, March 7, was Brainerd's seventieth birthday, and the family gathered in Summit before Brainerd made further fundraising visits in Baltimore and Washington D.C.

Big Helen left Summit for Crete in early April. A week later was Easter, and Edward came home for spring break. Easter weekend at the Twomblys' mixed the sacred and profane. Helen, Edward, and Uncle Harry attended a communion service on Holy Thursday evening at Central Presbyterian Church. On Good Friday Uncle Harry took a day of vacation, and they played golf. Saturday evening Helen and Edward went to New York to see the opera *Götterdämmerung*. For Helen, it was the visual display that captured her attention. "I'll never forget it. The scenery . . . water and mermaids and boats and fire, and all kinds of beautiful scenic effects."

The real adventure came afterwards. The performance, four and a half hours in length, ended just before midnight. Helen and Edward raced down Broadway, catching the elevated train connecting to the Hudson Tunnels, and arriving in Hoboken in time to see their train pulling out of the station. They passed the time happily at an ice cream parlor before catching the last train to Summit, only to find the house locked and Edward without his key. The pair went in search of a ladder to climb through a second-story window. The commotion woke Aunt Patty, who admitted the chastened miscreants. They made up for it by attending church in the morning, teaching Sunday school in the afternoon, and going to an Easter meeting at the mission in the evening.

Spring came late to Summit, with snowstorms lasting past Easter. But the appearance of May flowers signaled the changing of the season and the approaching end of Helen's stay. "I found my first white violets and wild azaleas, and swiped some lilac blossoms from Mr. Bennett's place."

May brought two weddings: Hal and Molly's in New Haven, and that of the Twomblys' Irish domestic, Mary, whose goal in coming to work for Aunt Patty was accomplished. Helen and Aunt Patty attended Mary's wedding, and Helen's impressions of the ceremony were unfavorable. "It was a quiet wedding and we were the only spectators. . . . I think the Catholic marriage ceremony is the limit. Just a monotonous Latin oration with a little Holy Water sprinkled in. . . . What on earth can a ceremony like that mean to anybody?" Helen was equally skeptical of a high church Episcopal service she earlier attended in New York.

> I had never dreamt that anybody but Catholics could have so much ceremony. There were candle-bearers and choir boys, and an orchestra, and a chorus of mixed voices in the gallery. . . . Then the priest or rector was dressed as

elaborately as the pope and had two men to hold up his gown and another to carry his hat. . . . [T]he rest of the ceremony, the robes and the candles and the incense and the bowing and crossing were too much for me.

Helen had not yet arrived at the point where church rituals were a part of her artistic outlook, a view she would develop with exposure to William Morris, the Gothic Revival, and the Arts and Crafts movement. The time would come when Helen would write in *Jean & Company* of visiting the Salzburg cathedral, where "the dim light filtering through the stained-glass windows, the people slipping softly in and out, the occasional priest moving around the altar, the flickering candles in the dusky chapels all made a deep impression on Jean."

Helen also demonstrated a degree of insensitivity, or simply immaturity, when it came to poor Mary: "She's going to keep on living with us, as her hubby hasn't a steady job yet. So, of course, we're delighted that her hubby *hasn't* a steady job." There is a similar tone-deafness in Helen's reaction to some of what she encountered at Neighborhood House. While trying to teach "the kidlets" a lesson about Moses, one small boy insisted on talking about the bedbugs at their house, and the best ways to kill them. "All of which sounds disgusting on paper but was really howlingly funny because it was told in such a guileless and confidential way. I am still trying to think what on earth the connection is between Moses and bedbugs." She later wrote of another incident wherein, talking about Gideon, she asked the children if they knew what fleece was. "And this was the answer: 'Like mosquitoes, only smaller!'"

Nevertheless, Helen's affection for the settlement children was evident. She supervised forty-eight children in planting a garden: setting beans, radishes, onions, carrots, lettuce, and corn in forty-eight garden beds. Uncle Harry's Sunday school boys came to the Twombly house, where "they've all had a dandy time shooting at targets and playing baseball, and racing, and particularly eating." To mark the end of the school year, volunteers took a hundred children on a picnic, piling them into three large horse-drawn wagons: flags waving, horns tooting, and children shouting at the top of their lungs. "I had two kidlets on my lap most of the time, with about six others to hold in, and the small boys standing on the back step, or hanging out over the wheel." At the picnic grounds Helen had her hands full, preventing children from falling into the river, pulling them out of trees, "and comforting at least three weeps a minute. . . . I guess all the teachers slept the sleep of the just that night."

In another portent of her future, Helen wrote about the festival held at Neighborhood House that spring. "The kidlets sang and the different nationalities dressed in their native costumes and there were beautiful rugs and tapestries and embroideries on exhibition."

For Helen, who had grown up on a college campus, the end of the school year was a season unto itself. Uncle Harry went up to New Haven for the twenty-fifth anniversary of his graduation. Edward joined him at the Class of '84 luncheon ("all the sons were invited"). Helen participated in Commencement events at Kent Place. The festivities demonstrated again how thoroughly Sarah Woodman Paul had adapted the rituals of the elite women's colleges to the school.[10] On Sunday afternoon, Helen attended baccalaureate services at the Episcopal church. The next morning, cousins Alex and Sophie's daughter Ellen, a fourth grader at Kent Place, coaxed Helen and Aunt Patty into picking daisies for the ceremonial Daisy Chain. In a description straight out of contemporary accounts of Commencement Week at Vassar, Helen wrote that she had never seen anything prettier than the acres of daisies in the meadow from which the three of them each picked a full bushel basket. Arriving at the school, Helen saw groups of students weaving the chain, decorating the lawn, and hanging lanterns. That afternoon was the Rose Festival, a combination folk festival and belated May Day celebration. The entire student body, dressed all in white, marched across the lawn carrying the Daisy Chain, taking their places in a circle marked off with poles and festooned with flowers. A senior girl was the May Queen. The smallest girls, wearing aprons and carrying milking stools and tiny pails, did a "hippity-hop milkmaids' dance." The middle-school students, including Ellen, in Colonial dress and powdered wigs, danced a minuet. Older girls performed a May Pole dance. Mr. Hamilton Mabie, the celebrated local author, delivered the commencement address, and the graduating seniors received their diplomas.

The celebrations occasioned a wave of nostalgia. "It seemed like our home Commencement," she observed, "only I wasn't in it. . . . There isn't anything that's quite so much fun as college, and college stunts, and college friends," she continued. "I read my scrapbooks over and over and . . . it will seem mighty queer to miss Commencement."

[10] See Helen Lefkowitz Horowitz, *Alma Mater: Design and Experience in the Women's Colleges from their Nineteenth-Century Beginnings to the 1930s* (Boston: Beacon, 1984).

As her time in Summit drew to a close, Helen went on three occasions to New York to see two English Shakespearean actors, Edward Sothern and Julia Marlowe, in *Hamlet*, *Twelfth Night*, and *Romeo and Juliet*. Sothern and Marlowe had already made several successful American tours; in 1909 they were at the height of their fame. The pair dedicated themselves to bringing Shakespeare to a wide audience. Tickets, Helen reported, ranged from fifty cents to a dollar-fifty. "It must be worthwhile to be able to give so many people so much pleasure as those two actors do. A beautiful play like that seems just like a dream or a fairy story to me, and I never want to wake up."

Summer arrived. Edward came home from Yale. Uncle Harry made vacation plans for his wife and his niece. Concerned about Aunt Patty's headaches and lingering heart problems, he decided that a stay at the seashore would be beneficial. After some consideration Uncle Harry chose York Cliffs, Maine, a resort catering to a wealthy east coast clientele. Helen and Patty would spend five weeks there, while Harry and Edward went fishing in Canada. Harry would join his wife and Helen at the end of August.

Helen and Aunt Patty arrived in York Cliffs in late July and moved into the Passaconaway Inn. All white shingles, towers, and turrets, the three- and four-story Queen Anne-style inn sprawled along the rocky Maine coast. If earlier Helen had fretted over the prices in New York, York Cliffs stirred in Aunt Patty some residual memory of her own thrifty Nebraska upbringing. Helen and Patty quickly dubbed the hotel "Pass-the-coin-away Inn." Aunt Patty insisted on changing their rooms, from a three-room suite to two, thereby "saving several gold bricks." Laundry service cost a dollar to three dollars a load, and led the two to the facetious conclusion that they would be better off simply buying all new clothes.

> [They] even charge you extra for a bath. What do you know about that? Consequently, we're beating the hotel out of as much writing paper as possible to relieve our feelings, and order as many things as we can on the bill of fare, without appearing greedy, just to get our money's worth. I'm so used to throwing tips around now . . . that I'll probably feed pennies to the chickens when I get home.

Nevertheless, Helen reported, she was having a wonderful time. She played tennis, went sailing, canoeing, and golfing, and dancing after dinner. The majority of the guests were "old maids or widows, and quite a few of them from Boston," so Aunt Patty was enjoying their company. In response to her mother's question as to whether there were no men vacationing there, Helen replied that there certainly were. "Three bald-headed ones . . . four little boys, and one or two that may attain to manhood in a few years." The bellboys, "colored" waiters, and the proprietors, she concluded, complete the male population. All this made cousin Edward, who arrived following the fishing trip, highly popular.

But Helen's thoughts increasingly turned towards Nebraska. She spent time alone, sitting on the rocks, reading, writing letters, looking out over the ocean, reflecting on the year gone by and on what lay ahead. "Just one month from today I shall be beating it for home," she wrote on August 1. Two weeks later she wrote, "I'm coming home and going to college and wild horses couldn't keep me away from you any longer."

Helen said her farewells to the Twomblys on the evening of Friday, September 3. By then Uncle Harry had joined his family, and they had all relocated to the Moorland Hotel at Bass Rocks, Gloucester, Massachusetts. The Passaconaway Inn was closing for the season, and Aunt Patty had decided to prolong her time at the shore until mid-September.

After dinner that final evening Uncle Harry, Edward, and Helen sat on the rocks overlooking the ocean in the moonlight for a long farewell talk. Uncle Harry and Edward kept up everyone's spirits by singing "all the fool songs" they knew. "We sat there until a big wave swamped us." Early the next morning Helen and Edward left without waking Uncle Harry and Aunt Patty, Helen desiring to avoid an emotional farewell. Edward went with her as far as Boston, where his cheerful conversation held off any "pathetic spasms." Helen boarded the train in Boston, headed for Chicago, making a detour to Grand Rapids before returning to Crete on September 15, "two days less than a year" from when she left.

But Nebraska, although Helen did not yet realize it, already belonged to her past. The year in Summit had changed her. Henceforth her compass pointed east.

Chapter 3
Transitions

Helen's return to Crete coincided with the start of the fall semester. The academic year began with the usual events, including a church service and reception. Big Helen entertained women students and faculty at a lawn party at The Grange. These traditions held firm, but the college to which Helen returned was in transition.

Several long-time faculty members had retired. New instructors and professors took their place. The curriculum in 1909 had been significantly altered from that of the college's early years. The preparatory curriculum, a function of an era when many students came to Doane without having completed formal high school education, had fallen by the wayside. Gone were the distinctions between the "classical course," the "English course," the "scientific track," and the "normal course." In 1907-1908 the college moved to an undifferentiated bachelor of arts degree, in addition to a bachelor of music. The trimester system was replaced with the semester calendar, one increasingly popular across the country. Greek and Latin, although still taught, were no longer graduation requirements. Juniors and seniors had latitude in choosing electives. In short, Doane College, under its longtime president Brainerd Perry, was modernizing.

And growing. Enrollment stood at 225 students. The twenty-three professors or instructors—the latter largely part-time, teaching music lessons—were a contrast to the college's first year, when Brainerd Perry functioned as professor, librarian, bookkeeper, and maintenance man.

Student social life was changing. The literary societies of the college's early years—Hesperia, Philomathea, and Palladian—all passed out of existence. The YMCA and the YWCA, however, remained active on campus. Members taught Sunday school at churches in and around Crete, and held social events at the college. Sororities and fraternities sprang up, along with discipline-specific organizations: the German Club and the Greek Club. *The Owl*, the college newspaper, continued, along with the college yearbook, *The Tiger*; and the *Doane College News Letter*, geared towards alumni. Sports teams—baseball, basketball, track and field—drew participants and attendance. Women played "lawn sports"—tennis and croquet—and competed on the rowing team. Football was reinstated after a two-year hiatus following the death of a player from an injury suffered during a game. "Going up the river:" boating, hiking, or taking a romantic stroll along the Blue, was an ever-popular activity.

A typical weekly calendar, published in *The Owl*, listed meetings of the Ladies Glee Club, Doane Players, the YMCA and YWCA, orchestra practice, Men's Glee Club, choir practice, and a Saturday afternoon football game. Sunday school preceded morning worship; the evening brought a meeting of the World Fellowship followed by another worship service. [1]

The college continued to respond to the presence of the Czech population in Crete and Saline County. In 1911 Brainerd wrote a letter to the president of the Chicago Theological Seminary, among others, stating that the college was "in search of a Bohemian to be a member of our faculty," with the goal of drawing in Czech students from the county and around the state. "We could give him work in Latin or Greek, or in Physics, or in English Literature and Roman and Greek History. . . . Now can't you tell us of the man who has tact and training and consecration such as would enable him to fit into our College work and be a power for good among his countrymen?"

Not only was the college in transition, but the Perry family experienced a major change. In October 1909, Brainerd and Big Helen bought a house in town, at 711 Grove Avenue, moving from The Grange, where they had lived for the whole of their married life. "All agog over selling place," Big Helen wrote in her diary on October 4. She and Helen spent days packing, measuring rooms and windows, and going to Lincoln to buy new furniture and curtains. "Your dear father was much opposed to the sale," Big Helen recalled in her memoir, "but he was always so good to me, and let me have my way." The new house had conveniences The Grange never did: electricity and a bathroom. The house also had a fireplace, instead of the wooden stoves which heated several rooms at The Grange. "Henry said he would keep and lay the fire always—though he sometimes resented having to do it for Helen's beaux, of whom there were many that year."

Helen threw herself back into the world of Doane College. She rejoined a sorority, the College Club, and the YWCA, teaching Sunday

---

[1] Don Ziegler, *A College on a Hill and Beyond* (Crete, NE: Doane College, 2007), 53-96.

school at the First Congregational Church. In 1909 she wrote the lyrics for the school's Alma Mater. With a revolving roster of suitors, Helen went "up the river," strolling or boating on the Big Blue. The senior class poem in the 1911 yearbook included the verse: *Helen C. Perry, so stately and fair / Lo many a suitor walked home in despair.* Nor did she neglect her studies. In her senior year, Helen took the capstone course, "Evidences of Christianity," taught by her father over the decades. At the time of graduation, Helen was valedictorian of her class.

Helen, 1911.

The year 1910 witnessed further transitions. That summer Carl surprised the family by coming home for the first time in the four years since graduating from Doane. Carl had completed his diplomatic assignment in Halifax and was being sent to the consular office in Calcutta. For all that he was the family member whose life took him furthest from Crete, Carl took the loss of The Grange the hardest, refusing to even go look at the house, saddened by the thought of another family living there. That autumn Henry, after two years at Doane, transferred to Yale. The move came at the insistence of his father. Big Helen wrote frankly in her memoir that Henry "was a spoiled lad at college; son of the President, and captain of the football team. His father thought it was wise for him to go east to school." Henry resisted, begging his mother to intercede and let him stay at Doane. "I felt pretty badly about it," Big Helen recalled, "but his father was wise. The first three months he would have come home if his pride had not held him. But after! He can never be grateful enough to his father for insisting on his going." In attending Yale, Henry followed his father, Uncle Harry, Uncle Harry's father and brother, and cousin Edward. He followed as well the Doane students whose admission to graduate and law school at Yale Brainerd facilitated: Fred and Hal Fairchild, and Cheney Jones. Henry made a success of his two years at Yale. He lettered in football and wrestling, and was admitted to the elite Wolf's Head society. Upon graduation, he followed grandfather Thomas Doane and brother Tom Perry into the field of engineering.

Henry came home to see Helen graduate. Commencement Week was steeped in tradition. The week, actually ten days, began with a service at the Congregational Church. That evening Brainerd and Big Helen entertained nearly 200 people at a lawn party at their new home. The week continued through a dizzying array of recitals, band concert, junior class play, sorority and fraternity banquets, YMCA and YWCA meetings and religious services, Baccalaureate, an alumni reunion and luncheon, a picnic for alumni and former students, and a reception at the Perry home, where Brainerd and Big Helen welcomed the sixty guests of the fourteen members of the class of 1911. Graduation day was Wednesday, June 21, with ceremonies held in the college's Lee Chapel. Standing before a portrait of her grandfather Thomas Doane, with her father seated to the side, Helen delivered the valedictorian address. Written in rhyme, and complete with obligatory references to ivy-covered walls, friends soon to be scattered, beloved teachers, and lessons learned, Helen's words nevertheless looked to a future far beyond Crete.

For this is not the end of all the best!
Ah; this is not the goal for which one strives.

'Tis the Commencement of the better part,
The opening of our larger, broader lives. . . .

God grant us patience in the long, hard way
And love and friends to sweeten all the strife.
God grant us joy in service; peace in pain;
God grant us all that broader, larger life!

The year 1911 marked Brainerd Perry's thirty-ninth year at Doane College. The end of Commencement Week brought with it another of the occasional challenges to the college's exercise of *in loco parentis*. Nineteen students violated curfew by going up the river, returning to the residence halls after 10:30 p.m. The following week, Brainerd sent letters of reprimand to the students, now home for the summer. The students' replies ranged from the sincere to the obsequious to the defiant.

Dear Sir: Received your letter Sunday, and was very sorry
to think I had caused you any anxiety. . . . [O]f course such
rules must be made and it is wrong to break them. . . . I am
very sorry to have caused you any trouble.

Dear Sir: In reply to your letter of a recent date . . . I have
thought of the matter carefully and I fail to see how this
incident should lower the morals of the students of Doane
or her good name and hence I cannot say truthfully that I
regret it. I do, however, see your point of view and take your
letter kindly in the spirit in which it was written.

Dear Mr. Perry: I received your letter concerning my
going up the river without permission and returning
to Hall late. . . . As long as I have been at Doane I have
thought that, to a large extent, rules were "off" during
Commencement week. . . . Then too, it must be taken into
consideration that during the last week everyone is too busy
to hunt up the preceptress and get her permission. . . . As
far as returning late to Hall, that has been done every year
and nothing said. In fact, the year that I was a Freshman
one of the nicest "old girls" told me that everyone who did
not stay out late the last night was considered a "squawk."

Dear Sir: I was off the river as required, and on my way, [when] I saw a crowd of students, including your son, and as I had no watch, I supposed they were on time so I returned to Gaylord with them. . . . Furthermore, I think it was Miss Meston's place to come to us instead of waiting until this late hour.

Brainerd had dealt with more serious challenges to authority over the course of his tenure, notably an episode in 1892. On that occasion he was away from campus on a fundraising visit when a student, accused of insulting a professor, was ordered to make a public apology in chapel before the student body and faculty. The student chose that sanction over the alternative: being sent home for ten days. But when the student stood to address the assembly, the entire student body walked out of the chapel in protest of the punishment. Returning to campus the following week, Brainerd found the place in an uproar. He called a meeting of the faculty, and expressed disappointment that the situation had reached such a point; the student should simply have been sent home. Brainerd then reassembled the students in chapel. Reviewing the facts, he ordered that every student "give satisfactory explanation," by that afternoon or "stand cut off by [their] own act," meaning expulsion. "We will never consent to let students act this way." By evening all students came forward with an apology. At the same time, and working with Margaret Thompson, his trusted dean of women and confidant, Brainerd launched an investigation into the matter. He met with students who witnessed the original event, and discovered that the instructor had made a remark to a female student which several deemed insulting, leading the male student in question to respond in kind. The instructor's contract was not renewed. [2]

That was twenty years earlier. Brainerd was now seventy-two. Margaret Thompson had married and left the college. For Brainerd, the toll of years of work and worry was increasingly apparent.

That autumn, following the start of the semester, Big Helen went east for three months, leaving her daughter to keep house and be a companion to her father. Big Helen spent a month in Grand Rapids with Tom and Ethel and their two children. With Ethel she attended a lecture on women's rights, making a point of wearing a white dress—

---

[2] Ziegler, 81-82.

the color of the suffragette cause. In late October Big Helen arrived in Summit. Henry and cousin Edward came down from Yale to see her. In November Big Helen made the trip to New Haven to see Henry play football against Princeton. Despite a broken bone in his hand suffered during practice, Henry was on the field for ten minutes of the game (Yale lost to Princeton, 3-0). Both boys returned to Summit two weeks later for Thanksgiving.

In Crete, Helen served in her mother's place as first lady of the college, presiding over the traditional social events. She continued to join in student activities: meetings of the College Club and the "Phi Sigs." But the anomaly of her position became increasingly clear to her. Helen was now twenty-three. She had outgrown college life—"stunts," in the slang of the day. Her contemporaries were moving on. Some were teaching, a career which held no interest for her. Others were getting married. Helen dutifully attended bridal showers and served as bridesmaid. But her mother's letters from Summit, full of news of meetings of the Fortnightly Club, trips into New York with Uncle Harry for shopping, the opera, and Hippodrome, served as a sharp reminder of her own time in Summit three years earlier.

Casting about, Helen learned that Columbia Teachers College offered a four-year technical program leading to a bachelor of science in Fine Arts. The program offered concentrations in House Design and Decoration, Fine Arts Education, Costume Design, and Illustration. These touched on Helen's interests: sewing, fashion, decorating. Costume design echoed her interest in the visual aspects of theater and opera, and recalled what she had seen of traditional garb among Summit's immigrant community at Neighborhood House. Fine arts education brought back the memory of her behind-the-scenes visit at the Metropolitan Museum of Art. And since Helen already had a B.A., she could complete the Columbia program in two years, while living in Summit and commuting daily, as Uncle Harry did, to New York City. Helen began to lay plans for a move to Summit in the spring, once her mother returned home and her father left on his annual eastern fundraising tour.

Big Helen came home to Crete in time for Christmas, and Brainerd prepared for his trip. Concerned at how weary her husband looked, Big Helen tried to dissuade him. Brainerd would not hear of it. Before he left, the two discussed the importance of making a significant financial pledge of their own: $1,000. "I couldn't see where the money was to come from," Big Helen recalled, "but it was his life, and he couldn't ask for gifts unless he did his own part. So, against my better judgment I agreed to his wishes and have always been thankful that I did, for he went away with a better heart."

Brainerd left Crete on January 10, a bitterly cold and snowy day. The previous afternoon, nearly 100 students, half the student body, came to a reception at the Perry home to wish their president well. Three days into the trip, traveling across Iowa, Brainerd fell ill. Noticing his discomfort, a conductor encouraged him to leave the train at Burlington, and personally brought him to a hotel. The next day Brainerd pushed on. In Chicago he met with mixed success. He was cordially received by one donor; another, with whom he thought he had an appointment, turned out to be spending the winter in Mexico; a third was ill and declined to meet with him. Now seriously ill himself, Brainerd telegraphed Tom from Chicago. Tom met the train in Grand Rapids and took his father home. Two days later Big Helen received a letter from Tom telling her that Brainerd had pneumonia.

"I have fallen into the very best of hands," Brainerd wrote to his wife two weeks later, "and am very grateful that I could find such a home, doctor and nurse. The doctor was called in soon after I reached here Monday night, January 15th, and he has missed but two days. . . . Ethel has been an ideal nurse, perfectly lovely."

Near-daily letters from Tom, interspersed with occasional ones from Ethel or Brainerd, brought conflicting reports and counsel. Brainerd's fever was higher; his fever had broken. He was coughing blood and was tested for tuberculosis; the test was negative. He came downstairs and sat in a chair for an hour; he was confined to bed. Twice Big Helen made arrangements to leave for Grand Rapids, only to be dissuaded either by reports of an improvement in her husband's condition or by Tom protesting the rigors of travel in winter. "The doctor today feels that there is nothing at all to call you on so far as father's condition is concerned. Of course, we'd love to have you here, if you would be more comfortable in your mind! ... But we question the wisdom of your coming now, with the consequent travelling expense. If any reason comes up will let you know by wire."

Uncle Harry wrote, offering words of encouragement. "Don't worry about Brainerd. . . . [A]ll he needs is a good rest, so as to recover from the drag of so much constant work. . . . If he does come East, we will put him at billiards, and sightseeing, or light and 'genteel' occupations till he is rested." Uncle Harry added that he and Aunt Patty "shall be glad to see Helen just as soon and whenever she can come to us."

Brainerd's letters to his wife alternated between concern for the worry he was causing his family and happiness at receiving news from them. He was delighted to hear of Carl's appointment as consul in Turin. "When does Helen want to leave for the east?" he asked. "Buy [her] whatever clothes she needs. I trust I shall reach home before she starts, but in any case, carry out those plans that she has had in mind." He was impatient to resume his trip. "If I am built up well and strong, I think I should push on and do what I can the next weeks or two months. If I am not in good fighting condition then I must continue to loaf. I hope for the best." Tom was more cautious. "Father is doing splendidly but was for the first days sicker than I think you realize. But he is coming out finely, although I think he never ought to work as hard as he has again. In other words, he must take life easier if he is to keep well and strong." Big Helen's brother John wrote to Brainerd in a similar vein.

> We learn through Helen of your illness and greatly regret that you have had such a disappointing time of it in the delay of the work upon your "new scheme," as Helen calls it. I do not know what the "new scheme" may be excepting that it must be a good one because it is yours, and I wish it all success, *but* you must now take care of *yourself* until your health and strength are fully established again. You are worth more to the college and your friends than any scheme can possibly be. Please be good to yourself. Your monument is now high enough, a splendid one to your forty years of devotion.

March 7, 1912, was Brainerd's seventy-third birthday. Doane students sent flowers, shipped by train from a florist in Lincoln, because, as Helen wrote to her father, "they think you would like Nebraska flowers" best. Greetings poured in from alumni across the country: from Oregon, California, Utah, Illinois, Wisconsin, Connecticut, New York, and New Jersey. One wrote from Paris. Another, from Albany, enclosed a picture-postcard of the high school "where I am trying to instill a love of the classics." Helen wrote to her father:

Dear Daddy: Here it is almost your birthday, and me not there to help you keep it. . . . I never can say the things that I want most to say, and just words can never tell how much we children all love you, and nearly worship you, and if we can only be worthy of you and mother even in a small way, we ought to amount to something. It seems to me that it is your perfect fatherhood and my love for you that has taught me the nearness and dearness of the Fatherhood of God, and more than that I cannot say. May God the Father bless my dear father. Lovingly, Helen.

"What to say, "Brainerd wrote to his wife, "in the presence of four score individual birthday greetings. . . . All spoke the same language of the heart, the mightiest as well as the most winsome object in the universe. . . . I would like it if I could say this to them individually and in person, but as this is impossible you might insert the above as a letter in the next issue of *Doane College News*, entitling it "Return Greetings."

A week later Big Helen received the wire that Tom had promised to send when circumstances warranted. She left for Grand Rapids the following day. Upon arrival, she found that Brainerd's condition was as bad as it had been at the lowest ebb of his illness. Still, as March turned to April, he seemed to gain strength. The doctor nevertheless recommended a period of convalescence at the Battle Creek Sanitarium, some sixty miles from Grand Rapids. On April 25, accompanied by his wife and son, Brainerd traveled by rented car to Battle Creek. The institution was made famous by its founder, John Harvey Kellogg, noted for his innovative, even radical, ideas about treatment and diet regimens.[3] Although Kellogg no longer ran the sanitarium, the place still drew a wealthy clientele. Brainerd, however, had a room in East Hall, formerly the nurses' dormitory, which now offered accommodations for patients who could not afford the elegant accommodations and spa treatments offered in the main building. Brainerd's condition continued to oscillate between improvement sufficient to raise his wife's hopes, and bad days, marked by severe bouts of coughing. Doctors treated Brainerd with codeine, injections of adrenalin, and oil massages.

---

[3] John Kellogg's brother William, at John's behest, invented Corn Flakes as a healthy breakfast alternative for patients at the sanitarium. William went on to found the Kellogg Company of Battle Creek.

On May 21 Big Helen wrote in her diary that "B. seemed very sick, tho Dr. did not so consider him. Read aloud till nine o'clock, then after his treatment and hypodermic he went to sleep + so did I." Just after midnight Big Helen awoke suddenly, in time to hear her husband take his last breath. "Telegraphed and did all the necessary things. Left B.C. with Tom at 4:30." Together they accompanied Brainerd's body home, traveling all night and through the next day, an unnaturally hot day for May, across the Midwest. Friends from Crete met the train at Lincoln. Henry, accompanied by Uncle Harry, arrived from New York.

The funeral took place on May 24, in the Congregational Church. The sanctuary was banked with flowers. Students from the college were seated in the galleries; family, friends, and townspeople filled the pews. All businesses in Crete were shuttered so that people could pay their respects. Brainerd was laid out in his academic robes, with a bouquet of lily-of-the-valley from The Grange in his hands. On the coffin was a spray of red roses, sent by the faculty and students. A soloist sang a setting of Tennyson's "Crossing the Bar," a poem which meant much to Brainerd during his illness. Following the service, the pallbearers—three trustees and three faculty members, including Arthur Fairchild, now acting president of the college—carried the coffin to a waiting hearse. The entire student body lined the route from the church to the cemetery, young men in dark suits, the women dressed in white. The senior class of 1912, in their graduation caps and gowns, walked as an honor guard on either side of the hearse. In Riverside Cemetery Brainerd was laid to rest next to the infant son and namesake who died so many years before.

Her father's death was, for Helen, a devastating blow. Big Helen, writing years later, acknowledged as much. "It was especially hard for Helen; she and her father adored each other, and she had wanted so much to come to be with him." Helen was constrained by the same considerations that held her mother back for so long: the rigors of train travel in winter, the crowded conditions at Tom's house and worry over being an additional burden, the expense of staying at the sanitarium in Battle Creek. The days immediately following her father's funeral were taken up with a stream of callers and tending to the letters that poured in. Tom left for Grand Rapids on May 27, his birthday. Henry and Uncle Harry returned east, Henry to a sad graduation ceremony at Yale.

The reality of life in Crete and at Doane without Brainerd sank in for Big Helen. The first Sunday service at the Congregational

Church following the funeral was "beautiful, but very hard." There was Commencement Week to be faced, presided over by acting president Fairchild. Helen gamely attended many of the week's activities and "class stunts," but the anomaly of her presence was ever more apparent. Both women were comforted by the arrival from Boston of Cheney Jones. Cheney, the former chore boy, came to Crete to attend the alumni reunion and memorial service for Brainerd held as part of Commencement Week. With him were his wife Nellie, a Doane alumna, and one-year-old daughter Frances. The sight of the little girl toddling around the house was a balm for Big Helen and her daughter.

The formal break with Crete lay a year in the future, but Big Helen recognized that an era had ended. "I could not live in Crete apart from the college. . . . I had promised the Doane people we would keep our home in Crete, and I would make my home there, but there was nothing for Helen, and while my life was gone, I must devote myself to her. I had seen so many cases where a young brilliant life was sacrificed in that of an older person." In July Big Helen rented out the house, and she and her daughter departed for the east. They spent the summer with a revolving roster of Doane relatives on Cape Cod: in Craigville, Barnstable, and Orleans. The latter recalled the happy summer when the entire Doane clan gathered on the Cape.

Among the people vacationing on the Cape was the Tener family, with a daughter, Edith, two years younger than Helen. Edith's brother Alex Tener had just graduated from Yale with Henry and cousin Edward. The connection with the Tener family would be a significant one for Helen in the not-so-distant future.

The arts program at Columbia Teachers College, which Helen entered in September 1912, marked another turning point in her life. Helen chose House Design and Decoration as her area of concentration. The curriculum included courses such as Household Art Design, Principles of Home Décor, Design in the Art Industries, and House Decoration and Furnishing. All dealt to some extent with the principles of design: space filling, line harmony, distribution of dark and light in a space, and simple color arrangement. Other courses allowed students to study principles of design in fabrics, metalworking, and woodworking.

Beyond the courses in her concentration, Helen had access to a range of classes in the technical arts program. She skipped those in the culinary sciences (as her later and limited skills in the kitchen bore out) but she did avail herself of classes in textiles and clothing. Those included History of Costume, Drafting and Dress Design, and a three-semester sequence in Textiles. All pointed toward Helen's future work. As a freelance magazine writer in the 1920s and 1930s, Helen would design clothing for both children and adults inspired by traditional European costumes. The focus on folk costumes would form a narrative through-line in *Jean & Company, Unlimited*. The catalog description of the Textiles sequence is a blueprint for the New Jersey Textiles Exhibition at the Newark Museum in 1916, the exhibit which served as the springboard to her career as a museum curator and director.

It was not only the program at Columbia which broadened Helen's horizons. In addition to belonging to a sorority, Helen joined the Art Students League. Located at 215 West 57th Street in Manhattan, the League was founded in 1875 by students, many of them women, dissatisfied with the conservative approach that held sway at the city's National Academy of Design. The League operated on the principle of complete freedom and autonomy for individual instructors, who leased studio space in the building and offered individual or group instruction. The Art Students League over time fostered the careers of some of the country's best-known artists, including Thomas Eakins, Alexander Caldwell, Jackson Pollock, and Mark Rothko.

Another organization with which Helen forged connections was the Three Arts Club. *The New York Times* covered the club's opening in a story in the May 15, 1904 edition, headlined "A Club for Girl Art Students." Modeled on an institution in Paris, and located two blocks from the Art Students League, the Three Arts Club provided safe, affordable housing to women studying painting, music, or the dramatic arts. "Thousands of young women come to this city to take courses in some one of these arts, and often arrive here utter strangers, with no knowledge of where to look for comfortable lodgings, or how to form suitable or congenial acquaintances." Such was not Helen's situation; she was living comfortably in Summit. But the Club, which by Helen's time had moved to a new location at 340 West 85th Street, a convenient distance from the Columbia campus, provided a haven to which to retreat after classes, a place to spend an occasional overnight or weekend in the city, and a source of new friends and acquaintances.

The most important of Helen's acquaintances at Columbia during this time, as it developed, was a fellow student in the House Design and Decoration program, John Morrison Curtis. John entered the program at the same time as Helen, in the fall of 1912. John was born in Jersey City in 1893, the youngest of the five children of Ben Kirk and Lide Owens Curtis. (John always regretted the fact that his parents had left Kentucky, where the family had its roots, and that he was born in New Jersey.) Ben Kirk Curtis worked for an uncle who ran a shipping business in New York and San Francisco. The job afforded the family a comfortable existence. John's oldest sister Clintie (Ann Clinton Curtis) once described the family home at 61 Summit Avenue in Jersey City as large and light-filled, with four bedrooms on the second floor and three more on the third. The yard was planted with fruit trees, and a stable provided "a fine play house" for John and his sister Dorothy, the Curtis child closest to John in age. In addition to the home on Summit Avenue, Ben Kirk Curtis in 1899 purchased thirty acres of land near Kingwood, West Virginia. A spring located on the land was a source of mineral water found to have medicinal properties. Curtis began bottling the water and selling it. So successful was this venture that it became the source of his livelihood.

John Curtis was initially, and for some time, no more and no less one of Helen's fellow students. Rather less, truth be told. In 1912 John was a nineteen-year old freshman, commuting to Columbia from Jersey City. Only in his second year, when he joined the Alpha Sigma Phi fraternity, did John move to campus. Helen was twenty-four, older even than many of her junior and senior-level classmates. But John could not help but notice the attractive, vivacious woman who shared his classes; a person who made friends easily, with her blend of Nebraska egalitarianism, New England propriety, and New York sophistication.

The intersecting worlds of Columbia Teachers College, the Art Students League, and the Three Arts Club not only brought Helen and John together, but introduced them to people who would become a part of their lives going forward. Those friends included photographer Clara Sipprell and painter and craftsman Jimmy Scott.

Clara Sipprell was born in 1885 in Ontario, but the family (Clara's father died shortly before she was born) relocated from Canada to Buffalo, New York. Clara's brother Frank opened a successful photography studio, to the point that conventional wisdom held that you were not anyone in Buffalo if you had not had your portrait taken by Frank Sipprell. Clara began spending time at her brother's studio, informally apprenticing there. Buffalo was home to a number of camera and photography clubs, a fact aided by the city's proximity to Rochester, home of the Eastman Kodak Company. The most prominent of the clubs was the Buffalo Camera Club. Women were not permitted to join, but Frank's stature allowed him to bring Clara as his guest. Clara's skill as a photographer in her own right was recognized when, in 1911, the Club invited her to exhibit her work. She soon achieved regional recognition.

In 1915 Clara moved to New York City, joining family friend Jessica Beers. Jessica was well-known in Buffalo as headmistress at the Buffalo Seminary and later as founder of the Elmwood School. Jessica came to New York to serve as principal of the Normal Training Department at the Ethical Culture School in New York City, a venture founded by Felix Adler. In New York, Clara joined Jessica and Jessica's mother, first at their apartment on W. 168th Street, later at 70 Morningside Drive. Clara was hired by the Ethical Culture School as a contract photographer. That same year, in 1915, Arthur Dow, head of the Fine Arts Department at Columbia Teachers College, invited Clara to mount a one-woman show at the college. Clara would go on to become one of the leading portrait photographers of her day. In a career spanning seven decades, she photographed such notable individuals as Queen Louise of Sweden, Robert Frost, Ilya Tolstoy, Albert Einstein, and Eleanor Roosevelt.[4]

Helen had graduated from Columbia by the time of Clara's 1915 exhibit, but John was still a student there. Helen, however, already had a connection to Clara. Jessica Beers traveled in the same progressive educational circles as Louise Connolly, former superintendent of the Summit public schools and friend of the Twomblys. Jessica Beers and Louise Connolly visited Helen, her mother, and Aunt Patty on Cape Cod in 1912, the summer the women spent there following Brainerd's death.

It was through the Art Students League that John Curtis met Jimmy Scott, who came to New York from Racine, Wisconsin. Jimmy's parents were born in Scotland, but the city in which they settled in 1888, the year before Jimmy's birth, was home to a sizeable population of Danish immigrants, so much so that Racine was known as "the most Danish city in America."[5] Immigrants flocked to Racine for the opportunities presented by the city's industrial economy. Thomas Scott, Jimmy's father,

---

[4] Mary Kennedy McCabe, *Clara Sipprell: Pictorial Photographer* (Fort Worth, Texas: Amon Carter Museum, 1990), 15-25.
[5] As late as 1930, Danish immigrants and their children comprised 11% of the population of Racine County.

worked as a machine hand. In 1902 he was killed in an accident at the shop, leaving thirteen-year-old Jimmy to support his mother and two younger sisters. Jimmy worked as a clerk in a hardware store, but was able to pursue his aptitude for painting and metalwork at a new venture in town, the Racine School of Fine Arts. The school was the creation of two Danish-born painters and silversmiths, Anders Andersen and Johannes Morton. Andersen studied at the Art Institute of Chicago before opening the school in Racine, seventy miles north of that city. In 1911 Andersen and Morton attempted to found an artist colony in Racine. That same year Jimmy attracted attention for work that he exhibited, along with others from the nascent artist colony. Jimmy also took second prize at the Wisconsin State Fair for one of his paintings.

The art colony in Racine failed to take hold. In 1912 Andersen and Morton reestablished it in the town of Milton in New York's Hudson River Valley, sixty miles from New York City. Reflecting the Danish heritage of its founders, the colony was named Elverhoj, "Hill of the Elves." Jimmy followed Andersen and Morton to Elverhoj, and at the same time studied at the Art Students League, where he and John Curtis established what would become a life-long friendship, one that expanded to include Helen.

In June, 1913, Helen and her mother returned to Crete. Tom, Ethel, and their two children (young Frances, who had so charmed Helen five years earlier, joined now by three-year-old Bretton) came from Grand Rapids, and Henry from Cleveland. Together the Perrys undertook the melancholy task of breaking up the household: sorting, crating, storing, selling furnishings, and giving things away. The *Crete Vidette-Herald* took note of "the gathering together of the children of President Perry under the roof of their mother. And it was the recognition of the fact that it probably is the last time this will happen that brought sadness to all their friends in town, college and state."

Helen returned to New York for the start of her second and final year at Columbia. A new job awaited her as well. Helen was one of a number of artists from the Art Students League hired by Albert Herter of the Herter Looms to paint the cartoons—life-sized designs—used in the weaving of tapestries. Herter, the son of the owner of the interior design firm Herter Brothers, studied at the Art Students League prior to going to Paris in the

1890s to further his studies. In Paris he immersed himself in the traditional craft practiced by weavers in France and Belgium. Herter brought forty craftsmen from the Aubusson Looms in France to the United States, where in 1909 he established the Herter Looms. Herter combined old-world skill with modern technology, allowing the Looms to create giant tapestries commissioned by wealthy Gilded Age patrons. Herter tapestries graced the walls of the Vanderbilt Mansion at Hyde Park, the Cranbrook Estate in Bloomfield Hills, Michigan, the residence of the Harriman family, and the McAlpin Hotel in New York City.

It was not only old-world craftsmen and techniques that Herter brought back from Europe. In England Herter encountered the work and philosophy of William Morris and the Arts and Crafts movement. Morris believed in the superiority of the cooperative form of labor found (if only in idealized notions) in the medieval guild and craft system, which Morris contrasted with the exploitative nature of industrial capitalism. An article published in 1914 in *Harper's Bazaar* highlighted the relationship between Herter and the Arts and Crafts movement:

> What Morris did for England with his revival in the art
> of tapestry weaving and the creation of beautiful textiles,
> Mr. Herter has done for America. As the whole revival of
> English decorative art in the eighties had its foundation
> in the protest of a group of artists against the commercial
> and conventional conception of art that obtained at that
> period, it is not surprising that we should now find in
> America a like protest against the modern machine-made
> fabrics which are almost universally used in decoration.
> Steeped in the lore of the old masterpieces of tapestry, the
> dim and exquisite tones of old textiles, and the harmonies
> of color seen in the priceless rugs of antiquity, Mr. Herter
> determined to make the effort to revive these arts. [6]

It was at the Herter Looms that Helen first encountered in a systematic fashion the thinking and products of the Arts and Crafts movement. While the style of the Herter tapestries echoed medieval designs, replete with unicorns, swans, peacocks, and flowers, many—

---

[6] Helen Lightfoot, "Tapestry Weaving: The Revival of a Royal Craft," *Harper's Bazaar* (May 1914): 25+65; also "Looms, The Aubusson : Where American Tapestries Are Designed and Woven by an American Artist, Albert Herter," *The Craftsman: An Illustrated Monthly Magazine in the Interest of Better Art, Better Work, and a Better and More Reasonable Way of Living*, 16 (New York City: April-September 1909): 226-232

including the *Harper's* author—overlooked the fact that Herter was in fact using modern machinery to produce the tapestries commissioned by nouveau-riche captains of industry. This contradiction marked both Herter's outlook as well as a strand of Progressive-era thinking about the relationship between craft and modern methods, between traditional and contemporary society. Helen, for all that she held progressive political views, proved susceptible to the Romanticism of Morris, John Ruskin, and others. This contradiction or tension would appear again as she curated the Textiles Exhibit at the Newark Museum in 1916. It would show up more perniciously when, traveling in Italy in the 1920s, Helen mistook fascism's cynical appropriation of the ideal of the organic, pre-industrial community for the genuine article.

After closing the house in Crete, Big Helen left for Oregon and California. Three weeks into the trip she received news of the death of her brother, Reverend John Doane, in San Diego. Big Helen hastened to be with her sister-in-law Alice. Changing trains in Los Angeles, she was met by nephew Everett and Lilla Perry, the young couple who had entertained Helen during her initial year in Summit. In 1911 Everett was named director of the Los Angeles Public Library, and was overseeing plans for the city's landmark new library building. Big Helen spent the next eight months in San Diego with her widowed sister-in-law. "Alice, at least, needed me."

Just when Big Helen and her daughter began to plan a trip to Europe is not clear. It appears to have originated in part with Big Helen's desire to visit Carl, now serving as consul in Turin. The family last saw Carl four years earlier, at the time of his visit to Crete. Big Helen's diary records the fact that she was taking Italian lessons early in 1913. By November she was taking a refresher course in French as well. In late March, 1914, she noted that she "wrote long letter to Frances [Aunt Patty] about trip abroad." She further discussed the idea of the trip with her nephew John Doane, Jr. A gifted musician and graduate of Oberlin College, John had spent the year 1912 studying in London.

A trip to Europe was a natural step. The tradition of the Grand Tour was long-established among the English aristocracy, such that a young man's education was deemed incomplete without travel to France and Italy. By the middle of the nineteenth century, the notion of the Grand Tour was becoming Americanized, democratized, and feminized. Legions of young scholars from the United States attended German universities, recognized as the best in the world, for advanced academic work. Brainerd had often spoken of his time in Europe—Heidelberg in 1867 for divinity studies, and time spent in Florence as well. More recently there was the example of John Doane's Jr.'s year in London. The first generation of academic women also embraced the idea of Europe travel. Jane Addams brought back the settlement house model following the second of her two trips to Europe in the 1880s, trips undertaken after her graduation from Rockford Seminary and a year at the Women's Medical College in Philadelphia.

In spring of 1914 Helen was graduating from Columbia. At twenty-five, she was eager to travel. Her fascination with European culture, sparked by encounters with the German and Czech communities in Nebraska and the immigrants with whom she worked at Neighborhood House, was heightened by her experience at Herter Looms and the introduction to the Arts and Crafts movement. Helen hoped to study in Europe, and perhaps secure an apprenticeship or employment at a decorating or interior design firm in England.

There was another incentive. Louise Connolly, Aunt Patty and Uncle Harry's friend, now living at the Twombly house, was working as the educational advisor at the Newark Museum. Connolly had recently published *The Educational Value of Museums*, a comparative study of American institutions. Knowing of Helen's interest in museums, sparked by her visits to New York's leading institutions in 1908 and fostered by conversations with Louise around the dinner table, Connolly suggested to Helen that she spend time while in Europe studying practices at museums in England and on the Continent, reporting back to Connolly. The status of the Newark Museum and Connolly's letter of introduction would provide entrée to museums across Europe.

Helen was also eager to see Carl. And the prospect of several months with her mother was appealing. The feeling was mutual. Big Helen missed her daughter during the time she spent living in San Diego. She noted, on more than one occasion, visits from Alice Doane's daughter Lois. "We had such a good time. . . . It made me homesick for Helen."

Big Helen left San Diego at the beginning of March, 1914. For two and a half months she visited family and friends along the way, including, as usual, Tom and Ethel in Grand Rapids. Big Helen arrived in Summit on May 18. The next three weeks were busy ones. Big Helen went into New York with her daughter to see an exhibit of Helen's work at Columbia. There was shopping to do. "We packed and sewed all day," Big Helen wrote in her diary. On June 12, accompanied by Uncle Harry, cousin Edward, and Tom—who came from Grand Rapids for the occasion—the two women took an early train to New York. The scene at the dock was typical of the joyful and frenzied send-offs that accompanied the departure of an ocean liner bound for Europe. "Friends of Helen gave us a merry send-off. We had two big baskets of fruit, flowers, candies and letters." The ship's orchestra played, people tossed confetti and streamers into the air, crowds on both the ship's deck and the dock cheered, waved, laughed, and cried. Tugboats busily nosed the *S.S. St. Paul* away from the dock, pushing and pulling the big boat into the Hudson River. The ship headed out into the broad Atlantic, and Europe beyond.

Chapter 4

Europe, and a World at War

Helen and her mother found their stateroom aboard the *S.S. St. Paul*, and went in search of their reserved steamer chairs on deck. At dinner they sat at the purser's table, where Helen, her mother observed, enjoyed "the most violent flirtation you ever saw." Tea was served on deck in the afternoons. There were games of shuffleboard for the young people, and evenings brought dancing in the ballroom. The latter proved challenging. Rough seas the first days out meant that people "collided violently, but everyone was good-natured, so we had a peach of a time."

Democratized the Grand Tour may have become, in comparison with its aristocratic antecedents, but only to a point. Americans sailing to Europe that summer came from the well-educated and the well-to-do; people with intertwined and overlapping social connections. "A jolly crowd of young people, girls from Vassar, Wellesley and further West," Helen reported, with a figurative wave to the vast reaches of the country beyond the eastern seaboard (and from whence she herself came). "Men from Yale, Harvard, Princeton and Cornell." Big Helen made the acquaintance of A. Ross Hill, president of the University of Missouri, and enjoyed long conversations. The two women met another mother and daughter, Bella and Winnifred Sibley. So much did The Helens (as they took to signing their letters) enjoy the Sibleys' company that they planned several days together in England. Big Helen befriended another mother and daughter, returning from visiting a son in New York. "They are interesting, suffragists, and have told us many things. Frances would enjoy talking to them."

Beyond meals and bedtime, Helen and her mother saw little of each other. Helen entered into another "typical boat flirtation" with a Mr. Allen. "Helen and Mr. Allen spent evening together." "Helen went to a concert with Mr. Allen and walked late with him." "Did not see much of Helen, she was with Mr. Allen all day 'til very late." Vying with Mr. Allen was a Mr. Hobson, who, despite the presence of his wife, was "also very devoted to her."

There were solemn moments. On Sunday, mother and daughter attended the Church of England service. At an altar draped with the American flag, prayers were offered for the president and for King George V and Queen Mary. And Big Helen noted in her diary on June 17: "Commencement Day at Doane. My thoughts were there."

The *St. Paul* docked in Southampton on June 20. Over the next five weeks, Helen and her mother cut a swath across England and Scotland. They spent a day on the Isle of Wight with the Sibleys, at a "charming and quaint inn, ivy all over the walls and house, and a wonderful view of the water." From there they went briefly to London, before embarking on a brisk itinerary: Windsor, and a Thames River cruise to Wallingford, Oxford, and Stratford-on-Avon. They went north to the Lake District, to Keswick, where they were the only guests at a small boarding house. Helen provided an evocative description: "The lake, Derwentwater, is just as pretty as its name. It is all surrounded by mountains, or high green hills. And the further away they get, the bluer they are, until they melt into the sky and play hide and seek with the clouds."

In Keswick Helen continued the tradition begun after her father's death: giving her mother red roses on July 3, her wedding anniversary. Every year, for the rest of her life, at least one of the Perry children sent their mother roses on that day. Helen assured her family at home that her mother (at age sixty making her first trip to Europe) was doing well; she "is more energetic than I am . . . but I haven't lost her yet!"

The vigorous pace of travel in unfamiliar surroundings was not without its challenges—even for such inveterate train travelers as The Helens. Big Helen wryly noted that "one has to watch always for change of cars, which seem to come every few moments, and for which there is never any notice; the names of towns are never called, though there is always a large and imposing sign just as one is *leaving* the town." Her daughter concurred.

This traveling in Europe certainly takes brains! No time-tables to be had, and the only way you ever get a train is to go to the station and sit there until one comes, going the right direction. Nobody at that station can tell you where you change. So at every station one sticks one's head out of one's window and politely asks a porter what place this is, and whether he advises one to change cars here. . . . The stations are never labeled except with the one word 'Bovril.'

We thought at first that all the train stations in Europe must be called that, until we discovered that all the back fences and street cars, etc. were called the same thing.

From the Lake District, The Helens went to Glasgow, Loch Lomond, and the Trossachs, "real Lady of the Lake Country." Next was Edinburgh, where they witnessed the arrival of the king and queen at their summer home, Holyrood House. "Some more pomp and style than we would have for the President," Big Helen observed, "but not much. Crowds lined the streets and it was raining, till just as they came. They are very ordinary-looking mortals." Her daughter concurred, comparing the king unfavorably to the military bearing of the head waiter at their hotel in the Trossachs, whom she dubbed "the Kaiser"—a term soon to have greater resonance. "King George wasn't half as impressive. He is short and not particularly good-looking and quite human." Nevertheless, "we were thrilled."

Returning to England, the two went to Durham, York, and Lincoln ("just at present our middle name is cathedral"). In York they walked the ancient Roman wall, from which they viewed the cathedral spires and the gardens of the houses clustered around it. For Helen it was the day-to-day of English life that captivated her. "The queer little houses and quaint narrow streets are fully as interesting to me as the cathedrals." They returned to London, where they again saw university president Dr. Hill, Mr. Allen, and "two more people who came over on the boat with us [and] are staying here at the same house." They received a call from a Boston couple, the Smiths, now living in England, friends of the well-connected John Doane, Jr., Mr. Smith wrote for *The Boston Evening Transcript*. Helen and her mother also reunited with the Misses White of Worcester, Massachusetts, two women they met in Oxford. "Charming women," Big Helen described them, "between forty and fifty years old. Know all about the Perrys and the Doanes and . . . so many people I do in Worcester." At their hotel in Edinburgh, The Helens found four American girls they first met in the Trossachs; "we told them about this place."

The recurring meetings with American tourists, women in particular, were not entirely accidental. Helen and her mother stayed at hotels recommended by the Women's Rest Tour Association, or W.R.T.A. The association was formed in 1891 in Boston to assist women "who might enjoy a vacation abroad if they but knew how cheaply it can be accomplished, and how easy the paths of travel may be made by confidence and common-sense." The association published a handbook and a listing of lodgings and pensions recommended by its members.[1] Big Helen described their accommodations in Oxford as "a W.R.T.A. place" set amidst "a solid group of houses where students live. . . . Apparently, a retired butler and a lady's maid have united their fortunes and keep this charming place." During the school term it was a boarding house for students, but "this being vacation they have tourists. . . . Five women of us at the house," including the two Misses White. In Glasgow, "we went to another W.R.T.A. place, where we were in a lordly mansion, the only guests."

Helen would return to England, in 1919, 1926, 1933, and 1936, but it was the 1914 trip that she fictionalized in *Jean & Company, Unlimited.* Passages in the book are drawn from the letters written by Helen and her mother. It was Helen, in the persona of Jean, who sketched Windsor Castle from the window of their hotel or drew detailed diagrams of the changing of the guard at Buckingham Palace. It was Helen and her mother who, like Jean, took "a last look at the gray towers and castle of Windsor, at the wide, green stretches and leafy shade of The Long Walk," before boarding a tiny steamer on the Thames River canal, gliding along "between mossy banks so close together that the branches almost met overhead, like a cool, green tunnel." It was The Helens who, at an inn in Wallingford-on Thames, like Jean and her mother, "took a candle from the table at the foot of the stairs and climbed up steps . . . worn by many feet, walk[ing] down a dim corridor where their own flickering shadows seemed the ghosts of ancient pilgrims, to a gabled attic room with two huge beds." And it was Helen and her mother, in a scene adapted to *Jean & Company,* who stood in awe at many-spired Oxford, under "a pearl-gray sky, with soft undertones of rose and violet and turquoise-blue melting into the gray background."

And everywhere, strawberries. Just as the pages of *Jean & Company* tell of lock keepers' children bringing wicker baskets filled with strawberries to the boat, so too The Helens described "strawberries nearly as big as one's fist," buying baskets of the fruit to eat on the train, or enjoying an afternoon tea of bread and butter, watercress, and strawberries.

Back in London, the two encountered the stark reality of the militant campaign for women's suffrage. The fight for votes for

---

[1] Women's Rest Tour Association, *A Summer in England, With a Continental Supplement; a Handbook for the Use of American Women* (Boston, 1900), 5.

women began in England in 1872, twenty-five years after the Seneca Falls Convention in the United States. In 1903, The Women's Social and Political Union (WSPU), under the leadership of Mrs. Emmeline Pankhurst and her daughters Christabel and Sylvia, came to the fore. By 1909 the WSPU adopted militancy as a tactic. Suffragettes wielding hammers smashed plate-glass windows in department stores and glass cases in museums, and even, on one occasion, the case containing the crown jewels in the Tower of London. Pictures in art galleries were slashed; at the British Museum mummy cases were smashed. Suffragettes cut telegraph wires and tossed incendiary devices into mailboxes. A bomb was discovered at St. Paul's Cathedral. The orchid house in Kew Gardens was vandalized and the teahouse burned down. In June 1913, before a horrified crowd, suffragette Emily Davison threw herself in front of the king's racehorse at the derby at Epsom and died of her injuries.

Reprisals were harsh. Over 1,000 women were arrested, and jailed in Holloway Prison. Suffragettes embraced the tactic of the hunger strike. The government retaliated with force-feeding, a procedure amounting to torture. Worried lest it create martyrs, Parliament in April 1913 adopted the Temporary Discharge for Ill Health Act. Critics called it the "Cat and Mouse Act." Suffragettes weakened by force-feeding were released from prison until their health improved, then arrested again, the cycle of hunger-striking and force-feeding resuming as well.

Discussion of women's suffrage was a recurring theme in The Helens' letters. They were alert as well to evidence of women's equality or accomplishments, commenting on a sign in York advertising the office of a woman architect and surveyor. In Edinburgh they met Dr. Elsie Inglis, "a very prominent suffragist and a very skillful surgeon." The description scarcely does justice to Inglis's accomplishments as a crusader for women's rights and maternal health. Her greatest accomplishments, however, lay ahead, in ways the Helens could not yet fathom. [2]

Public places were on alert against possible attacks, interfering with Helen's intention to study museums. Time and again she met with locked doors: St. George Chapel at Windsor Castle, Blenheim Palace, and the National Gallery, closed "because a Suffragette chopped up a

---

[2] Elsie Inglis led the creation of the Scottish Women's Hospitals for Foreign Service Committee during the First World War. Women's suffrage organizations funded the creation of all-female-staffed hospitals in Belgium, France, Russia, and Serbia during the war. For Inglis's efforts in Serbia, improving sanitation and reducing typhus, she was regarded as a second Florence Nightingale, earning the title "Lady with the Torch." Inglis died in November, 1917, with the war still raging in Europe, a day after returning to England from Serbia.

portrait there yesterday." At the Tower of London they had to surrender their purses before entering; at York Minster the crypt was closed to all visitors "on account of disturbances." There are times, Helen wrote, "where I'm almost an anti-. But never when I'm conversing with an Englishman; It's too much fun to 'sic' them on by disagreeing with them on every point, and standing up for the militants. I think mother must be ashamed of me most of the time."

Nevertheless, they managed a number of visits, Helen reporting her findings to Louise Connolly. At Edinburgh Castle they saw the regalia of Mary, Queen of Scots. On her own, Helen went to the city's art museum, "much more interesting and up to date than the last Academy Exhibition in New York." In London they went to the Victoria and Albert Museum, the Houses of Parliament—albeit hurried along by policemen—and the British Museum to see the Elgin Marbles and Rosetta Stone, this after "being vouched for by our landlord as American women with no suffragist tendencies." Helen, however, had an experience at the art museum in Glasgow which delighted her:

> At last I've been taken for a Suffragette, so I'm perfectly
> happy! The guard . . . not only walked in front of me and
> behind me, and all around me, he even bumped into me two
> or three times. To see if I'd rattle, I suppose, with concealed
> weapons. I'd have loved to have roused his suspicions a little
> more, but I don't suppose Mother would enjoy talking to
> daughter thru the bars.

Regretfully, Helen passed up an opportunity to hear a speech by Mrs. Pankhurst. The evening ended in a riot and Pankhurst's arrest, "so for mother's sake it was just as well we didn't go, I guess. But I'll get there yet. And so will mother."

Interested as she was in museum work, Helen's goal was a career in interior design. In London she visited several firms, cultivating contacts with the hope of returning to London to work. She visited a firm where one of the partners remembered Helen from her visits to its New York studios. The firm did not employ women, she was told, but the partner gave her addresses of other businesses to contact. Helen was invited to tea one afternoon at the home of a designer, a woman to whom she had a letter of introduction. These visits raised her hopes about returning to London in the fall.

During their final days in England, The Helens attended the Ballets Russes in Drury Lane, sitting in the top balcony on wooden benches, for performances of "Daphnis and Chloé" and "Scheherazade." Big Helen pronounced the first beautiful, the latter "the vilest thing I ever saw." They went to tea with the Smiths, the American journalist and his family, at their home in Golders Green. With the Smiths they traveled by "tube" to a Soho restaurant "in the foreign quarter," where Big Helen drank a glass of wine: "don't ever mention it!" (Brainerd had been a supporter of the temperance cause.) On their final night in London mother and daughter took a ride across town on the top of a double-decker bus. "All so different from ordinary sightseeing."

One event went unremarked. On June 28, while The Helens were in Oxford, the Austrian Archduke Franz Ferdinand and his wife Sophie were assassinated at Sarajevo. As Helen and her mother repacked their bags at the end of July, lights burned late in the chancelleries of the Great Powers. Austria issued an ultimatum to Serbia, Germany issued the "blank check" to its Austrian ally. Russia signaled support for Serbia. France and Great Britain watched nervously. Helen and her mother purchased their tickets and headed for Paris.

"Here, at least, is one fix that we never dreamed of getting into," Helen wrote on August 3, 1914. England's ultimatum to Germany, demanding the withdrawal of troops from Belgium, expired at midnight. England and France declared war on Germany.

The Helens arrived in Paris on Saturday, July 25, after a short but uncomfortable train ride from London to Folkestone in a second-class smoking car. The Channel crossing was rough and choppy. They compensated by going first-class from Boulogne to Paris, eating dinner in the dining car, arriving in Paris at 9:30 p.m. Big Helen, a cheerful traveler in England, was unnerved. "I felt like a stranger in a strange land." Her mood lifted somewhat at the sight of the letters awaiting them at the Hotel Cecilia from family at home. A letter from Carl, however, upset her deeply. "Very bad news from Carl," Big Helen confided to her diary. "He's in debt again and wants me to help him out. Sent cable [to] Tom and wire [to] Carl. Very blue and depressed. It all seems so sad and disgraceful for my boy."

That first Sunday afternoon, The Helens strolled the Champs-Élysées, saw the Arc de Triomphe, and sat in the Tuileries Gardens, watching children roll hoops down the paths and sail small boats in the pond. "And the French children *talk French!*" Helen exclaimed. "There is nothing particularly original about being surprised at the fact that even the little children talk French, but I am just as much so."

They took breakfast in their room, "but after four solid English meals a day, we nearly starve with only coffee and rolls for breakfast, and no tea." The quantity of the food was not the only thing Helen found to criticize, as she cast a decorator's eye at their surroundings in the "horribly dressy" Hotel Cecilia. Parlors were done in "French style:" soft colors and rose-colored draperies, "tottery chairs," and "enough mirrors, or rather whole glass walls to drive you wild. The first day I kept walking into them, thinking there were more rooms beyond." On the whole, she opined, English design, with its solid paneling and substantial furniture was superior. "Oh, for a job in London! Here's hopin'!"

During the ensuing days they visited the Louvre, the Eiffel Tower, and Notre Dame. "Helen thinks it the loveliest of all the cathedrals." The meals more than made up for the continental breakfasts: four-course luncheons and six-course dinners. And, as in England, there were American travelers, by now old friends. The Sibleys came for tea. "Some Columbia girls" stopped by for a visit, as did three young men from the *S.S. St. Paul*, also recent graduates from Columbia. But a warning note crept into Big Helen's letter of July 31: "We're all very much excited over the war scare, and the city is full of crowds of people. . . . [I]f we had had our visit with Carl I should be tempted to go home. Helen says no." Plans, however, were in flux. "We shall have to give up our trip through Germany and Austria now, and go down through Switzerland to Italy."

Even with the heightened tension of the days leading to it, the declaration of war caught people unprepared. Scenes of panic ensued among Americans who suddenly found themselves in a combatant nation. Lines formed at embassies and banks, where only limited amounts of cash were given out, leaving many short of funds. Wire transfers were cut off. Helen described people abandoning baggage in the rush for train depots; clothes torn from bodies in the mad crush as people desperately scrambled to board trains. Many who reached French ports were denied passage across the Channel unless they could prove that they had reservations on a ship sailing from England to the United States. Tourists who had rented automobiles had them confiscated in order to provide transportation for military officers.

After some initial panic, The Helens regained their equilibrium. "We cabled Uncle Harry this morning, 'Safe in Paris,'" Helen wrote. "We also registered with the *New York Herald* in order to have our names published in the New York edition as being safe." In part their resolve stemmed from the realization that any attempt to return to England would have been futile. With their open-ended travel plans they had not booked a return voyage. Instead, Helen and her mother witnessed the transformation of the city they had so happily begun to explore days earlier. "We are no longer the City of Paris. We are Camp Paris, with cannon on the Eiffel Tower and the Tuileries." Shops and galleries closed; local trains and subways ceased operating. A 10:00 p.m. curfew was enforced, and gas and electricity were curtailed. The Helens attended a meeting of several hundred stranded Americans at the Grand Hotel, where those present approved a resolution asking the American government to send transports to take them home. But The Helens were determined to get to Italy. Helen reassured family at home: "Mother is a good sport, and is very brave, and I feel that we are personally perfectly safe. . . . We are still determined to get to Carl if we can, and perhaps in a few weeks, things will blow over. . . ." Big Helen was resolute. "I can't bear to come home without seeing Carl." And she offered a practical reason: "Our two trunks are there! and we have only three suitcases with us."

Helen and her mother moved from the Hotel Cecilia to a pension run by two English ladies, Miss Galloway and Miss McTavish. Among the guests at the pension were President Woodrow Wilson's sister, Annie Wilson Howe ("a charming woman"), her twenty-three-year-old daughter Anne Cothran, and two-year-old granddaughter, Josephine. The Helens' move was necessitated by the closure of the Cecilia for lack of staff. French workers were conscripted. German staff, of whom there were a surprising number, were arrested and sent south to do agricultural labor.

The reality of their situation was brought home to Helen as she and her mother joined the queue to secure a *permis de séjour*, required of all non-nationals remaining in Paris. "If anybody had told me when we started that mother would one day be sitting on the cold hard stones in a Paris alley with the rain coming down on her defenseless head, and that I should nearly weep over losing half a roll in the gutter, I shouldn't have believed it!" All fifteen of the residents of the pension, accompanied by Miss McTavish, rose at 5:00 a.m. to line up at the prefecture, where they found people already waiting. Despite repeated promises, the doors remained closed. An elderly woman fainted and was carried home. At 9:00 a.m. someone prevailed upon a waiter from a nearby bistro to bring them "cups of very bad coffee and a roll each. The coffee saved mother from fainting." People spread coats on the pavement, and the older ladies took turns sitting; the younger people forming a protective cordon to keep anyone from stepping on them. Matters worsened when it began to rain. "It was then that I dropped my roll in the gutter, and could have wept." Ruefully Helen reflected on the fact that only days earlier she had complained about the coffee and rolls at breakfast. Finally, early in the afternoon, Helen and her mother obtained the *permis* and returned to the pension, "tired, cross, and frightened."

Compounding the anxiety was the absence of reliable news, despite—or because of—being so close to the war. News from the front "was kept entirely out of the papers," Helen wrote, "so we don't know how much real news we are getting.. . .You probably know much more about the fighting here than we do. The press here is very cautious, and we get only the good news." Unawares, Helen identified a dangerous portent: wartime censorship, propaganda, and misrepresentation of facts would inject a poison into postwar European political life.

The situation heightened the sense of alienation Big Helen experienced upon arriving in France. "I hate to go out evenings in this heathen place. . . . The cab drivers are such horrid-looking men." "Mother," Helen wrote, "has an idea that everybody in Paris will either kidnap me, or rob her, or stab us both, but it's simply a state of mind brought about by all this war scare. She doesn't realize that everybody is too busy with their own troubles to trouble anyone else." Contributing to Big Helen's anxiety was the fact that they were receiving no mail from home. She attempted to make light of it, writing that "Helen and I have threatened to advertise for each other so it would appear as if someone was interested in us."

But, with a Nebraska-bred practicality, Big Helen organized the women in the pension to sew shirts, knit socks, and roll bandages. In two weeks, they turned out two dozen shirts and sixty-five yards of gauze dressings. The landladies affectionately dubbed Big Helen "General Joffre." Helen and Katherine Jackson, another American at the pension, attended first aid classes at the Red Cross. The lack of staff at the pension required guests to pitch in and help. "This morning I have been with Miss McTavish to market," Helen reported. "Four of us went. . . . [We] carried great bundles of vegetables and meat and fruit . . . and loaded up for a long time. But we are asked not to waste a particle of bread even, and much of the time we have no butter."

As the days passed, Helen grew more enthusiastic. "Hurrah for little old Belgium! Liège still holds, and the French have crossed the frontier. I'm getting positively blood-thirsty and should like to do to the Emperor what [the suffragettes] wanted to do to [Prime Minister] Asquith." Elsewhere she wrote: "This morning we watched several regiments marched out of Paris, and if I had been a man, I should have been wild to go. Lots of American students, from the Latin Quarter are volunteering, and Katherine Jackson and I are going to get into Red Cross work as soon as we can." In part her enthusiasm was born of the belief that the war would be of short duration. She predicted, erroneously, that the United States would join the war "inside of a week," and "the sooner the better, as the more nations [go] after Germany the sooner the fighting will stop." Above all, she was thrilled at being part of history. While Big Helen wrote that she would prefer a "more peaceful, quieter way of getting information," Helen reveled at being at the center of events. "This is certainly going to be an interesting experience and I'm glad I'm here. . . . I would rather be in the midst of it than anywhere else. But *it will be the last war!* There can never be another one, I firmly believe."

Although they were receiving no letters, The Helens would have been reassured had they known that theirs were arriving at the other end. "Are you getting all this literature I'm sending you?" Henry scrawled on the back of a letter forwarded to Tom. Sending a later batch, he wrote,

> I was very much relieved to get this bundle of letters tonight from Mother and Helen and learn that they are safe for the time being. I do wish they were well out of Europe, though. Still, I guess there's nothing to be done. Helen is taking her usual optimistic view of the situation and is, I think, well able to take care of Mother. I'd like to be over there with them and take a rap at the Kaiser myself.

The Helens could also take comfort in the steady stream of friends and acquaintances in Paris. Helen and Katherine Jackson went out together during the daytime ("I am afraid to let Helen out of my sight unless she is with someone," her mother wrote). A woman from Boston at the pension had been in a sorority at Boston University with Tom's wife Ethel. The Helens met two American men who had just come from Italy; "anyone that looks like an American is a long-lost friend." One was an instructor at Yale, and knew Hal and Fred Fairchild. Other visits brought troubling news. One of the Columbia graduates, an architect, was mobbed and nearly beaten when he was sketching outdoors, the crowd believing him to be a spy. He reported that other artists were being arrested on the same suspicion. Helen gave up sketching. Still, the architect fared better than another American who was taken for a German in a town outside Paris "and was nearly beaten to death before he could be rescued. His face is all black and blue now."

Despite everything, Helen resolved not to miss out on Paris. "This week we have really braced up to do a little sight-seeing, but nothing but the gardens and churches are open." She went shopping, purchasing a coveted Paris hat and blue silk dress. She and her mother returned to Notre Dame, visited smaller neighborhood churches, and took a boat-trip up the Seine to St. Cloud. Evenings, Big Helen went for walks with Miss McTavish or Miss Galloway. One afternoon The Helens took Miss Galloway on a drive through the Bois du Boulogne. "We are making the best of little old Paris while we are here!"

Slowly the pension emptied out. Katherine Jackson and her mother left for England. The Sibleys came to say goodbye; they too were returning to England, and then home. President Woodrow Wilson's sister and her family had already left, with a car and escort from the American Embassy. Their departure was hastened as much by the death of Wilson's wife Ellen on August 6 as by concerns for the presence in Paris of close family of the American president. "Hundreds of Americans are leaving Italy, France and England every day," Helen reported. "From the estimates given of Americans at different cities in Europe, we conclude that the whole population of the United States must have been spending the summer over here, and that if Germany had only known she might have declared war on us at the same time." But their determination to get to Italy remained firm. "It's 'Turin or bust,' and we aren't coming home without seeing Carl!!!"

The Helens left Paris, headed for Marseilles, on the evening of August 26. The more direct route was out of the question, as Switzerland was limiting entry and transit. Instead they went south, and from there along the Mediterranean coast to Italy, arriving in Turin three days later. Under normal circumstances the trip took sixteen hours. Before leaving Paris, Helen stood in long lines, first to secure a *permis de départ* (for which a letter from Carl proved invaluable), then for train tickets. At the station they joined forces with Charlotte Nevin, an American working with the YWCA in Italy, thus fluent in Italian, and Mme. Schaleck, a Frenchwoman married to a German-born naturalized Englishman living in Turin. Eight people crammed into a compartment intended for six. Helen and Charlotte Nevin spent the night walking or sitting in the corridors. Arriving in Marseilles at noon the next day, they went to a YWCA hostel, securing rooms for the night. Next morning there was more paperwork—"the history of our lives to the third and fourth generation"—before they were permitted to board a train for Italy. Another all-night journey, this time with Helen and Charlotte taking turns sleeping on the compartment floor, as the corridors were filled with soldiers. At Genoa they saw the sunrise, before changing trains again for the trip north to Turin.

After traveling for two months and living out of suitcases, The Helens were happy to settle in at Carl's spacious flat, and be reunited with their trunks ("good to see some things we had longed for all summer"). Helen slept until noon the first day, but, once recovered, she took in their new surroundings, and assessed Carl, whom she deemed to be "splendid, looking so well and fine!" (His mother wrote that he had "aged somewhat.") The consulate occupied space in an apartment building where Carl's flat was located as well. Helen wrote that she and her mother "have a nice bedroom next to his, and a beautiful big bathroom, and a whopper of a living room back of his office." There was a kitchen, with a cook and a maid provided at government expense. Although Carl had been at the consulate since 1912, Helen considered the rooms to be still "a little bare . . . [they] will only need a few touches to look homelike."

For his part, Carl was relieved to have his family safe in Turin. It was one less worry in a situation where he found himself working through a list of nearly 300 Americans believed to have taken refuge in Italy, fleeing Austria, Germany, France, or the Balkans. Letters and telegrams flooded the consulate, needing to be forwarded to other parts of Italy or Europe.

Having gotten his mother and sister safely to Turin, Carl cautioned against further travel until the situation became clearer. Italy, although a member of the Triple Alliance with Germany and Austria, had declared its neutrality. But feelings on both sides ran high. Helen chafed at the inactivity. "If it wasn't for me, she would go back to Paris for some sort of work," Big Helen wrote. "It is a good thing she has the responsibility of a mother, I think." Carl did his best to keep the two women occupied, introducing them to members of Turin's expatriate community: Mrs. Poole; Florence Botsford and her "very charming and refined daughter" Rosamond; Mrs. Weinske, "a divorcee, young and pretty, and plenty of money;" and Mrs. Kind, "a pleasant English woman" whose husband was in the Swiss army. Mme. Schaleck, who shared the journey to Turin, was a frequent visitor for tea; The Helens in turn were invited to her home. Mrs. Weinske invited the three Perrys to the cinema (Turin, The Helens learned, was the center of the Italian film industry), after which all four "drove out to a lovely park café and had ices and a charming drive home."

Although Big Helen noted with admiration the ability of the people they met to speak several languages—"most unusual to us Americans"— she offered a revealing insight into the lives of the American women living abroad:

> I am more thankful every day that I am an American living
> in America. The circle of women we meet have so little in
> their lives, I feel as if I have gone back twenty-five years or
> more. Of course, we have the war to talk about, but aside
> from that, there is nothing but people and clothes to discuss,
> and one grows rather bored by it all. Oh! Yes, I forgot, dogs.
> The women are bright, conversational, and attractive, but
> it all amounts to so little. . . . No clubs, no church work, no
> philanthropies. The women are good housekeepers, but have
> no visible husbands, most of them. One is in America, one in
> the Swiss military, one in service in Africa.

Big Helen's final observation was poignant: "They think Helen is wonderful because she means to do things" with her life.

Ever the organizer, Big Helen put the women to work sewing for the Red Cross. "Have had two meetings of English and American ladies to sew and knit for the soldiers, about thirty here each time. . . . Our own little circle of friends, and then people from stenographers to countesses, governesses and people of wealth." The work carried on for the duration of The Helens' time in Turin. "They are all crazy about mother," Helen reported, "both for herself, and also because she gave them this opportunity. . . which the wife of the English consul herself refused. But evidently said lady has profited by the good example mother set her, for since then she had given a very nice Xmas tea for all the ladies who are working here."

Helen also turned to the familiar: volunteer work and study. She spent a day a week at the Red Cross office. She met an Italian woman, fluent in French, who wanted to learn English, so they agreed to trade lessons. "After Christmas I hope to take up a little Italian too." And Helen resumed sketching. She attended a fashion show and saw some "very modern gowns, light fitting waists and long tunics." She discovered that Turin was renowned for its chocolate, "and chocolate is my favorite article of diet!" Mother and daughter were introduced to unfamiliar foods by Maria, the cook: risotto, eggplant, mushrooms, and "sixty different kinds of macaroni." They marveled at the bouquets of flowers in the shops, surrounded with chiffon and ribbons, "just as formal and ornate as the Italians themselves." Their building had a garden plot, maintained by a gardener who worked for the countess in the apartment above. Daily he left flowers on the windowsill of the consular offices and their apartment: roses and geraniums and heliotrope. The two maids brought bouquets for Helen and her mother as well.

The Helens were delighted with Turin, surprised at the width of the streets, the spaciousness of the city squares, and the outdoor shops, tucked under the arcades, selling a variety of silk and leather goods. Two things jarred them: the number of beggars ("one never imagined so many forms of mutilation") and the way that Italian men "stare and ogle one in most unpleasant ways, stop and turn around, and follow one. It makes Helen cross. . . . Even an old woman like me doesn't escape it."

"The Helens" in Turin, 1915.

One afternoon Carl took Helen to the Martini and Rossi winery and vermouth plant, a half hour's drive from Turin. "Carl had done something for them in a commercial way, something about their export to the U.S., so they invited us all out to see their factory. Mother didn't feel like going, so she missed a wonderful day." The company owners drove Helen and Carl past "red and white villas on the green hills, and wonderful vineyards planted in step-like terraced gardens." The facility employed 400 workers, a village unto itself, with "miles of big, airy wine cellars" lined with hundreds of vats. The owners, four brothers, invited Carl and Helen to lunch; Helen describing it as a twelve-course meal, served by a liveried butler on beautiful silver and china, with five different wines to sample. "I endeavored to be polite and pretend to drink them, but it's a wonder I wasn't carried out on a stretcher. I hate wine so, that I don't usually attempt it at all, but under the circumstances I had to make the endeavor." Two weeks later the winery sent Helen a dozen bottles of wine. "The reason for the gift was that I admired some of the cunning jugs and pretty vase-like bottles, and they sent me a collection, but all *full!* Tell Miss Connolly I wish she were here to help me get rid of them." Big Helen, meanwhile, broadened the range of her experience by celebrating her birthday with a glass of champagne: "My first taste of champagne! I felt much puffed up and very wicked."

As the autumn progressed, the political situation in Italy calmed. The flow of displaced persons slowed, and Carl's workload abated. He and his sister spent more time together, going for walks around the city. Carl, conscious of the aggressive behavior of Italian men, did not like Helen to go out unescorted, much to her chagrin. They went to afternoon tea dances at the hotels, and to the cinema. Big Helen was happy to see the two spending so much time together, "it rejoices my heart". But to her diary she confided her nagging concern: "Carl out in p.m." "Carl out late till all hours and I didn't sleep." "Carl was out very late at night. Slept scarcely any."

With political tensions eased, the Perrys embarked on some weekend travel. By train and bus, they made the three-hour journey to Courmayeur at the southern foot of Mont Blanc. They drove through villages consisting of a single narrow street; chickens and donkey-carts everywhere in evidence; women coming from the surrounding fields carrying loads of hay on their heads. "I think the national motto of Italy must be 'Let the women do the work.'" Helen compared the scenes to paintings by Millet. Each village had "square gray mossy bell towers" atop the church, and "always the tall gray-green poplars beside them. I like to think of the poplars as the church-spires of the open fields." Mont Blanc came into view as they exited the railway tunnel. "It was just at sunset, a shiny white peak against a red sky." The area was popular with hikers in summer; in winter it was a ski resort. The Perrys arrived between seasons, "so we had the hotel all to ourselves. Carl's room had a fireplace and we certainly appreciated it, for the nights are cold." They awoke in the morning to the sound of cowbells, "soft and musical, like the echoes of chimes." Wandering the town, Big Helen marveled at the cleanliness of the Dora River which flowed through the Aoste Valley, and at the domestic uses to which water directly from the river was put: washing vegetables, cleaning and scrubbing pots, cleaning wooden shoes, and doing laundry, all in the open. "Every few blocks would be a big tank under a shed with washing slabs and there the women were washing and gossiping, slapping, soaping and rubbing the clothes." In the afternoon, before heading back to Turin, Carl and Helen climbed the paths at the base of the mountain, exploring back streets of the town, while their mother waited below.

In mid-October, Helen fulfilled her wish to see Venice. It was "the place above all others" she wanted to see. Carl accompanied them as far as Milan, where they visited the Duomo and saw Leonardo da Vinci's "Last Supper" in the Dominican convent of Santa Maria delle Grazie. From there Helen and her mother went on to Venice. Helen's descriptions were rapturous. "I wonder who originated Venice!... It's the quaintest, prettiest, and watery-est place I've even been in, and everything about it is just the same as it was centuries ago." Twenty years later, even after visiting the city another three times, she lifted passages directly from letters written during this first visit and used them in *Jean & Company*: descriptions of vermilion sails, shining white domes, crimson cushions in black-painted gondolas, gondolas that served as moving vans and vegetable carts.

Venice, Helen observed, was the first place they had been where galleries and churches were not closed either on account of war or militant suffragettes. They toured the Doge's Palace, and went to the outlying island of Murano to visit its glass factories. They went shopping at the Lido, where Big Helen wanted to buy everything she saw: "laces, beads, jewelry and glass, beautiful beyond compare." Mrs. Carroll, wife of Carl's counterpart in Venice, invited them to tea. Returning to their hotel by gondola one evening, Helen described the lagoon at sunset as

a golden path, with the sun a great golden ball, setting behind the faintly purple hills at the edge of the opalescent sea. It made you fairly ache with the beauty of it all. And last night I hung out of my window at the hotel and listened to the soft lapping of the waves against the gondolas, and the singing, and watched the red and orange lights hanging between the black sky and water.

Late October and November in Turin brought chilly, foggy weather. "Sunny Italy is a misnomer!" There was no heat in their building until mid-November, and Carl and his mother came down with colds. They bundled up in layers, wearing overcoats inside the house and taking hot water bottles to bed. Carl and Helen located a small petroleum stove, which they wheeled from room to room. Late October brought an earthquake tremor, sending crowds rushing into the streets. "Europe is certainly putting herself out to entertain us, isn't she?" Helen wrote; Big Helen adding, "I believe now robbery is about the last thing to come to us."

In late November, Helen and her mother experienced the melancholy sensation felt by Americans abroad on Thanksgiving Day, as the rest of the country "went peacefully on her everyday way, and never knew it was Thanksgiving at all." It was strange, Helen wrote, not to have a big family gathering, with turkey and cranberry sauce, but they invited a dozen expatriate friends in for a big dinner, followed by dancing, "everything from the Virginia Reel to the Fox Trot." Those assembled drank a toast to family and friends at home in America. "Then we had American ice-cream and American cake, and sang Auld Lang Syne, and had just a nice home-y time all together."

Christmas arrived. Helen went to the home of one of their American friends to decorate the Christmas tree. "It was a real American Xmas tree, and just loaded with droll little toys. . . . At Xmas time I always wish I was six years old!" On Christmas Eve Helen attended Midnight Mass with Maria, the cook. Carl went to a dinner at one o'clock Christmas morning, and was out all night. Helen and her mother gave each other tickets for the upcoming opera season. Christmas night the Perrys invited a few of the expatriates to dinner; others joined afterwards for dancing. "It was a very jolly party, and what we thought would be a lonely Xmas turned out to be a very gay one."

The festivities continued the next day, with Rosamond Botsford's wedding, to which Carl had devoted much time and paperwork, given the circumstances of the marriage of an American citizen to an Italian. The Perrys attended the church wedding and went next to the *Municipio* for the civil ceremony. "I was a bridesmaid," Helen wrote, "which fact was denoted by a bouquet and nothing else. We all just stood there, until two or three men rattled off some Italian, and then everybody signed their names. Nothing particularly solemn about it, but it's a good tight knot, as divorce isn't recognized in Italy." After a luncheon at the home of the groom's family, the couple were given "a regular American send-off," with rose petals, rice, and a bouquet of white roses tied to the car. "It was all new to the Italians and they enjoyed it a lot!"

Year's end brought a sober realization. Jubilant crowds in August had cheered the troops with slogans that they would be "home by Christmas." Helen's thoughts were a marked contrast to her earlier enthusiasm. "Heartsick," she wrote. The adopted son of Mme. Schaleck, with whom they had traveled from Marseilles to Turin, was killed at Verdun. "That brings the war near to us." "The killed and wounded count up to many thousands," Big Helen wrote, "and the present generation of men seem likely to perish from the earth."

Helen worried about her future as well. "I wonder when I'll be earning a salary again? Work in London doesn't look at all promising since the war, and I wonder if business won't be pretty slow in New York, too." In November she had written that, much as she would miss Turin, she looked forward to getting back to work and was hoping to hear from Mr. Dahler, the director of Herter Looms. Shortly before Christmas she learned that Mr. Dahler had left the company, and "there is nothing doing in New York for this winter." She persisted in her errand on behalf of Louise Connolly: learning as much as she could about museums, "but most of them are closed for repairs, and when they are open, I seem to be the sole visitor. Nevertheless, I am getting at the directors by writing letters to them, and visiting all the places I can find."

January in Turin was cold and snowy. Big Helen's diary records a monotonous routine. "Home all day." "Sewing." "Saturday went for tea." Helen and Carl, along with some young people, went on a skiing trip to Gressoney-Saint-John in the Aoste Valley; Helen happily sporting a new "mountain suit" of trousers, short skirt, and jacket.

And then something happened. Big Helen's diary breaks off from February 15 until April 6—this from a person who daily kept a diary from 1909 until just before her death. There is also a gap in the letters sent home. But a close reading of the diary entries in the four weeks leading up to mid-February gives some clues. Fifteen of those entries concern Carl. "Carl out all night." "Carl opera, late, out [until] four o'clock." "Carl out for lunch & dinner & home at ten, fell into window in door and cut forehead and fingers." The next day's entry reads: "Carl and I went to Mrs. Poole's for tea. He pretty seedy after fall. Opera in evening and then he stayed home to please me." The next three entries, however, indicate that Carl resumed his late nights. Then the diary breaks off. When the diary and letters resumed, mother and daughter were in Santa Margherita on the Italian Riviera. Helen wrote that "Mother is eating to beat the band, and has slept nearly twelve hours each night." She referred to the "busy time getting away from Turin . . . Mother was just getting well enough to go out a little. . . ." Three weeks later, in a letter from Rome, Helen wrote about the enjoyable time she is having. "I've been lonesome since [Mother] and Carl were both sick."

Did Carl's problems, now apparently escalated to heavy drinking, cause Big Helen to become so ill or distraught that she was unable to write any diary entries or letters? Was the trip to Santa Margherita, followed by several weeks of travel through Italy, an attempt to put distance between the two women and Carl's problems in Turin? A clue comes from Big Helen's memoir, wherein she summarized the year in

Europe in a single paragraph.

> In June, 1914, Helen and I went abroad. She was graduating from Columbia and wanted to study abroad, and to see Carl in Turin, Italy. We had a wonderful year in England, France, and Italy. The World War was declared. I was desperately ill. We spent eight months at the Consulate in Turin where Carl was consul. Very tragic, distressing months.

At first reading, "tragic, distressing months" appears to refer to the war. A more careful parsing of the paragraph suggests that the reference is to Carl and his situation in Turin.

Between April and early June, Helen and her mother traveled through Italy. In Rome they were taken under the wing of an American, Rose Morrow Previtali, who had lived in Summit and knew the Twomblys. In 1909 Rose married an Italian physician she met in New York. She now divided her time between Rome and the family estate in Bergamo. Rose insisted that Helen and her mother stay at the Hotel Boston, where she had rooms. Rose, Big Helen wrote, has been "a god-send to us, she has introduced us to many pleasant people, has been about with us a great deal, and is in herself charming."

Like all first-time tourists in Rome, The Helens took in the sights, Helen even venturing into the Catacombs, "to which depths," her mother wrote, "I refused to go. Helen was glad I didn't, as it was dark and spooky." The Sistine Chapel was a disappointment, "more admired when read about than when seen." The crowds in St. Peter's Basilica recalled for Big Helen a story once told her by Brainerd: he attended a service there, fainted due to the bad air, and came to still standing on his feet. The Coliseum inspired awe. "One is taken back at once to the days of Nero." From Rome they went down the coast to Pompeii. "I've gotten interested in archeology since our stay" in Italy, Helen wrote. The museum at Pompeii "shows the life of the village, the real people, instead of just emperors and their palaces and ruins." Everywhere it was the everyday aspects of life she found most interesting: Naples, where cows and goats were brought right to the front doors of buildings and milked on the spot for customers. The narrow streets of the slums, "women combing their own and children's hair in the doorway, and every possible domestic thing being done out of doors." The way the attendants in a salon were awed by her mother's white hair and gray hairpins: "nobody has white hair over here, either a wig or dye, very many wigs are worn."

From there to Tuscany, where in Florence they visited the Baptistry outside the *Duomo*, its bronze doors the work of the Renaissance artist Lorenzo Ghiberti. Everywhere they found Americans with connections to home, or people from earlier in their trip, confirmation of the democratization of the Grand Tour and the limits thereof. In Rome Helen met, according to her mother, "some charming American artists . . . all interested in the same kind of work Helen is . . . attractive fellows. They have been at Columbia and know many of the same people she does." Helen spent a good deal of time with them. "They came for her after lunch and she has been out with them ever since. Just coming in now to tell me she was going out to dinner with them." Reporting from the pension in Siena, Big Helen wrote that two of the twelve women there had connections to Summit. In Florence, they ran into Charlotte Nevin, with whom they shared the harrowing train trip from Marseilles a year earlier. With the leisure to sit in a café over coffee, they discovered that Charlotte's older sister was married to the writer and diplomat Amos Wilder, a classmate at Yale of Uncle Harry's. Charlotte had met Uncle Harry on several occasions in New York. [3]

But the situation in Italy was growing daily more tense. The German Embassy was located just around the corner from their hotel in Rome. Heavily guarded, it was the scene of near-daily demonstrations. The Kaiser was hung in effigy. At every train station between Rome and Siena they saw crowds of men and women saying goodbye, kissing and weeping; people gathered for miles along the tracks to wave and cheer as the trains carrying soldiers passed. Big Helen described the scene in Florence:

> As we came home from the *Duomo* this noon, hundreds of soldiers passed us, marching to the train. Roses and rose petals were showered upon them from the windows, and there were many tears and sad faces. I stood with the tears running down my face to see those young boys marching to death. It is all harrowing, but it seems a certain way of shortening the war.

Italy entered the war on May 23, 1915, on the side of England and France, lured by promises of territory at Austria's expense. Helen

---

[3] Amos Wilder's son was playwright Thornton Wilder, whose fame lay in the future.

declared that this time "I am going to help!" A friend of Rose Previtali talked of opening her villa as a hospital, and Helen hoped she might go there to work. "I should go mad just sitting and doing nothing, in the midst of so much suffering and misery!. . . And who knows, America may be putting her finger in the pie soon!" Observing that President Wilson's protest over the sinking of the *Lusitania* two weeks earlier was all well and good, she wondered: "will it have force enough? Wish we could really be a *power* in settling things."

The Helens returned to Turin on June 2, where Big Helen prevailed in her insistence that they return to the United States. Carl's counterpart in Genoa was taking his family home at the end of the month; the two women would join them. Big Helen feared that, with Italy in the war, opportunities for sailing would be fewer, and the journey less safe. It was time to go home.

Helen and her mother booked passage on the *Duca degli Abruzzi*, sailing from Genoa on June 28. The American expatriate community in Turin turned out to bid them farewell. The first nights at sea the boat sailed in darkness, a precaution against German submarines. The mood on shipboard lightened as passengers put ever more distance between themselves and the war-torn continent. The Fourth of July saw a festive celebration. On July 10, at twilight, the ship entered New York harbor. Some twenty years later, it was this first homecoming that Helen described in *Jean & Company:*

> . . .they stood side by side leaning over the rail, as they came up the river again to New York. Once again they passed Fort Wadsworth, Ellis Island, the Battery, the Aquarium. It was the most beautiful hour of the day, just at sunset, and the towers of the great city were bathed in gold. The sky behind them was opalescent, shimmering. Twinkling lights shone here and there in the tall buildings.

Big Helen wrote that she wanted to kiss the ground. "Closed our adventure."

Chapter 5
Homelands

Uncle Harry and Edward met the *Duca degli Abruzzi* at the dock in New York. Back at the Twombly home The Helens were greeted by Aunt Patty, along with cousins Alex and Sophie. The women rested up, and unpacked their trunks. Helen went to New York City to catch up with friends and to find an apartment for herself and her mother. The first weeks at home were a re-entry experience, including resuming connections with people from Europe. Mrs. Botsford, who went home to New York after her daughter Rosamond's Christmas wedding in Turin, came to visit Big Helen, the first of many visits back and forth. Helen went to a suffrage meeting in Summit. In September she and cousin Edward attended a rally in New York City. Women's suffrage was on the ballot in New York in November. Helen served as an usher at the rally; Edward sold tickets at the door.

Big Helen confided to her sister and brother-in-law the story of Carl and their time in Turin. "Long hard talk about Carl's affairs. . . . Told Frances the story and was very ashamed of it all, nearly sick all day. Harry was lovely to me."

Meanwhile, Helen began a new job. With the change in administration at Herter Looms, and with the interior decorating business, as she feared, at a low ebb, Louise Connolly stepped in and offered Helen a short-term position at the Newark Museum, assisting with the upcoming New Jersey Textiles Exhibition.

Louise Connolly was educational adviser to John Cotton Dana, the revered director of the Newark Library and—following its creation in 1909 as a separate institution—the Newark Museum as well. [1] Connolly was appointed to her position in 1912, following a contentious firing from her post as superintendent of public schools in Summit, a job she held from 1906 to 1910. By a six to three vote, the all-male school board voted not to renew her contract. The board's president claimed that the "prevailing impression . . . was that the public schools in New Jersey

---

[1] The Museum Association, as the separate institution was called, was still housed in the Newark Library. For simplicity's sake, the Museum Association is referred to herein as the Newark Museum.

were becoming too 'feminized,'" and that "the schools here require the businesslike administration which a man Superintendent could give."

Summit's club women, including Aunt Patty's Fortnightly Club, rose to Connolly's defense. Seven hundred people signed a petition; the board refused to consider it. The *Summit Herald* offered a misogynistic analysis of the protest. "If the unwarranted personality and intimidating influences of the women, who for the past few weeks were engaged in a contest in the interest of retaining one of their sex in her position as school superintendent, is any evidence of what would be the result if we had women suffrage, may the good Lord deliver us from such a misfortune." [2]

Following Connolly's termination as superintendent, and until her appointment at the Newark Museum, she worked as head of the Elementary Text Book Department at D.C. Heath & Co. In 1912 she moved into the Twombly home as a boarder. Connolly was still living with the Twomblys when Helen and her mother returned from Europe.

Louise Connolly was another of the influential people Helen was fortunate in befriending. Connolly was representative of the "new woman," a college-educated, reform-minded individual steeped in the values of the Progressive Era. [3] Born in 1862, she came from a family of ardent abolitionists. She earned both a bachelor of science and a master's degree from George Washington University in 1888 and 1898 respectively. Connolly was an ardent suffragist, teacher, and administrator. She was involved in the settlement movement in New York City, and taught courses at lower Manhattan's Judson Memorial Church, whose mission it was to serve African Americans and newly arrived European immigrants. Connolly first met the Twomblys at Summit's Central Presbyterian Church (Connolly was raised in that denomination); that connection led to her involvement with Neighborhood House.

Louise Connolly's *The Educational Value of Museums*—whose findings she hoped Helen could augment by visiting European institutions—advocated for a new kind of museum, one rooted in and serving the community. Everything, from the architecture to the exhibits to a staff grounded in pedagogical methods, should provide a welcoming experience to visitors. Connolly singled out the Smithsonian

[2] "Summit is Rent by a School Dispute," *New York Times*, February 19, 1910; Edmund B. Raftis, *Summit, New Jersey: From Poverty Hill to the Hill City* (Seattle: Great Swamp Press, 1996), 187-188.
[3] Carol G. Duncan, *A Matter of Class: John Cotton Dana, Progressive Reform, and the Newark Museum* (Pittsburgh, PA: Periscope Publishing, 2009), 107.

Museum in Washington D.C. as an example of a museum that failed in every regard. The building was a "castle with forbidding towers," its location "far removed from man's daily life," its "repellant" interior and display of objects leaving children with "museophobia—a horror of museums." Citing John Dewey, she argued that children learn best through hands-on experience. [4]

Louise Connolly's "museophobia" concept anticipated John Cotton Dana's 1917 critique, *The Gloom of the Museum*. He charged that the traditional museum kept objects in splendid isolation, far from the life of the community in which it was located. [5] "A great department store," Dana wrote, "easily reached, open at all hours, is more like a good museum of art than any of the museums we have yet established." [6] Dana is rightly considered to be the most innovative library and museum director of the era. He shifted the focus of the museum from a storehouse of European Old Masters to an institution that championed the American arts. He sought to break down barriers between art and the artifacts of daily life.

Louise Connolly was instrumental in the realization of Dana's vision. Art historian Carol Duncan states that "over the fifteen years they worked together, [Dana] became increasingly dependent on Connolly in the running of the museum. It is certain that without her the Newark Museum would not have been the vibrant, innovative institution it became." [7] Dana worked well with women in a professional capacity. He supported women's suffrage. He cultivated philanthropic support from women's clubs in Newark and environs (Summit's Fortnightly Club, for example). Historian Marjorie Schwarzer writes that while many saw library or museum work as an acceptable hobby for a genteel lady, Dana encouraged women to think in terms of a professional career. Women, Dana wrote, "were less likely to embroil themselves in ... showmanship and more likely to care about educating people." [8]

The role of women as educators and nurturers conformed to the social feminist or "difference feminist" ideal of the day, i.e. women *were* different from men, and thus could make a difference in society.

---

[4] Duncan, 108-109.

[5] Art historian Ezra Shales states that "with a master's degree as well as a college education, Connolly had more professional training than that of the rest of the staff, including Dana." See, Ezra Shales, *Made in Newark: Cultivating Industrial Arts and Civic Identity in the Progressive Era* (New Brunswick, NJ: Rivergate Books, 2010), 90.

[6] Chalmers Hadley, *John Cotton Dana: A Sketch* (Chicago: American Library Association, 1943), 68.

[7] Duncan, 108.

[8] Marjorie Schwarzer, *Riches, Rivals and Radicals:100 Years of Museums in America*, (Washington D.C.: American Association of Museums, 2006), 177.

Connolly and her colleagues at Newark, part of that first generation of female college graduates, saw themselves as social reformers, and library work as a calling. Connolly once told the Newark *Sunday Call* that "there is no profession which demands so fine a quality of self-abnegation as that of the librarian." [9]

For Helen, museum work recalled the female society she experienced during her visit in 1909 to the Metropolitan Museum of Art; staff members gathering in their cozy basement lunchroom. Moreover, Helen's Columbia University training matched the Newark Museum's plans for an upcoming exhibit on New Jersey's textile industry. Research for the exhibition was the first project to which Helen was assigned. The textiles exhibition was modeled on the success, a year earlier, of the Clay Products of New Jersey exhibit (New Jersey was the nation's largest manufacturer of clay products). The exhibit showcased everything from antiques to factory wares, teapots to toilets and sewage pipes, and was, according to art historian Ezra Shales, "a deliberate strategy for upsetting hierarchies within the arts, breaking down precise definitions of art and industry." Industrialists, artisans, and clubwomen lent objects to the museum; the latter opening their china cabinets, bringing out cherished antiques, transforming "private possessions into public culture." Louise Connolly wrote scripts for the docents, including the line: "Be it known to you that the first person who tried pottery was a woman!" This statement constituted, for its time, a "stridently feminist point of view, and aligned with [Connolly's] espousal of women's suffrage." [10] The Clay Products exhibit drew 28,000 visitors during the two months of its run, twice the total museum attendance of the previous year.

The Textiles Exhibition, planned for February and March of 1916, was destined to be an even bigger success. Fully one quarter of New Jersey's workforce was involved, directly or indirectly, in the textile industry. This represented an enormous base from which to draw donors and visitors alike. Dana described his vision for the exhibition in *The Newarker*, the museum's magazine. The show would feature the art of weaving in New Jersey, "from the bark mats of the Delaware Indians and the homespun stuffs of our Colonial grandmothers, to those silks and tapestries of our own day which rival in beauty the best products of the looms of Europe." Striking the theme of community

---

[9] Shales, 18-19.
[10] Shales, 117, 153-154, 158.

participation, Dana noted that "manufacturers, craftsmen, educators, club women and school children are all co-operating to make this undertaking a success." He highlighted the museum's educational mission: raw materials, production, and finished products would be shown in sequence, and phases of production would be explained to visitors. "In this way . . . publicity can be given to the manufacturer, and at the same time the public can be educated to a better knowledge and appreciation of home industries." [11]

New Jersey Textile Exhibition; Newark Museum, 1916.
The Sunday Call, *Newark, NJ, January 30, 1916.*

Over fifty firms were represented in the exhibit, which was organized according to categories: cotton thread, knits, silk ribbon, tapestry, woolen garments, and hat making. The latter was a major provider of jobs in Newark: a dozen millinery firms employed 5,000 workers, ten percent of the city's workforce. [12]

Helen's responsibilities included corresponding with businesses and factories to solicit the loan of products. The silk industry's trade magazine listed nine firms which, "through the direct efforts of Helen Clark Perry, a member of the museum staff," agreed to participate in the exhibit ("Helen's exhibit," as her mother always referred to it in her diary). [13] Months earlier, Helen was in contact with The Commercial Museum in Philadelphia, requesting assistance with an exhibit of live silkworms. "It would be quite possible," the curator wrote to Helen, "for

[11] John Cotton Dana, "Textile Industries of New Jersey," *The Newarker* (January 1916): 50.
[12] Shales, 194.
[13] *Silk* 9:1 (New York: Silk Publishing Industry, January 1916): 38. https://babel.hathitrust.org/cgi/pt?id=n-yp.33433107853131&view=1up&seq=42, accessed 25 February 2020.

you to get the eggs and hatch them, feed the worms and show the entire development from the laying of the eggs to the cocoons." Not, however, without challenges.

> It would be necessary . . . to have sent to you, this occurring in the winter, fresh leaves from the mulberry or one of our allied plants, the Osage orange. In a limited way, if you prepared for it now, you could transplant in tubs several small trees of Osage orange which are very common for hedges, and in that way support your worms, making a live exhibit. . . . I should think it would pay you to come over to The Commercial Museum some day and see the silk exhibit and in that way more definitely determine how you would set up [yours].

The Textiles Exhibition drew 50,000 visitors over the course of its six-week run. Three hundred groups, from women's clubs to school children to the staffs of department stores, attended. Demonstrations of a traditional spinning wheel to a modern knitting machine attracted attention. Visitors wrote expressing their appreciation. One letter, in the neat handwriting of a teacher, conveyed the sentiments of the children:

> On February 29th we all went to the Textile Exhibit. . . . We first saw the moving pictures of silk, wool, cotton, flax and all sorts of things. Then Miss Perry showed us the different exhibits. Most of us liked the silk best. We saw combs for combing the flax and spinning wheels for spinning it. Miss Perry showed us how to spin. There were some copper rolls for printing cloth. They came from the mills at Paterson. We saw three looms, two for weaving rugs and one [for] ribbon. Miss Perry explained how they worked and wove a little for us. The exhibit was very large and we could not see everything that day because we had to go back to school for lunch.

Another letter, addressed to Dana from Jane Fales, director of the Textiles and Clothing Department at Columbia Teachers College, and one of Helen's former professors, expressed the "very great pleasure of seeing, under Miss Perry's kind guidance, the splendid textile exhibit you have arranged at the Newark Public Library, and I cannot resist writing to tell you how valuable an exhibit my textile students and I thought it. It seemed to me to combine to an unusual degree the extremely practical and extremely artistic." Helen replied to Miss Fales: "I am very glad you thought our exhibit was worthwhile. . . . We are now taking it down, which is rather the 'cold grey dawn of the morning after.' I hate to see things go."

Helen also wrote to those who had loaned artifacts, thanking them and making an additional request.

> We are now asking manufacturers if they are willing to give to the Museum any or all of their exhibit to be used as the basis of a permanent industrial museum that we are planning. We believe that a museum should be not only a storehouse of rare and costly paintings, objects of art, but an institution which brings to the attention of citizens the things used in everyday life, by exhibiting them in an interesting and uniform manner.

A component of the Textiles Exhibition was the Homelands Exhibit, highlighting the contributions of Newark's immigrant population. (Two-thirds of Newark's residents in 1913 were foreign born.) The Homelands display was so popular that the museum expanded it into a stand-alone exhibit during the summer of 1916, part of a series of city-wide events celebrating the 250th anniversary of Newark's founding. Along with textiles, the new exhibition included pottery, wood carvings, leather-work, jewelry, toys, furniture, and cooking implements. Dana put Louise Connolly in charge; she in turn set up a committee, the Homelands Association, representing women's clubs and ethnic associations. Museum staffer Alice Kendall oversaw the execution of the exhibit.

The Homelands Association gave the widest possible connotation to immigration. "The city will celebrate not only the coming of the first strangers 250 years ago, but their continued coming ever since; not only the sterling qualities of the first English or New England settlers, but the constant addition of skill, talent, virtue, knowledge and taste made by settlers from many lands." The Homelands Exhibit fit with

Connolly's interests. She was passionate about welcoming Newark's immigrant population into the library and museum. Her commitment was an extension of her earlier settlement house work, and, inasmuch as the Homelands Exhibit included Newark's African-American population as immigrants, it was an extension of her work at Judson Memorial Church as well.

Connolly's inclusion of immigrants contained an element of gender politics. Speaking to members of The Contemporary, a Newark civic organization, she argued that men and women experience the city and immigration differently.

> The American man is awake to the fact that there are 'furiners' over the border. So he is putting on his war togs, rattling his terror-rousing drum. . . . The American woman is waking to the fact that there are foreign-born women within the border. So she is exchanging recipes, presenting baby clothes, giving advice about the croup, and setting up that subtle service of sisterhood which her mother and grandmother knew before her, unto the nth generation of those that suffered and loved, according to the universal custom of women.

Connolly further elevated the purpose of the exhibit, contrasting it to the conflict raging in Europe: "Thus the contribution of our women to our 250th Anniversary is one of peace. . . . While Slav, Teuton and Celt redden the fields of Europe with each other's blood, here in Newark . . . their daughters battle only in a friendly rivalry as to which shall add most of that knowledge and skill brought from the homelands of their birth to the comfort and pleasure of this best Homeland of their choice." [14]

Earlier, in gathering artifacts for the Homelands portion of the Textiles Exhibition, the museum worked through the public schools. So successful was this strategy (immigrant families submitted so many items that some schools held their own exhibits) that efforts at working with the schools were redoubled. The Homelands Association sent a letter to schools, describing plans for the summer exhibit and

---

[14] Untitled manuscript by Louise Connolly, Newark Museum archives. The content is similar to a speech delivered before The Contemporary, and quoted by Duncan: "The male Newarker who meets a Swede, an Italian, a Japanese, a Negro, queries, 'How can you serve in my business, [or] how will you function in the political life of the city?'" By contrast, "The thoughtful women in Newark. . .think: 'How do you live? How do you feed and clothe your children?'" The manuscript is likely the text for speeches given by Connolly to civic organizations and women's clubs in Newark. See Duncan, 135-136.

requesting that children ask their families for the loan of items that will "reflect credit on the good taste and the skill of the people from your nation."

Museum staffers recognized that personal contact would be even more effective, and assigned Helen to the task. During the spring of 1916 she visited public and parochial schools, asking children to encourage their mothers to open cupboards, trunks, and storage chests and lend items for the Homelands Exhibit. She went further, inviting children to bring their mothers to school in the late afternoons or evening so she could meet and assure them of the museum's interest in their offerings, and guarantee the safe return of cherished family possessions. It was Helen's responsibility to manage the paperwork: a form for each item lent so as to assure return to the proper owner.

The Homelands Exhibit opened on July 5, 1916 and ran for a month. It took place not at the museum but at the Burnet Street School, the largest elementary school building in Newark, one boasting a large auditorium. Nineteen ethnic groups were represented, and admission was free. The exhibit was open six afternoons a week, with extended hours on Tuesday and Friday evenings. Special performances, at ten cents admission, took place in the auditorium: a Ruthenian choir, Russian dancing troupes, a "Negro choral club," mock weddings in traditional costumes, plays, skits, and tableaux vivants. A Chinese restaurant hosted a reception and banquet. Representatives of different nationalities, mostly women, demonstrated traditional methods of spinning, weaving, embroidery, and lace-making.

The Homelands Exhibit drew 5,000 visitors over the course of the month. Attendance was hurt by a summer heat wave and fears resulting from an outbreak of polio in the city. Nevertheless, the Homelands Exhibit was the best-attended event of the several marking the city's 250th anniversary. The exhibit was publicized with banners in city parks, flyers in twenty languages, and extensive coverage in the Newark and New York City newspapers. The *New York Evening Post* of July 16, for example, carried a story headlined: "Newark Proud of Homelands Exhibit / Old Customs of New Americans There on View." The article stated: "If nothing should come of the all-summer Newark celebration but a closer union between the different peoples who live there, and a quicker amalgamation of all nationalities into Americans who still keep the best of their life in the old countries, the celebration would be worthwhile."

The phrase "quicker amalgamation of nationalities" surfaces a tension at the heart of the Homelands project. Scholars debate the extent to which the exhibit was a celebration of ethnic diversity, or a manifestation of curiosity for the exotic. Ezra Shales points out that while the earlier Textile Exhibition was organized according to methods of manufacture, the Homelands section as well as the standalone exhibit organized artifacts ethnographically, each nationality given its own room. No attempt was made at distinguishing the work of an artisan from that of an amateur. "While the sampler from 1834 [in the earlier main exhibit] was credited carefully to a ten-year old . . . broad cultural labels such as 'Russian,' 'Jewish,' 'Romanian,' and 'African,' were used to classify Homelands artifacts. . . . The 'primitive' arts of foreigners comprised a benchmark to confirm the rest of Newark's progress, and establish a course for immigrants' future refinement." Shales goes even further: "The subdivision of Homelands artifacts followed the conventional emphasis on national identity . . . and on race[found] in natural history museums and world's fairs. . . . The decision to classify all immigrant textiles by race and nation in this manner was an aspect of the Homelands Exhibit that reveals its intellectual origins in nineteenth-century imperialism." [15]

The Homelands Exhibit likewise invites comparisons with the critique of the Labor Museum at Chicago's Hull House, which displayed and demonstrated traditional crafts and methods of production. [16] There was a strand of thinking in Progressivism that yearned for the restoration of the harmonious social order found (or imagined) in the pre-industrial community of craft shops, as opposed to that of the modern factory. Revulsion at the exploitation of human labor in modern capitalism was an element at the basis of the Arts and Crafts movement and the writings of William Morris. Adherents admired and embraced handiwork as superior to the product of the machine. John Cotton Dana was an early admirer of the Arts and Crafts movement, although he came to believe in the co-existence of the two systems: handicrafts could

---

[15] Shales, 199-200.

[16] There is also a comparison between the gender politics expressed by Louise Connolly in her speeches promoting the Homelands Exhibit and the ideas of Jane Addams. In her autobiography, first published in 1910, Addams contrasts the "first generation of college women [who] had taken their learning too quickly, [and] had departed too suddenly from the active, emotional life led by their grandmothers and great-grandmothers." While the educated daughter is "only at ease when in the familiar receptive attitude afforded by the art gallery and opera house," her mother is back at the pension, "using her inadequate German with great fluency, gayly measuring the enormous sheets or exchanging recipes with the German *Hausfrau*." What this passage says about Addams' ambivalence regarding her own status as a college-educated woman would make for a fascinating study. See *Twenty Years at Hull House* (New York, Macmillan, 1951), 71-72.

enrich modern manufacturing, and vice versa. [17] Others at Hull House and at the Newark Museum romanticized the handicrafts. Art historian Carol Duncan writes that "the Arts and Crafts and the settlement house movements shared enough convictions and aims to look like two sides of a single phenomenon." Jane Addams' close friend Ellen Starr spent a year in England learning bookbinding from Thomas Cobden-Sanderson, founder of the Doves Press and publisher of William Morris. Helen knew of William Morris, John Ruskin, and the Arts and Crafts movement from her work at Herter Looms, where traditional craft and design were adapted to modern techniques of production.

In 1916 John Cotton Dana and Frances Doane Twombly—Aunt Patty—collaborated on a book, *The Romance of Labor*, for which Helen did the illustrations. ("Helen to Summit to do Frances' book," reads a typical entry in Big Helen's diary that spring.) Dana and Aunt Patty cite Louise Connolly as the inspiration for the project; they write in the preface that the book's purpose is to help guide young people "to the places in the workshops of the world to which they are best fitted." [18]

The Romance of Labor is, in the judgement of Carol Duncan, "a curious little book." It consists of excerpts from sixteen novels. Only two of them (Upton Sinclair's *The Jungle* and Henry Sydnor Harrison's *V.V.'s Eyes*) deal with modern factory labor, and are labeled by Dana and Twombly as "not recommended for children." The remainder, according to Duncan, "depict jobs that, if not technologically obsolete, were beyond the reach of working-class youth." In the latter category are stories of deep-sea fishing, logging, harvesting hemp, or building a desert highway. The category of the "technologically obsolete" includes excerpts from *Marietta*, a romantic tale of fifteenth-century Venetian glassblowers, and *Brunel's Tower* by Edna Phillpotts, set in an English pottery shed. "The book's supposition," Duncan writes, "that pot throwing and glassblowing are gratifying occupations to which one could still aspire, was seriously misleading."

Duncan also critiques Helen's illustrations. Referring to Helen as "a member of the museum staff" (missing altogether the fact that she was Frances Twombly's niece), Duncan writes that

> judging by [Helen's] work, she too was uncomfortable with
> the subject of labor. She kept it completely out of sight

---

[17] Shales, 129-130.
[18] Frances Doane Twombly and John Cotton Dana, *The Romance of Labor* (New York: Macmillan, 1916), v.

in her drawings for the Sinclair and Harrison excerpts.
The cigar factory is seen from the outside and set within
a picturesque street scene, enlivened by playing children
(in the lower right), although in the book the street is an
appalling slum. Her illustration for *The Jungle* reduces the
abattoir, meat-packing plant and stockyard buildings to
vague shapes on the horizon. Instead of the sick animals
and filthy, brutal carnage Sinclair's book excoriates, we are
shown something like a western roundup in which healthy
animals appear under an invigorating, cloud-filled sky. It
is not that Perry was unable to represent human figures.
Although she did better with landscape, many of her
drawings depict figures at work or, to be more exact, figures
involved in a craft—a potter at his wheel, for example, or a
young Venetian blowing glass. Where the work in question
was industrial, she averted her gaze. [19]

Helen's work on the Homelands Exhibit had a profound effect
on her. It drew together various strands of experience: her exposure
to the immigrant communities in Nebraska and her work at
Neighborhood House in Summit, where "the kidlets sang and the
different nationalities dressed in their native costumes and there
were beautiful rugs and tapestries and embroideries on exhibition."
Now she met with immigrant women, choosing from their offerings
the clothing and artifacts for the Homelands Exhibit. Helen's interest
in folk costumes and crafts would one day form a significant part of
her work as a freelance writer and clothing designer. A decade hence,
she would publish drawn-to-scale patterns for women's and children's
clothing based on European peasant and folk costumes, copied from
items loaned to her by the Newark Museum (the museum purchased
some of the items lent to it for the Homelands Exhibit). The framework
Helen used for *Jean & Company, Unlimited* had her alter-ego, "Jean's
mother," traveling Europe researching folk costumes. Helen's sunny
and romantic view of a Europe of peasants and aristocrats, of colorful
costumes and crafts, was nurtured in the experience of the Homelands
Exhibit and was consistent with her attraction to pre-industrial arts
and crafts.

---

[19] Duncan writes that "Perry, who must have had some training as an artist, handled much of the correspondence for the 'Textile Industries' show and went on to a post in the Trenton State Museum." Duncan, 121-123; n. 38, 206.

For its part, the Homelands Exhibit would be imitated at museums in Albany, Buffalo, Rochester, Cleveland, and in 1917 at the New Jersey State Museum, under its new director—Helen Perry.

By the time the Homelands Exhibit opened in July, 1916, Helen was in Trenton. A year earlier, the legislature mandated the reorganization of the State Museum. Founded in 1895, the museum was badly in need of revitalization. Housed in a single large room and adjacent corridors on the third floor of the statehouse, the museum was, in the words of its critics, "far from being up with modern methods and standards and was not the least calculated to inspire visits or study on the part of children or adults." The room was cluttered, poorly lit, its exhibits showing signs of wear, labels unintelligible to the ordinary visitor. [20]

True to his reputation for encouraging women in their careers, John Cotton Dana advised Helen to apply for the directorship and take the competitive civil service exam. Helen scored a 97.7, the highest of any applicant. She assumed her new post on June 1, 1916. Helen and her mother gave up their apartment in New York and moved to Trenton, into a boarding house in the Cadwalader Place neighborhood, a tree-lined enclave designed in the 1890s by Frederick Law Olmsted. "We like our boarding place very well," Big Helen wrote in her diary. "Pleasant big house in beautiful part of the city. Pleasant people and nice room. Big porch where everyone sits." Meals were served to residents in the dining room, freeing both women—one a working professional, the other who had spent much her life as the official hostess of a small college—from that domestic task.

Helen threw herself into her new job. The museum closed for six months so that she could carry out a complete overhaul. Helen had the help of several Newark colleagues. John Cotton Dana gave Gertrude Koch a two-month leave of absence to work with Helen. Louise Connelly, along with Beatrice Winser, one of Dana's trusted confidants, spent time in Trenton. John Cotton Dana made recommendations regarding headings and captions for display cases; the state's chief geologist and forester gave advice as well.

Helen and her colleagues began by stripping display cases of their "gingerbread and other decorative parts," painting them a soft gray.

---

[20] *The Sunday Call*, Newark, January 14, 1917.

They banished moldy specimens to the basement. Artifacts received a thorough vacuuming and cleaning. Helen spent weeks in the "down cellar vaults" of the capitol building, sorting through thousands of objects long stored away. She took files home to review. Nights, while Helen worked, her mother sat and read aloud to her.

The museum reopened to acclaim on January 16, 1917, coinciding with the inauguration of New Jersey's new governor. "New Idea Now Reigns in State Museum," the headlines read. "Jersey's New Departure in State Museum." "New Jersey's Products 'Put on the Map' by Energetic Western Girl." Visitors found the third-floor room and its adjoining corridors beautifully furnished: with rugs, tapestries, and decorative pottery on loan from New Jersey manufacturers. Reading tables were stocked with materials corresponding to the displays. Exhibits were systematized, simplified, and contextualized. Rather than grouping birds by genus and species, Helen created a display entitled "Bird Homes," showing specimens in characteristic habitats. In so doing, she recreated the exhibit which made such an impression on her eight years earlier at the Museum of Natural History in New York. In another exhibit, "How Birds Feed," she posed specimens with the plants and animals that were their prey. Louise Connolly wrote "a jolly, popular story" to accompany each display. Helen planned to change the display cases to show birds and animals, trees and flowers in the different seasons, altering them to reflect their appearance in spring and summer, fall and winter.

As in Newark, the museum showcased the state's natural and commercial resources. Two display cases explained New Jersey's commercially important trees. Other exhibits featured the United and Globe Rubber and the Cook Linoleum companies of Trenton. Another display traced the story of cotton thread from the boll to finished product: spools from the Clark Thread Company of Newark. Yet another showed the production of wool from its raw state to finished fabric, with sample goods provided by the Botany Worsted Mills of Passaic, New Jersey. In an echo of Newark, clay products made in the state were also displayed.

Following the Dana and Connolly vision of the modern museum, Helen reached out to the schools in Trenton. Teachers brought students to the museum for classes. Charts and photographs of exhibits were loaned to schools throughout the state. The involvement of school children would be reciprocal. Children were encouraged to find and bring to the museum flowers and fruits growing in certain months of the year, and to submit reports on the birds, insects, and small mammals that they saw. [21]

Over the course of the first year, Helen included previously overlooked groups. A display, whose vocabulary and rhetoric unfortunately evinced the thinking of the times, told the story of New Jersey's Vineland Home for the Feeble Minded, and displayed products made by residents in its training school. Another exhibit featured crafts made by the blind. According to the *Trenton Evening Times,* arrangements were in place for special days on which the sight-impaired could visit, and "Miss Helen Perry, director of the Museum will have a number of the cases . . . open so that the blind people may 'see' the birds and fishes and other interesting pieces."

In Trenton, as she had in Newark, Helen maintained a busy social life, enjoying more than her share of male company. Her mother's diary records the comings and goings of numerous suitors. "Helen long walk with Mr. Hughes in evening." "Helen canoeing with Mr. Raff." "Leap Year Dance, Helen and Ted. Young people home at 2:00." "Helen dinner with Mr. Kee." "Canoeing with Mr. Raff and walking with Mr. Hughes." "Helen concert in Princeton with Raff and Hughes."

One name appeared with regularity, only to fade and reappear again: John Curtis, Helen's former classmate from Columbia. In her memoir, Big Helen wrote that "John Curtis appeared on my horizon for the first time. A handsome, attractive man." The first mention of John in her diary is on July 11, 1915, eleven days after The Helens returned from Europe. "Helen dined and theatered with Mr. Curtis. Stayed in New York." Helen's mother does not mention John again until February of 1916, but then regularly thereafter. "Mr. Curtis, friend of Helen's, here to call." "Mr. Curtis—dinner-dance—McDowell Club. Really good time. Helen home 1:45 a.m." "Helen and Mr. Curtis tea at McDowell Club." "Helen and Mr. Curtis dance McDowell Club."

Big Helen's memoir described her daughter as "a very pretty, attractive girl." Helen described herself as a "tomboy . . . a general harum-scarum."[22] She played football with her brothers, golfed, and rode horses. The canoe in which she went on outings on the Delaware

---

[21] *The Sunday Call,* Newark, January 14, 1917; *The Philadelphia Record,* January 28, 1917; *Trenton Evening Times,* February 16, 1917.
[22] *American Girl* (November, 1933).

River was her own. "Helen got her canoe," her mother wrote in her diary a month after the move to Trenton, "and she is a very happy girl." Helen regularly paddled the canoe the short distance from home down the Delaware River to reach her job at the museum. At the same time, she loved the arts, especially the theater. The arts were a bond between her and John Curtis. They had, after all, met in the arts program at Columbia. They were both members of the Art Students League. The McDowell Club of New York, where John and Helen went to dances, was part of a network of clubs founded to perpetuate the legacy of American composer Edward McDowell. In short, Helen's wide range of interests drew the attention of many suitors.

But Helen was not interested in marriage. She loved her work at the museum, and envisioned a career modeled on those of her Newark colleagues: Miss Connelly, Miss Winser, Miss Cook, and Miss Kendall; or Miss Morris, presiding over her cozy lunchroom at the Metropolitan Museum. Ambitious women. Career women. Single women all.

But Helen's life was about to take an abrupt turn. The war, which Helen and her mother saw declared in Paris in 1914 and in Siena in 1915, now reached the United States. It was with a sense of resignation that Big Helen noted simply in her diary: "War declared," as America on April 6, 1917 entered the First World War.

Within days, Big Helen was at work as a volunteer at Red Cross headquarters in Trenton. In April of 1918, Helen returned to Europe, this time as a volunteer with the YMCA.

A number of factors motivated Helen's decision to go to France. Her first impulse in Paris in 1914, after all, was to join the war effort. Now the war was drawing some of the people closest to her into service. Helen's brother Henry enlisted in November, 1917. Barely a month later, he fell ill. Big Helen went immediately to Camp Sherman in Chillicothe, Ohio, arriving on December 21 and remaining at Henry's bedside through Christmas into the new year. Henry's illness, along with his impending departure for Europe, had one salutary effect. Evelyn Hollister, a young woman from Cincinnati and the sister of one of Henry's Yale classmates, agreed to marry Henry before he went overseas.

Evelyn was the daughter of Judge Howard Clark Hollister, appointed to the federal bench in 1910 by fellow Ohioan and member of the Yale Class of 1878, President William Howard Taft. Evelyn's name featured prominently in the pages of Cincinnati newspapers, often as a bridesmaid at society weddings. By contrast, Evelyn and Henry had the kind of wedding that was increasingly the norm as the number of men heading overseas grew. The *Cincinnati Enquirer* reported that the wedding reception following the ceremony at Seventh Presbyterian Church would be a small affair. "There will be no invitations issued for the house, a few intimates only being asked verbally to look in for a moment after the ceremony to wish the happy pair God-speed." The *Inquirer* further noted that "the best man and the groomsmen will all be army men, and the selection will not be known until their request for leave of absence is accorded by their commanding officers. . . . The only disappointment of the happy day is the fact that none of the bride's brothers, all three of whom are in the country's service, will be able to be present." [23]

Cousin Edward Twombly was also headed to France. Edward's marriage to Mildred Hadra, a Summit girl, had been in the offing since they announced their engagement in June of 1916. But given Edward's rank as a lieutenant in the Reserve Corps, and anticipating an early call-up, the wedding was moved up to April 14, 1917.

Little wonder that, in the midst of all this, Big Helen wrote, "Helen and I went to church and I wept during most of [the] service. Things are so dreadfully out of shape now."

Helen had another reason to make a dramatic change in her life. She was encountering difficulties in carrying out her work at the State Museum. The museum lacked the legislative support and funding necessary to carry out Helen's ambitious agenda. With the departure of the Newark colleagues, loaned to her at the outset by John Cotton Dana, Helen was left to run the museum with only one or two staffers, and was forced to rely on help from her mother and her friends. "Down town and helped Helen at Museum all A.M.," reads a typical entry in Big Helen's diary. "Helen very tired and went to bed early." "Helen slept all A.M." on a Sunday rather than joining her mother at church.

There was a third reason motivating Helen. Her personal life was deeply unsettled. She was spending more and more time with John Curtis. The two went to dinner and the theater together in New York City, often weekly, and John regularly joined Helen for skating parties, dances, and canoeing on Sanhican Creek. But Big Helen was troubled

---

[23] *Cincinnati Inquirer*, March 2 and March 3, 1918.

as she observed her daughter with John. "I like him, but Helen does not, sufficiently, to suit him. I am very sorry for him!"

Helen continued to see other men. "John W.—another victim," Big Helen wryly, or despairingly, wrote in her diary. The days leading up to Helen's birthday on February 17 precipitated a crisis. John Wimmer sent flowers on Valentine's Day. Two days later John Wimmer and John Curtis both telephoned, with invitations to dinner and the theater in New York. Helen ducked a decision by going to Summit to celebrate her birthday at the Twomblys'. But evasion was not that easy. Soon her uncle and aunt and even Edward were weighing in, in favor of John Curtis. "Ed thinks it is a go, and so does Frances. . . . Helen says she is going into a convent!!"

In a move perhaps calculated to force Helen's feelings, John Curtis volunteered for service with the American Ambulance Field Service in France. In so doing, he joined over 2,500 volunteers—many of them students or alumni from the Ivy League—who drove ambulances in France in the years before the United States entered the war. Motivated by family ties to the allied countries, or stirred by a sense of altruism or adventure, these volunteers served, until April 1917, under French army command. Over one hundred Americans in the ambulance service died while evacuating 400,000 men from the battlefields. Despite initial doubts on the part of the high command, the Field Service demonstrated the effectiveness of motorized ambulances, and created a model adopted by the United States Army. [24]

As it happened, John's departure for France came just days before the United States declared war. "Helen in N.Y. to say good bye to J.C. who sails for France on Saturday for Ambulance work," Big Helen wrote in her diary on March 29. "Helen home at noon. Really blue at having J.C. go." Not *too* blue, apparently. The diary entry for March 31 reported that Helen attended a party. "Mr. Hoyt new man."

But true to the proverb, John's absence had an effect on Helen's feelings. One factor may have been the danger John encountered on his way to France. His ship, the *S.S. New York*—a civilian ship, as it left port before war was declared—was struck by a mine in the Irish Sea on April 9. All passengers made it into the lifeboats, were rescued by a British steamer, and taken to Liverpool. [25] From there John sailed to LeHavre, arriving in France on April 17. Two months later, traveling to

---

[24] Arlen J. Hansen, *Gentlemen Volunteers: The Story of the American Ambulance Drivers in the First World War* (New York: Arcade, 1996, 2011).

[25] *New York Times*, April 10, 1917; *Poughkeepsie Eagle News*, February 5, 1918.

Crete with her mother to attend a college event there, Helen admitted that "she cares very much for J.C." Stopping off in Grand Rapids to visit Tom, Helen read aloud to her family John's letters from France.

Only one of those letters survives. Dated July 27, 1917, is is headed "Letter #7," and John indicated that he was awaiting the arrival of her Letter #15—an indication that Helen's feelings for him were indeed growing. John wrote matter-of-factly of mechanical problems with the ambulance, of coming under shelling, and a false alarm of a gas attack. Most of the letter, however, deals with a description of the villages through which he was traveling, of the "dreamy old Gothic Churches, mossy tile-roofed houses, and the beautiful lazy lifeless Marne twisted all through it." In one passage, appealing to their shared love of art and design, John described a farmhouse where he went in search of breakfast for his crew.

> I wish you could have seen the kitchen where I sat. A broad group of windows at one end, opposite a bare wall with a huge walnut chest against it, browner than the bronze walls. There were yellow milk jars on top of it, Helen, with blue lids. Can you see that bit of color? The other half of this wall was filled with a blue and white tiled oven and sink with shiny brass and copper kettles in neat rows above it. . . . The big thick-topped table with two stools on either side was set right under the windows and the rosy faced woman in her simple neat clothes finished the homey picture.

An opportunity to escape her various dilemmas came in the form of a suggestion from Helen's friend Edith Tener that they go together to France with the YMCA and work in a canteen serving soldiers of the American Expeditionary Force. This was the Edith Tener Helen had met during the summer on Cape Cod following her father's death. Helen and her mother spent several days in the late summer of 1916 with the Teners at their seaside home in Gloucester. The Teners were a prominent Pittsburgh family. George Tener was an industrialist and owner of copper mines. Edith's uncle, John Kinley Tener, served a term in the US House of Representatives, followed by four years, 1911-1915, as governor of Pennsylvania. Edith's brother Alex was a classmate of Henry Perry and cousin Edward at Yale. Edith's comings and goings were duly reported in the society pages of Pittsburgh's newspapers, but by 1917 Edith sought a more meaningful life. In New York City she enrolled in a practical nursing course, where she was alerted to the possibilities of volunteer service in France. [26] Moreover, her father was a supporter of the American Ambulance Field Service—the same organization with which John served. Edith's mother, Annie Fallbush Tener, chaired a local committee of the American Fund for French Wounded, providing relief to wounded soldiers and civilians in France. [27]

Helen had a connection to the YMCA, beyond her affiliation with the campus chapter at Doane College. In 1863 her father, David Brainerd Perry, then a divinity student, spent two months with the YMCA's Christian Commission as a chaplain on Civil War battlefields and in hospitals. [28] Father and daughter, Civil War and World War I—an example of what Dorothy Wickenden calls "the breathtaking brevity of America's past." [29] Helen alluded to her father's YMCA service only once, in a letter written within days of her arrival in France: "If I was sure I wanted to do this thing before, I am ten times surer now. . . . I *know* that I am doing what my father would most want me to do."

Helen's announcement that she was going to France created an uproar. Big Helen was opposed, as was John. So alarmed was he upon learning of her intentions that he sent a telegram—for dramatic effect it arrived at midnight—telling her not to go. Big Helen wept and pleaded until "we were all emotionally worn out." At one point, in the face of concerted opposition, Helen, "heartbroken, gave up the plan." But a decision by the state legislature in December was the final straw. Lawmakers announced that visits of school children to the museum would be limited to two days a week. This struck at the heart of Helen's plans to make the Trenton museum part of school curricula, and to involve children in hands-on experience. "Helen all upset," Big Helen wrote. Three days later, Helen went into New York and was accepted by the YMCA for service overseas.

That winter, while awaiting her departure, Helen completed plans for exhibits at the museum and worked with the assistant who would serve as interim director in her absence. [30] Her departure was preceded by a round of parties. In addition, The Helens made a quick trip to

[26] *Pittsburgh Daily Post*, December 21, 1917.
[27] http://archives.nypl.org/mss/73, New York Public Library Archives and Manuscripts.
[28] David Brainerd Perry papers, 5/2, President Perry, D.B. File 02-2, Doane Archives [DA].
[29] Dorothy Wickenden, *Nothing Daunted: The Unexpected Education of Two Society Girls in the West* (New York: Scribner, 2011), xi.
[30] *Trenton Evening Times*, March 13, 1918.

Cincinnati where Henry's hastily scheduled wedding (he gave his family a week's notice) took place on March 9, 1918.

At almost the last minute the YMCA venture was cast into doubt. Edith Tener wrote to Helen on February 19 to say that her father was ill, and "she could decide nothing yet." A week later Edith canceled her plans for France. George Tener was indeed seriously ill (although he would live another five years). But in a happy surprise, days before her departure Helen received a check from Mr. Tener for $2,000, money he would have given Edith, to finance Helen's trip and expenses while on service with the YMCA. This was significant, because the YMCA initially expected volunteers to provide much of their own funding.[31] The amount of money given by Mr. Tener was staggering; it amounted to a sum well over the average household income in 1918. "If by any chance," Mr. Tener wrote, "you are called home before you have used all of this you can return me any balance unused. On the other hand, should your stay in France be longer than expected and you need more money I shall expect you to call on me. This," he continued, "is purely an affair of business and I know you will look on it in that way. Permit me to say that I am proud of you as my personal representative in this work in France, and with Edith I will feel that we are doing something as nearly personal as possible."

On April 3, 1918, Helen and her mother left Trenton on the 9:22 train. They met Uncle Harry in New York for lunch, after which mother and daughter bade each other farewell. It was left to Uncle Harry to escort Helen to the dock. That night Big Helen wrote in her diary: "I sent my precious daughter across the water. It was heartbreaking for me and a great joy for her."

Helen was headed back to Europe.

---

[31] The YMCA even required women to buy their own uniforms until it became clear that this expense was a barrier to a number of potential volunteers. Uniforms were then provided to all participants.

Chapter 6
"The Touch of a Woman's Hand"

O nce aboard the *S.S. Espagne*, now converted to a troopship, Helen located the stateroom she was to share with two other women. "Living is a trifle congested, but we get on very nicely." The stateroom faced outward, but this was to little advantage. Rough seas dictated that the porthole be kept shut against high waves; at night all windows on the ship were heavily curtained lest any light shine through.

"We have a wonderfully interesting crowd on board," Helen wrote to her mother, "the steerage full of soldiers, second class full of sailors, and first class full of people going for Y.M.C.A., Red Cross, Ambulance, Reconstruction, Motor Corps, and a number of other organizations." It was an early indication of the kind of class distinctions to be encountered in the months ahead. Helen again demonstrated her flair for meeting and befriending notable individuals. She reported the presence on board of "Mabel Boardman, the head of the Red Cross, . . . Anne Morgan . . . and last, but not least, Mary Gardner. . . . [I]f worst comes to worst, I'll be in good company, as me and Anne Morgan and Mary Gardner always retire to our bunks whenever the weather is in the least unpleasing!"

Helen's casual mention of the women indicates how widely known were their names. Mary Sewall Gardner was the founder of the National Organization for Public Health Nursing. In 1918, she was chief nurse of the American Red Cross Tuberculosis Commission for Italy, responsible for training Italian women as nurses. Anne Morgan's name was likewise well known. The daughter of financier J.P. Morgan, Anne was a founder of the Colony Club, the first women's social club in New York City. The club embraced Progressive-era causes, including giving financial support to striking shirtwaist workers in the garment district, even joining working women on picket lines. Long a Francophile, Anne Morgan in 1915 founded the American Fund for French Wounded—the same group with which Edith Tener's mother was affiliated. In 1917, with the French government providing better care to its wounded, Morgan established the American Committee for Devastated France, known by its French acronym, CARD. At the recommendation of General John J. Pershing, Morgan and her friend, doctor Anne Murray Dike, focused their efforts on the region of Picardy, recruiting other American women as volunteers. Participants were required to speak French, know how to drive and repair a car, and—in a model inspired by the settlement house—live and work alongside civilians and displaced persons in a war zone. Between 1917 and 1924, when CARD ended its work, some 350 women joined in Morgan's effort. Anne Morgan traveled back and forth to the United States on fundraising tours during the war. [1]

The crossing was rough, and Helen battled seasickness. "I haven't been 'actively sick'. . . but there have been times when it seemed fifty yards to the rail and fifty miles to my room, and when I hoped we'd be torpedoed in a hurry!" Safety, however, was no joking matter. There were daily lifeboat drills, and passengers wore lifebelts at all times. Despite assuring her mother that "nobody seems to be at all concerned about submarines or danger," the reality of the situation unfolded in Helen's letters. "Our decks are always totally dark at night, and every window in the salon is heavily curtained. No one is allowed to light a match on deck, so it's all very spooky and mysterious, but very thrilling." A few days later she wrote: "The other night, when we were in most danger, I woke up suddenly, and you were standing by my bed, so I know you are with me, watching over me, all the time. I want you to want me to do what I'm doing, and be proud of it."

Days on board were busy. There were meetings and lectures about the work of the Red Cross and the YMCA. In the afternoon, volunteers attended French classes. In between there was time for fun. The mix of male and female volunteers, along with sailors from the second-class deck, brought predictable results. "Edna Phillips and I started to walk around the upper deck . . . the first thing we knew we were simply surrounded by sailors. One of them, a quite gentlemanly lad who had had six years at college, said we were the first women he had spoken to since the fifteenth of December." Four days later Helen reported: "We've had some dancing on deck to the tune of my little old Victrola, but at night now we aren't allowed to make a sound."

As the distance from home increased, Helen's spirits lifted. Recalling their trip together in 1914, Helen speculated that "perhaps you'll come

---

[1] Alan Govenar and Mary Niles Maack, *Anne Morgan: Photography, Philanthropy & Advocacy* (2016); "Anne Morgan's War," English version of film, 2018

over after the war, who knows, and we'll have another wonderful trip together; me and my disposition will be more pleasing than it has been these last few uncertain months. I should think it would be a blessed relief to get rid of such a bad-tempered person for a while."

After ten days at sea the *Espagne* docked at Bordeaux. The volunteers spent the night in a hotel, where Helen noted the wartime privation. "Three of us slept in a room not much larger than our steamer stateroom. The couches were improvised and sheets were un-hemmed, unbleached muslin, and the hotel was overflowing with soldiers, sailors, and YMCAers. No butter or margarine is served with any meals, and only a small piece of bread." The next day they set out for Paris; Helen vividly describing the unfolding landscape: hilltops crowned with chateaux, red-tile-roofed villages clinging to the slopes. Walled gardens and flowering fruit trees surrounded the cottages. "It is springtime in France."

But it was also wartime, a fact impressed upon the volunteers at orientation meetings. "We are instructed to forget the names of every town in France, except Paris. We are to know nothing and say less." Helen subsequently found ways around the censorship, and it is a commentary on the censorship that she got away with as much as she did. Learning of her assignment, she wrote: "I can't tell you where I'm going, but the next time you see Hilda, ask her where it was that Vernor Henry has been most of the time. It's the same place." And upon arrival at her post: "I can't tell you where it is, except that it's the general headquarters in France, and for that reason perhaps one of the most interesting places I could possibly be. It's one of the loveliest hill cities in France. The city itself is on a hill, with an old, old wall around it, wonderfully picturesque with its towers and quaint roofs and chimney-pots."

In their orientation meetings, the volunteers learned about what lay ahead of them. "I had no idea," Helen wrote,

> the extent of the Y work in France. It runs the Canteen
> or store in camp, and it provides physical directors,
> entertainment, movies, practically all activities not covered
> by the army or Red Cross, and . . . vacations as well. It . . .
> encourages sports, and gives the boys the most wonderful
> playtime of their lives, as many of them have said. They are
> doing everything possible to make the boys feel 'at home,'
> as much as that is possible in a strange land. And they are
> keeping them all out of Paris.

The involvement of the YMCA in war work was the result of efforts by Raymond Blaine Fosdick (1883-1972), one of the "young idealists trained in the doctrines and spirit of progressivism in the decade preceding World War I."[2] At Princeton, Fosdick belonged to the group of self-described acolytes of the unconventionally charismatic professor, later college president, Woodrow Wilson.[3] Following graduation, Fosdick went to New York City, working at the Henry Street Settlement while attending law school at night. In 1908, Fosdick was hired by the city to investigate prostitution and human trafficking. He met John D. Rockefeller, Jr., destined, along with Wilson, to be a long-term mentor. In 1913 Rockefeller hired Fosdick to lead a study for the newly created Bureau of Social Hygiene, addressing the evils of poverty, prostitution, and venereal disease. Fosdick eventually headed the Rockefeller Foundation.

In 1916 the United States sent troops to the Mexican border to counter raids led by Pancho Villa. Fosdick served as an aide to General Pershing, surveying conditions in military camps with attention to the problems of alcohol, prostitution, and venereal disease. When, a year later, the United States entered the war, Pershing asked Fosdick to chair the War Department's Commission on Training Camp Activities for the Army and Navy (CTCA). Fosdick's wartime efforts aligned with Progressive-era beliefs. "The idea that misbehavior could be prevented and human character trained in desirable directions was a basic tenet of ... reformers."[4] Such measures were needed all the more with American boys so far from home. France "figured in the American imagination as a place of special dangers: Catholic, foreign, and sophisticated, a land of wine and 'fast' women." Wholesome recreational activities to counter the lure of French bars, bistros, and prostitutes were essential.[5]

To this end, Fosdick coordinated the efforts of the YMCA, the Salvation Army, the Knights of Columbus, the Jewish Welfare Board, the Red Cross, and the American Library Association, placing them under the umbrella of the United War Work Council, assigning particular tasks to each organization. The Red Cross would care for the sick and wounded. The YMCA and Salvation Army, along with the Catholic Knights of Columbus and the Jewish Welfare Board, would address, along denominational lines,

---

[2] "Raymond B. Fosdick Dies at 89; Headed Rockefeller Foundation," *New York Times,* July 19, 1972.
[3] Wilson would become a mentor to Fosdick, appointing him in 1919 undersecretary of state to the League of Nations, a position Fosdick held until the US Senate a year later rejected membership in the League.
[4] Susan Zeiger, *In Uncle Sam's Service: Woman War Workers with the American Expeditionary Force 1917-1919* (Ithaca, NY: Cornell University Press, 1999), 54-55.
[5] Zeiger, 55.

the recreational and spiritual needs of the troops. [6] By war's end, the YMCA operated 1,500 canteens in the United States and France, maintained 4,000 "huts" for recreation and religious services, and raised more than $235 million for relief work. A total of 3,198 women volunteered with the YMCA, most of them in canteen work. [7]

Fosdick's efforts were augmented by the work of a group of wealthy American women with Francophile sentiments. Referred to as the "heiress corps," their ranks included Mrs. Vincent Astor, who opened the first canteen for American sailors at the port of Brest in 1917; and Anne Morgan, with whom Helen sailed to France. Two other "heiresses" involved in war work in France were Mrs. Theodore Roosevelt, Jr., and Martha McCook.

Eleanor Butler Alexander Roosevelt was born in 1889 into wealth and prominence in New York. She married Theodore Roosevelt Jr., son of the former president, in 1910. In 1917, when her husband went to France with General Pershing, Eleanor joined him. She opened a YMCA canteen in Paris, and taught French to American soldiers at night. Eleanor would be one of the organizers, in August 1918, of the Women in War Work Congress in Paris, attended by more than 1,000 volunteers, including Helen. It was Eleanor who "put an end to the prevailing notion that a woman's place was in the Y kitchen," freeing them for broader responsibilities. She was instrumental in having the term "canteen worker" replaced with that of "secretary." [8]

Eleanor also designed the uniform worn by the YMCA canteen workers:

> a gray whipcord jacket and skirt . . . capacious pockets
> and a powder-blue collar with the YMCA triangle insignia
> embroidered in scarlet silk. The blue hat had a small brim
> and the same insignia. Instead of an overcoat, we copied an
> Italian officer's cape in dark gray-green blanket cloth with a
> blue collar to match that on the jacket. Long and circular, it
> proved far better than an overcoat, as we could roll up in it
> when sleeping in camp or on unheated trains." [9]

---

[6] Lettie Gavin, *American Women in World War I: They Also Served* (Niwot, CO: University Press of Colorado, 1997), 129-130.

[7] http://www.ymca.net/history/1900-1950s.html.

[8] Gavin, 130.

[9] *Day Before Yesterday: The Reminiscences of Mrs. Theodore Roosevelt, Jr.* (Garden City, NY: Doubleday, 1959), 85, quoted in Gavin, 131.

The uniform was no trivial matter. It set YMCA women apart from civilians, and minimized class differences.[10] Helen noted that "our uniform is recognized everywhere we go, is usually saluted by officers, and is a great protection from annoyance in a French town like [Chaumont]."

Martha McCook, another of the heiresses, was head of the YMCA's Canteen Division. From her seat in the audience at orientation sessions, Helen described Miss McCook as "pretty as a picture . . . looks about twenty-five, but she certainly has ability. I can just see her winding the whole American army around her little finger if necessary." Born in 1883 (making her thirty-five years old), Martha was a girlhood friend of Alice Roosevelt Longworth, daughter of Teddy Roosevelt. Martha enjoyed a life of social activity and travel, including five trips to Europe during the decade prior to World War I. Her wedding in 1920 would make headlines:

Helen in her YMCA Uniform; April, 1918.

The first wedding of prominence to be affected by women's acquisition of the right to vote . . . is that of Miss Martha McCook . . . to Mr. Eliot Cross which was set for September 14 but on account of that being primary day the wedding has been postponed to the following day. Miss McCook has been working with the Republican state executive committee, hence her determination to allow nothing, not even her marriage, to interfere with her political duty and that of her friends that day, as she believes every good suffragist should be free to cast a vote.[11]

---

[10] Prints and Photographs, Library of Congress. http://hdl.loc.gov/loc.mbrsmi/trmp.4088)
[11] *Evening Star* (Washington DC), August 29, 1920.

The work of the heiress corps was decisive in reshaping Fosdick's plans. He initially sought to recruit "virile men:" college coaches and recreational directors to run programs for the troops. But he changed his mind. A woman worker, he wrote, is "worth three or four men" because the soldiers "are homesick, and the thing they want more than anything else is the touch of a woman's hand and the sound of a woman's voice." [12]

In Paris, the reality of war asserted itself. "We heard the bombardment," Helen wrote, "as we were sitting there before an open fire, drinking tea." Three days later she described her first air raid.

> Bells rang in our hotel, warning us all to go downstairs, and in a minute or two all the lights in the city went out. We all grabbed our coats and flashlights and anything else we could think of, and came down. Now we're all sitting around on the floor . . . the only place where there is light. . . . Some are knitting, some are writing, some lying on the floor sleeping.. . . . Afterward the church bells all over the city began to ring. . . . We went out on our balcony and listened to them, and it was only then that we began to realize what we had probably escaped.

There were reminders of that earlier time in Paris, in 1914. Helen drove with three other women in an open carriage up the Champs-Élysées. The Bois de Boulogne, she wrote, was more beautiful than ever, "with its spring foliage, lovely lakes and drives, and gay parties and picnicking, with uniforms added, but the restaurants were all closed." In the markets she saw violets and forget-me-nots. "Isn't it French to have flowers, even though they are going without sugar and butter and bread!" A visit to Notre Dame, its statues banked in sandbags, recalled "our first glimpse of it together, mother, and then the fête day with the wonderful procession." She described seeing a wedding, with a "shy pretty bride and a very pleased-looking bridegroom" leaving the Church of the Madeleine; a day later there was a funeral procession descending the same steps; on yet another day a First Communion procession. "France is certainly a country of contrasts!"

---

[12] Zeiger, 55

On April 24 Helen left for Chaumont, 130 miles and "about a half day trip" from Paris. She was one of three women sent to the town, joining three already there.

> The six of us serve the Canteen, the Officers' Club and the hospital in this huge city of soldiers. I am to be in the Canteen for enlisted men, I'm happy to say, as I think that's by far the most interesting and necessary work.. . . The only other American women here are the nurses in the hospital . . . and a few telephone girls. We are the only women to whom the privates can talk. Nurses have the rank of second lieutenants, telephone girls are taboo. [13]

Professor John Bennett was also in Chaumont. One-time chore boy at The Grange and alumnus of Doane College, Bennett was dean of men at the college when, in December 1917, he took a leave of absence to join the YMCA's war work. Before she left home, Helen wondered if she would see Professor Bennett in France, and his presence in Chaumont was another reason she was delighted with her assignment. She surprised him by arriving unannounced, and Bennett was equally happy to see her. Bennett's job was that of director of educational activities. He lived in a small room off the canteen's kitchen, and, impressive title notwithstanding, his duties included starting the fires in the morning, counting the money, and closing up the facility at night. The coincidence of two people from Doane College was but the first of a number of reunions that would take place in the coming months.

The women assigned to Chaumont lived in two rooms in a house in town, an illustration of the grafting of war onto civilian life. Their "duplex," as Helen called it, consisted of two rooms, rented from two of the building's four tenants, on two separate floors. The upstairs room served as a bedroom for four of the women; the downstairs room Helen arranged as a living room, which served at night as a bedroom for herself and the remaining woman. Helen took the sofa as her bed. Their landladies took turns serving the women breakfast. Helen's landlady

---

[13] The telephone girls, or "Hello Girls," were recruited through the joint effort of AT&T and the US Army. Upon arrival in France, General Pershing was dismayed at the state of communications and decided that skilled female telephone operators were needed. The women took an oath upon joining the Signal Corps, and assumed, therefore, that they were members of the US Army, with rank. Following the war, they were told that they had merely signed a contract, thus were not veterans and not entitled to benefits. The legal battle to secure veterans' status ended in 1977 when President Jimmy Carter signed the necessary legislation. See Elizabeth Cobbs, *The Hello Girls: America's First Women Soldiers* (Cambridge, MA: Harvard University Press, 2017); and the documentary film, "The Hello Girls," 2018.

invited her in to lunch on days off. Helen sat with the woman's husband and little daughter at a table spread with a red and white checked oilcloth, a luncheon of *pommes de terre au gratin*, brown peasant bread, jam, and coffee. A litter of kittens provided entertainment.

Their rooms overlooked the valley and the river, beyond which a vine-covered wall and chateau rose above the town. A garden plot for each of the families in Helen's building provided fresh vegetables and flowers. Helen described the living room where she slept: an open fireplace, brass candlesticks on the mantel, vases of fresh flowers from the garden on every table, colorful lampshades. She fashioned a window seat by covering her steamer trunk with a rug and adding bright chintz pillows.

The women quickly settled into a routine. Given the prominence of Chaumont as the headquarters of the American Expeditionary Force, and the fact that the canteen served not only those stationed in Chaumont but in some twenty small towns and camps nearby, the facility was a large one, a so-called double hut. "In half of it the boys may gather to read, write or eat at the big tables. The other half is an auditorium, where there is some sort of a program every night. The counter where we sell things is at one end of the first room." Hours were from nine in the morning until eight at night. Two secretaries worked the counter in two-hour shifts. Helen compared it to "running a sort of combination grocery store and soda fountain . . . standing behind a counter, and selling coffee, chocolate, cigarettes, cookies, toothbrushes, shoestrings and the like to several thousand boys a day." When not at the counter the women were busy with other projects. "We have been here only a week, but already we have made costumes for theatricals, drawn a map of the Philippines for a lecture, indexed books for the library, worked on the bulletin boards, mended clothes, and a thousand and one other little items."

Those "thousand and one other little items" consisted in no small part in providing a listening ear, the figurative touch of a woman's hand. "It's astonishing," Helen wrote to her mother, "how many things you can fit in with serving chocolate and selling cigarettes!" The women listened to "stories of the men just back from the front, the little things that they like to talk about, the pictures of their wives and sweethearts, and sometimes children, the things they tell us because they just have to tell a woman, and we happen to be the only ones handy." The men sought advice as well. One soldier with two girlfriends at home asked Helen (of all people!) to read his love letters and advise him as to which woman he should marry. The men's confidences, Helen confessed, sometimes made her want to cry, and other times laugh. "But always what they tell us seems sacred, because it is what they would so much like to be saying to some other woman."

Socializing with the enlisted men was not confined to the canteen. There was a reason behind Helen's efforts to make their rented rooms as homelike as possible. "We want it to look like a little bit of America when the men come to see us." This plan was—not surprisingly—met with misgivings on the part of the landladies, requiring Helen and her colleagues to "painfully explain . . . that we expect to have men here occasionally, but that we are nevertheless perfectly respectable young persons. After our first caller the other night we fully expected to be asked to move, but my very nice landlady said that she knew I had a good heart . . . and whatever I did would be all right. Another case where the uniform helps."

In sending women to France, the YMCA walked a line, aiming for wholesome "big sister types" on the one hand, and women attractive enough to make the men want to frequent the canteen on the other. "The girls recently coming over under your auspices are splendid," General Pershing wrote to Elsie Mead, head of the Women's Bureau; "'dangerously attractive,' which is just the way the A.E.F. likes to have them. Pulchritude helps."[14] The insistence on the part of official sources in portraying canteen workers as mothers and big sisters highlights the demographic profile of the volunteers. Only three percent of the Y's female volunteers were under the age of twenty-four. Fifty-one percent were between the ages of twenty-four and thirty-one. (At age thirty, Helen fell in this category.) Thirty percent of the women were thirty-two to thirty-nine years old, and sixteen percent were in their forties and fifties.[15] Helen wrote about a soldier who had not heard from anyone at home in a long time, and who "comes and talks to me because I look like his sister."

Historian Susan Zeiger states that many of the soldiers who patronized the canteens "seemed to adopt the sentimental view of women auxiliary workers.... Homesickness, fear of dying, and the horrors of combat might well have prompted American soldiers to turn to female auxiliary workers for the homey comforts of hot chocolate and conversation."[16] The role, however, could be burdensome. YMCA

---

[14] Zeiger, 58.
[15] Zeiger, 35.
[16] Zeiger, 62.

volunteer Marian Baldwin described a typical day: canteen duty from 9:00 to 10:30 in the morning, followed by two hours playing tennis with three different soldiers. Back at the canteen from 2:00 until 5:00, and then a walk with a soldier from 5:00 until 7:00. From 7:00 until 11:30 p.m. the YMCA hosted a dance. "You have no idea," Baldwin wrote, "how strange it is to do things like these 'by order' and to know that even if you . . . cordially dislike some of the men you are dated up with, you have to do it just the same and start off with a beaming smile, to laugh, talk, and joke yourself and them through three or four hours on end." [17]

Helen's experience was similar. "We are overwhelmed with invitations. . . . Sunday, I had eleven invitations to walk, two to dinner, and one to the movies." Of course, she wrote, "I couldn't accept either of the latter, but I managed four or five of the former in my spare moments. And that is about an average day." On at least one occasion she displayed a flash of impatience. "Miss Thomas has just come in after an evening with one of these bi-weekly souls in agony. We have both of us reached that state of mind . . . where we occasionally wish the whole American army in the deep blue sea, except a congenial person or two, who has never had a tragedy in his young life, or if he has, doesn't insist on telling it." She allowed that "this state of mind has been brought on by an unusual dose of sad confidences, and by tomorrow we shall have recovered. Once in so often we just go off with somebody because we like them, and then we feel better." And the plan to invite soldiers to their room proved successful: "One of the men who was in the other night told one of the secretaries when he got back, 'Gee, we had an open fire and I sat in a big chair and stretched out my legs and the girls sat there and sewed or something, and it was just like home!'"

Helen devised another plan.

We are trying to have the men meet our landladies, and their children, and get interested in the garden and the rabbits, and see a little bit of the lovely home-life here in France.. . . Our big family here, including four children and the kitten, play together every night and our soldier friends enjoy them too. So many of them have met only the girls who run the streets, and the storekeepers who charge them outrageous prices, and it's no wonder they do not admire the French as a people.

[17] Marian Baldwin, *Canteening Overseas 1917-1919* (New York: Macmillan, 1920), 87.

Her efforts were reciprocated.

The children in our street now have learned that we like
flowers, and they come running with . . . bouquets in their
little hands to give us. The older people all nod to us as we
pass, and sometimes ask us in to their gardens. The other
day I overtook the dearest little old lady in the park. . . .
It was market day and she was struggling along with a
great basket full of vegetables. She would not let me take
the basket alone, but I took hold of one side, and we must
have made a funny picture, the tiny bent old lady and my
own enormous self, carrying the basket between us down
the main street. She asked me in to her lovely old house
and showed me her little garden. The garden used to be
of flowers, she told me, and the house was cared for by
several servants, and she had apparently lived prosperously.
But now this little seventy-year old lady does her own
housekeeping, plants, and cares for her own vegetable
garden, and is as spry as you please. *C'est la guerre!*

The first two months in Chaumont saw constant rain. "I don't think
it has missed raining a single day since I have been here." The women
wore their capes and struggled to keep their one wool uniform clean.
Helen described the ubiquitous mud as "the color and consistency of
soft fudge." The metaphor was an apt one. Much time was devoted to
making fudge or hot chocolate, the latter in a boiler which heated a
thousand cups at a time. "It would do your heart good," Helen wrote,
perhaps a bit naively, "to see how they clamor for hot chocolate, and
would apparently rather have it than all the things they can get in the
cafes down town."

As May wore on, and the weather improved, Helen explored the
town and did some sketching—for which she received permission only
"after having had my ancestors and posterity and all my connections
on both sides of the family investigated." From the chateau high above
the town with its sweeping view over the valley she watched a flaming
sunset. Other expeditions led to the discovery of a stately home, its gate
ajar. "There is a long lane through the woods that leads to the house . . .
a peacock and a meadowful of buttercups, and a farmyard in a wall-
enclosed courtyard, and an orchard . . . and lagoon full of goldfishes.. . .

Although it's within a stone's throw of one of the camps you would never dream there were soldiers, or a war."

But the war was never far away. "Last night," Helen wrote, "for the first time I heard the big guns. It must have been a very quiet night, as they are a long way off. We are very military here, with changing of the guard, wonderful bugles and drums for marching music, a splendid band, bugle calls at all times of the day and night, gray automobiles whizzing back and forth, and a city full of soldiers."

Two weeks later, Helen attended her first military funeral, a soldier who died in the hospital in Chaumont. A chaplain led a horse-drawn caisson carrying the flag-draped, flower-covered casket, followed by a few soldiers and some French civilians. "The little graveyard where all our American boys here are buried is near a tiny church in the valley. Our men are buried in squad formation, in simple graves marked with crosses and names in inverted glass bottles, which will be replaced sometime by stones, I suppose." The chaplain read the Episcopal service, followed by the hymn "Nearer My God to Thee," and then taps and a three-gun salute.

> I think I have never heard anything so exquisitely beautiful as that bugle call, on the quiet hillside, beside that simple grave. It just brought your heart into your throat. I should have liked to have written to the boy's family, and said so to the chaplain, but he explained to me that there is a very wonderful woman at the hospital who visits the men, writes home for them while they are sick, and to the families if they die. I am so glad to know that there is someone to do that.

The funeral, appropriately, took place on Decoration Day, as Memorial Day was then known, and the day took on added meaning. The cemetery next to the church was decorated with flags and flowers, the latter brought by French civilians from town. It brought "the war home in a very real way," Helen wrote, "and although we ourselves do not yet know of any of our friends who have gone it makes us heartsick to think of losing sight of these boys of whom we have grown so fond, and never knowing, perhaps, what has become of them."

The end of May marked the first major American engagement on the Western Front, the Battle of Cantigny. Helen noted that those behind the lines were sometimes the last to know, relying instead on rumor and circumstantial evidence. "I have no more idea how the war is going than if I had never heard of it. . . . We know that there is a great battle raging, and that men are going up all the time, and that some nights many are brought into the hospital here. . . . But those who know don't tell, and the rest of us settle the battle daily to our own liking." Despite being on the same side of the Atlantic as so many of the men in her life, Helen relied on reports from home for assurances of their safety. "I haven't heard yet from any of the boys in France, I mean Ed or Henry, or Donald Rice. But army mail is slow. . . . I supposed John is in Ireland by now, but I haven't heard from him on this side yet."

Mail was another responsibility that fell to YMCA workers. Helen was struck—as her father had been during his Civil War service—by the number of soldiers who were illiterate. She wrote letters on their behalf, and in turn read those received from parents, children, and sweethearts. Some were poignant, others humorous. "I have written a letter to a local Red Cross Chapter in America, asking them to investigate the wife of a man over here who has not heard from her or of her for months, and is terribly worried. Neither of them can read or write much." She told of writing a letter "to another wife, just to tell her that her husband is looking well, and is terribly proud of her and the new baby, and that . . . he is keeping straight for them."

Other letters fell into the "sometimes to laugh" category. "I wrote a love letter the other day for a man who cannot write and [I] discovered afterwards that he already has a wife. He certainly could dictate fluently and entirely without embarrassment. I was the only one who was embarrassed!"

Many soldiers wrote to Helen after they were sent to other camps or to the front. The letters are further evidence of disparities in social class and educational attainment among the troops. Sgt. H.W. Peltier wrote to Helen, in a letter nearly devoid of punctuation: "Dear Miss Perry, Your card and then the nice cigars and chocolate all the same day, say but if I was over there I would really I believe kiss your hand so kind of you and a million thanks from me and the Sgt. as we always go 50-50 you know." Peltier's letter concluded: "Now I hate to trouble you Miss Perry but you are such an obliging Miss, that if it isnt too much trouble could you repeat the cigars, now you see, its a lot of comfort to be able to lie down on your bunk at night and smoke a nice cigar especially when you do a lot of walking."

In a letter drawing a sharp contrast, Robert Tabley wrote: "I have so often interrupted you when you were reading your mail that it is with some compunction that I attempt to borrow your ears, eyes, or attention (to use the Marc Antonian phrase) for the perusal of this letter." After relating news of examinations at the Army Intelligence School, Tabley continued: "Alas, after the final exams, certain post-finals remain. Friend Kates surmises that we have crossed the Rubicon but it still remains to be discovered who was drowned." Tabley promised to send Helen a copy of *The Light That Failed*, Rudyard Kipling's semi-autobiographical novel. "If it becomes burdensome just stick it in some library after you have read it."

Maintaining a library was another responsibility. The canteen had some 1,500 books, "and our shelves are invariably almost empty, which is the best recommendation for a library that I know." Reading led some of the men to wonder about the country where they found themselves, and Helen did her best to answer questions about France's history. Other soldiers wrote poetry and sought Helen's opinion. Yet others took to sketching. On another occasion, and again reflective of class differences, "two men, one a Harvard graduate and the other a University of Michigan man, walked in five miles in a pouring rain to see me, as I was the first girl they had had a chance to talk to for months." The two men noticed a copy of the *Boston Cook Book*, "spotted first by the Harvard man, of course, and they amused themselves most of the evening by reading their favorite recipes aloud."

The library was the setting for another of Helen's encounters with a famous person, although she didn't realize it at the time. "Last week as I sat on the floor . . . painting a chair, someone in civilian clothes came and talked to me for a long time. After he had gone, I found it was Mr. Fosdick, the head of the whole Fosdick Commission. But he looks just like anybody else."

July came. Helen and her colleagues exchanged their wool uniforms for light blue chambray dresses with white collars. Lemonade replaced hot chocolate. Helen decorated the hut with summer flowers, "yellow jugs full of goldenrod on all the tables, and great branches of Mountain Ash with its orange berries against the walls." Summer brought weekly picnics. "Mrs. Whiting and I took half a dozen men on a real American picnic, with white bread sandwiches, lemonade, etc., and we had a real white linen tablecloth to spread on the grass."

Helen, second from left; France, 1918.

The picnics were an opportunity to evade strictures of class and rank.

> We have tonight four or five college men, one or two officers
> among them, officers who have risen from the ranks and
> are therefore looked upon with leniency by the privates.
> We cannot all walk thru town together, but the officers will
> meet us at the picnic place, as it were, accidentally, and after
> that all rank will be forgotten.

Even more intractable than class barriers were those of race. Not only were the military services segregated, but the organizations—with the exception of the Catholic Knights of Columbus—maintained separate facilities for the races as well. [18] Helen's only references to black soldiers while in Chaumont were to "negro minstrels" or "a colored jazz band"—this on an occasion when "negroes in Khaki" served at a dinner for officers, with tables spread with "real linen, china and flowers." [19]

The languorous heat of summer contrasted with the increased tempo in military activity. On June 9 the German army launched an offensive aimed at Paris; American and French troops successfully counter-

---

[18] Addie W. Hunton and Kathryn M. Johnson, *Two Colored Women in World War I France* (1921, reprinted Big Byte Books, 2015).

[19] While on shipboard, in words jarring to contemporary ears, Helen described "a jolly entertainment, with funny speeches and some duets and choruses. You should hear the darkies join in on the southern songs."

attacked. Between July 15 and 17, the Germans attacked Reims, again countered by the Allies. And on July 18, French and American armies launched the Second Battle of the Marne, the beginning of a series of Allied counter-offensives on the Western Front. "The news is wonderful today," Helen wrote, "and we are all very happy over it, in spite of the fact that the wounded are pouring in and the hospitals are full."

Heightened military activity brought more Americans to the vicinity of Chaumont, including Helen's brother Henry, whom she had last seen at his hastily arranged wedding in March. Henry was stationed twenty miles from Chaumont, "right in our own Y.M.C.A. district. So I telephoned the secretary there, and he found Henry for me." Henry told Helen that for the last three days he had been sent for by various officers and walked "miles" to their offices, "only to be told that they had just seen his sister." Consequently, "everybody in both our towns became much interested in our getting together, not a simple matter . . . at present, especially as Henry's little town has no railroad." By happy coincidence "we were sending a speaker out there for Sunday night by automobile" so Helen was able to catch a ride. "I had several hours with Henry. . . . I saw him just one day over three weeks from the day he sailed [for France]."

Helen and Henry managed several visits over the following weeks. Henry came to Chaumont from his post at Montigny-le-Roi, and Helen showed him around the canteen. They spent the Fourth of July together, thanks to an officer who invented a reason to send Henry to Chaumont. Even after Henry's assignment in September to officers' training camp at Le Mans, Helen managed twice to visit Henry. [20] "I got out to Henry's camp about four o'clock, and found him coaching a football team. . . . He went in to ask his captain if he could have permission to take his sister out to dinner. The reply was that if said officer had a sister, he should take her out to dinner, permission or no permission."

Cousin Edward, Helen learned, was in Baccarat, near the front— "but it is very quiet there just now." Cousin Leroy Doane, Alice's son, was among the wounded in the military hospital in Chaumont, and Helen lightheartedly reported, for the benefit of those back home, that he "came hobbling out on crutches, very much amused at his costume, which consisted of pajamas and a blue dressing gown such as you Red

---

[20] Observing censorship requirements, Helen used an APO mailbox and indicated locations by writing the first letter of the name of the town, followed by a number of dashes corresponding to the number of letters in the name of the town. An exception to this were the letters she wrote to her mother from her three visits to Paris in July and August. In those she told her mother that she was in Chaumont, Edward in Baccarat, etc.

Crossers make, mother, and apparently taking the whole business as a big joke." Leroy had waited five hours on the battlefield to be rescued. His shin bone was shattered by a piece of shell, and the doctors were keeping the wound open, but "three days after he was wounded, he was wandering around on crutches, so you can see he is getting on splendidly." Through her mother, Helen sent further reassurance: "By the way, Aunt Alice, when I was out at the hospital . . . a boy came up to me and said: 'You know I'm from Fremont, and used to go to school with Roy Doane.' Whereupon I said that Roy was here now, and sent him over to see him. . . . Isn't it funny, a coincidence like that?"

Nor were these the only familiar faces Helen encountered. "I looked up from the counter yesterday to see Ted Kenyon coming up to it. Ted has seen Edward recently and told me exactly where he was." "Sunday, when I was very busy, I saw a hand stuck across the counter and looked up to see Charlie Drake." "The division to which John Wimmer and Frank Korab belong is coming in near here." "Professor Bennett and I found two or three men who had been to Doane, among them the Mr. Sally who married Arda Watson." "Colonel Arrowsmith, who was military instructor at Doane is coming here." "Two more girls have come in here, one of them Ethel Tener, Edith's cousin." "Someone else said I looked awfully familiar, and asked me where I was from. I said Nebraska. He said, 'So am I.' I said Crete. He said 'So am I!'" Brother, cousins, neighbors, friends—the web of relationships transplanted to France by war.

John Curtis, now serving in the US Navy, was in Ireland. Going to France had not, after all, provided escape from Helen's romantic dilemma. She reported that "John writes such nice fat letters, and they keep coming along quite often." Earlier she had had to contend with her mother, Uncle Harry, Aunt Patty, and Edward weighing in on her personal life; now the military censorship took up John's cause. On one of John's letters, in which he lamented that he was not receiving enough mail from her, the censor scrawled "Right-O." Helen confided to her mother, "I'm just as unsettled as ever in my mind, but I'm not worrying about anything these days. Every day is enough for itself over here, and I'm just living from day to day, never knowing what new interest or work the next may bring."

July and August brought three opportunities for visits to Paris, the first two involving opportunities for a new assignment. That Helen would be considered for an administrative position was not surprising. She was a college graduate, with administrative experience. In

Chaumont she was the only secretary who spoke French. Helen wrote to her mother, during the first of these Paris visits, about the possibility of the new assignment. "I . . . will probably be one of the eight regional woman secretaries. It's an entirely new position and will be awfully interesting to develop." But she hesitated. "Of course, I won't have as much contact with the men, day in and day out . . . but I can spend more time in various canteens all over my region . . . and in this way get in touch with a greater number of places and people. . . . This is the army, and I'll go where I'm sent." [21]

Three weeks later she returned to Paris for a meeting with Martha McCook, the woman she had so admired from her seat in the auditorium back in April. Helen was indeed offered the position of regional secretary for women's affairs. She would be responsible for dealing with the personal problems of women volunteers, and working with the Women's Bureau at YMCA headquarters to resolve any troubling issues. With understandable pride, Helen wrote to her mother that "I was the youngest of the eight women chosen, except Mrs. Vincent Astor." But it would mean "constant travel, the sorting out of difficulties of all kinds . . . and all kinds of advisory work," and would rule out almost all personal contact with the men, "which is what I am here for." She further demurred, adding that she felt that the position demanded an older, more experienced woman. "I told Miss McCook that I would rather stay with my own men."

Martha McCook replied by letter, offering Helen the job of director of activities at the YMCA hut in Chaumont. "We are most anxious," McCook wrote, "to make such an experiment in order to prove that a woman can do it, and do it well! . . . Will you talk it over with Mr. Gethman and . . . let me know." Helen happily accepted, and immediately began making plans. "I'm to be the first woman hut secretary in charge of all the activities in a big hut, so it will be lots of fun to work things out by myself, with no traditions to follow. I'm to have charge of all the entertainments, work up local talent plays, pageants, and concerts . . . organize clubs, run the library, redecorate the hut, build on a big, new room, etc."

The trips to Paris gave Helen an opportunity for some genuine R&R. On the first occasion, she wrote that she had "a real BATH . . . the first for several months." After sleeping until 10:00 the next morning,

---

[21] Zeiger cites a study of women canteen workers showing that fifty-seven percent of them had some level of college education or were college graduates. College education introduced another social distinction between the YMCA secretaries and the average enlisted man. See Zeiger, 37, 70.

she went to a hairdresser for a shampoo, manicure, and facial massage. In the afternoon "I promenaded on the boulevards," window shopping and admiring "all the pretty civilian clothes and even some hats in the windows, and imagining myself in them." Lunch, alone, in a restaurant, was a special treat. "You can't imagine what a heavenly sensation it is not to have to talk to a single soul!!!" Helen ordered "all the American things I wanted to eat—creamed chicken and fruit salad and ice cream—and then I was a new woman, ready for anything." On her last night in Paris four soldiers from Chaumont turned up. The five donned civilian clothes, "had a real dinner all together, and went joyriding in a real taxi. . . . We all forgot we were soldiers and had a wonderful time."

The return to Chaumont, this time by automobile, was memorable. The party left Paris in the evening, but their driver got lost. A Frenchman on his bicycle led the car part of the way. "As a result of all our wanderings we reached C-------- at six the next morning, very sleepy, but it had been a wonderful ride. It was the first time I had come out by motor, and it was brilliant moonlight all night long, and we saw a wonderful sunrise over the hills."

In late August Helen returned to Paris for the Congress of Women War Workers. One thousand women, representing Belgium, Romania, Serbia, Italy, France, England, and the United States, gathered to celebrate the work of women volunteers. Organizations represented included the Red Cross, the YMCA and YWCA, reconstruction workers, motor drivers, and munitions workers. The women wore their respective uniforms. One afternoon they were fêted at the home of Mrs. Theodore Roosevelt, Jr., Helen's third personal encounter with a member of the heiress corps. The following day French president Raymond Poincaré hosted a reception at the Élysée Palace. Helen cast a decorator's eye on her surroundings, describing walls of "pale ivory and gold, with hanging chandeliers of glass, and beautiful tapestries on the wall." The gardens made an even greater impression: "real Elysian fields...lovely sloping lawns, with winding paths...and unexpected bits of statuary."

The message of the Congress was that of the social feminist, or "difference feminist" ideal. "I wish you could have had the thrill," Helen wrote to her mother,

of seeing all those wonderful women together and feeling
that they were all working together, standing behind

the manhood of the world, preserving, and binding up
and building up, until the war shall be over. That was
the keynote of the whole meeting, woman's instinct for
preservation, the preservation of people and ideals. . . . And
the most wonderful part of the whole thing to me was that
in it all there was no crying for independence, only a quiet
spirit of helpfulness and cooperation in the work of the
men, as if women had always and would always stand beside
them as equals. So many things have settled themselves in
this war, for all time.

Even as the Congress took place the final phase of the war was
unfolding. The Hundred Days Offensive began on August 8 with the
Battle of Amiens and culminated in the Meuse-Argonne Offensive.
From September 26 to the Armistice on November 11 the operation
involved 1.2 million American soldiers, the largest battle fought by the
American Expeditionary Force. It was also the second deadliest battle
in US history, with 26,000 American fatalities to 28,000 German
deaths, and an unknown number of French losses. With the offensive
Helen at last got her wish: assignment to a unit at the front.

Helen left Chaumont on September 27. Her departure was an
emotional one.

I was a little homesick, leaving C------, because I've got such
a lot of good friends there. . . . One night the men gave me
a serenade in my garden. Imagine the setting, moonlight,
garden, serenade, all with a French flavor. Afterwards they
came in and we had a party in front of the open fire. The
same evening . . . the cooks came to call on me in a body,
and wish me good bye. . . . The little old lady in our street,
who always gives me flowers, called me in to have a glass of
her choicest wine, which I had a terrible time pretending
to drink. A little girl in the same street brought me a huge
bunch of flowers.

Helen went by train with the 89th Division, passing "shell-holes, and
dugouts, and trenches, and ruins." On October 1 she was in Récicourt,
ten miles west of Verdun. Helen and two other women camped out in
a ruined building, with sheets of canvas for doors and rain coming in

through the ceiling. They kept a primitive stove—sheet iron laid across stones—fired up to feed the few hundred American soldiers and officers who remained in the town, along with returning French refugees. "Today we even fed a horse, and on bread. It was a gassed horse that had to be used, but it was pitifully thin and ravenously hungry. We had nothing but bread-crusts to feed it." Even in the midst of this, 'there were light-hearted moments. "Last night we had a Nebraska reunion, thirty of us, in a little kitchen. We had chocolate and doughnuts and cigarettes and a wonderful time. I never had a nicer party."

The three women were moved to Épinonville, two kilometers from the front. Riding in an automobile, along muddy roads, they passed columns of marching soldiers, trucks, ammunition trains, tanks, officers' cars. They drove through villages leveled to the ground, only cellars and piles of stone remaining in a sea of mud. Planes flew above, shells burst around them, and everywhere was the roar of the big guns. In Épinonville they set themselves up in the "only house left standing in the village," with doors and walls riddled with shrapnel holes and all windows broken.

> In the daytime we stack our baggage and folding cots
> against the walls and serve hot chocolate. Sometimes we
> have ten or a dozen people in this tiny room, sitting around,
> talking and getting warm. . . . We sleep in our clothes and I
> want nothing so much as a bath. . . . The big guns boom all
> day and all night, especially at night. The biggest ones shake
> the building. At first, they kept me awake, but now I hardly
> hear them, except as my heart hears them, and hopes they
> are ours and not the enemy's.

A steady stream of ambulances passed, returning from the front where "our men have been in the line for two days now . . . and casualties are heavy." The horror of the war struck her forcefully. "Isn't it unbelievable that all of us here, just ordinary kindly and generous and tender-hearted, should be deliberately trying to cut each other's throats with equal sincerity and patriotism and devotion on both sides." The only thing that made the sacrifice worthwhile "is that our children may never see the like again."

Épinonville nightly came under shellfire, and on one occasion warning of a gas attack sounded. "Not much came over, and we soon went to sleep again." Another night the shelling was so heavy that the group took refuge in a dugout, led "in a queer little procession" by one of the male volunteers. Helen described the dugout as an "unspeakable mud-hole" in which they sank up to their ankles. The beams were so low that they could scarcely sit erect; the ceiling dripped moisture down their necks. A single candle provided the only illumination. "We stuck it out a little while and then decided that being blown to pieces above ground was preferable to dying ignominiously in a mud-hole."

Ahead of the final Allied assault Helen and her female companions were evacuated to Vittel, some 150 kilometers south of the front, and from there back to Chaumont.

> We started from the front sitting on our baggage in the back of a big army truck, covered with camouflage. You can't imagine the sensation of rattling along through the night, without lights, having other moving things loom up before you, pass and disappear, a steady stream of trucks, horses, guns and ammunition. Now and then . . . soldiers would climb over the back of the truck and ride with us a little way. We heard their voices but could not see their faces.

Helen was in Chaumont on November 11, Armistice Day. She did not write again until November 17. By then the immediacy of the Armistice was overshadowed by descriptions of her posting in the ruined town of Dun-sur-Meuse and news of her brief reunion with Henry, "disgusted at not having a chance in the lines. But I am selfish enough to be glad he wasn't." YMCA worker Marian Baldwin, whose letters were published in 1920, provides a poignant description of Armistice Day:

> Peace! Somehow, I didn't feel like yelling. It all goes so deep and the great relief and joy make one silent. We closed up the canteen and walked home. The soldiers were buying up all the champagne and other wine in the village for a mammoth celebration. We found our French family back home, heads bowed, crying. It was a realization of the price that has been paid.

For Helen, the reality of war's end slowly began to sink in. "You can't imagine what a blessed thing it is to say 'Good bye' to a lad without the fear in your heart that he may not come back safely. Troops are marching through here all day long on their way to the border but we know they are going to comfortable hillsides and not to muddy trenches, and that makes all the difference." Dun-sur-Meuse, she wrote, must have once been a lovely village, but now there were only shell-holes, mud, and temporary bridges across canals, bridges hastily built by American soldiers as they retook the town.

Thanksgiving Day was November 28. Dinner was jelly sandwiches and hot chocolate, "but everybody was jolly and we didn't have time to be homesick." In the first week of December the 89th Division crossed into Belgium. Helen and Penelope Parkman were the only YMCA women accompanying the division. On December 9 the division entered Germany. "This is a most astonishing world," Helen wrote.

> Here we are in Germany . . . and I can't see that the
> landscape is particularly different, or the people startlingly
> wicked, or any of the things I expected. I was prepared to
> hate the people and everything connected with the name
> "German," but here we are living with a fluttering old lady,
> in a funny old house, with a red plush upholstered parlor,
> and a heavenly view of picture-book country from our
> windows. . . . Nobody has put poison in our food, or refused
> to serve us. The children hang around the door of the
> canteen . . . they are much like children the world over.

The YMCA workers traveled between companies, dispensing hot chocolate and selling cigarettes. "We rattle along the road like a tank corps going into action," Helen reported, carrying "pails, kettles, tin cups, cases of cocoa and condensed milk. . . . Our boiler holds enough to make a thousand cups, and only takes an hour to heat, so we can set up in no time at all." They celebrated the first Christmas in peacetime in Prüm. "This is regular Christmas card country—fir trees and quaint little houses and snow and candlelight—a perfect setting." On Christmas Eve the women decorated the canteen: Christmas trees tied with red bows and decked with candles. Santa Claus arrived in a dogcart pulled by two soldiers. Five hundred packages of YMCA candy and gum were distributed, and the party ended with hot chocolate. "When we woke up Christmas morning the ground was covered with snow and I have never seen a lovelier sight."

Later that afternoon Helen and Penelope arrived in neighboring Schönecken bei Prüm. "Here I am in a convent at last. I always knew I'd land in one sooner or later!" The two shared a tiny cell with a high window, two iron beds, a table, and a single chair, "the idea . . . being, I suppose, that at least one of us should be continually on our knees!" By now two months of constant travel had taken a toll. "We are never in one place long enough to have our washing done . . . and sometimes have to go several weeks without. We only have a suit apiece." By trading clothes and with much mending the two women coped, "but the time is fast coming when only one of us can appear in public at the same time." In fact, the plan for the following day was for one of them to stay in bed while a suit was cleaned; the next morning the other one would do the same. "We have the same old shoes mended by the army cobblers. Penelope's hair is coming out, and I have chilblains."

Helen spent three weeks in Schönecken, allowing her to observe something of Germany's nascent democracy. Germans "do not seem to be particularly concerned about the Kaiser and are very busy being friendly with our American soldiers, many of whom speak German." But there were discordant notes. Helen was struck by the lack of physical destruction. "It seemed strange to see fields without shell-holes again, homes with roofs on and glass in the windows and civilians and children in the towns." It would not be long before demagogues would parlay the absence of an invasion of German territory on the Western Front, the absence of fighting on German soil, into the "stab in the back" legend, claiming that Germany was winning the war, but socialists, Jews, and pacifists betrayed the country and signed an armistice. Helen witnessed several political meetings in a theater used by the YMCA as a canteen. One of the meetings was "a suffragette one . . . only ladies present," except for the "three priests [who] addressed them and the women said nothing as nearly as I could make out." Helen noted that "the Catholic republican party is very strong in this part of the country and it's 'down with the socialists.' But I can't see that the Germans are being allowed to do their own thinking any more than before the war. The priests are dictating how they shall vote."

The death of former President Theodore Roosevelt, on January 6, 1919, was marked solemnly. "We went out with one of the batteries last week and watched it fire the salute for President Roosevelt. . . . It seemed very strange to be saluting [him] in the country where he was so admired and feared."

Helen's thoughts increasingly turned toward home. "I'll be glad ... when this time of waiting is over. It's so much harder fighting the Armistice than it is fighting the war." She recognized how fortunate her family was. "I'm trying to look up several cases now for families of men who were killed over here, to learn the circumstances of their deaths and where they were buried. And I keep thinking how wonderfully fortunate we have been not to lose any of our own lads. But I should have been mighty proud to have them go that way."

Helen's last surviving letter from Europe is dated January 15, 1919, although she did not return home until April 27. A letter written to Mr. Tener upon her return accounts for her movements during those final weeks. Helen remained in Germany until March 1, with Penelope Parkman, running a mobile canteen and organizing canteens to be continued after their departure. From March 1 to March 10 she was traveling, ending in Paris, where she joined Mr. Bennett. Over lunch he showed Helen a telegram asking him to become president of Doane College. Sitting together in a Paris café, the daughter of Doane's first president helped the soon-to-be third president of the small-town Nebraska college write his letter of acceptance. [22]

Helen was in England for ten days until March 20, "for which I paid from my own funds." She returned to Paris, where plans for sailing were twice canceled due to the numbers of soldiers and civilians returning home. She made use of the next four weeks, working at a Paris canteen and traveling to Biarritz to assist there. On April 16 Helen boarded the *S.S. Chicago* for the voyage home.

Helen's letter to Mr. Tener provides a scrupulous accounting of how she used his $2,000 check, everything from her travel expenses to buying food and cigarettes for the wounded in hospital.

> I have tried to ... spend the money as I thought you would
> want it spent. .... You will notice that during the six months
> I was with the 89th Division I had practically no personal
> expenses, as we ate at army messes, and lived either in
> ruined French villages or German billets. But I used the
> equivalent of what my expenses might have been, and even
> more, in buying special things for the enlisted men, such

---

[22] Thomas Doane Perry, ed., *History of Doane College 1872-1912* (Crete, NE: Doane College, 1957), 248.

as flour, sugar and chocolate for doughnuts and fudge, for plants and curtains to make our canteens gay.

Her expenses for the year were $1,750. "I am enclosing herewith a check for the balance of $250." The past year, Helen wrote, was "the most wonderful year of my life."

I wish I might tell you in some way just what this year has meant. Have you ever wanted to do anything so much that nothing in the world seemed to matter? Well, that is just how I felt about going to France—and you sent me. It's no use trying to thank you, because I never could.

Chapter 7
Marriage and Motherhood

Helen arrived home, sailing into New York harbor on April 27, 1919. She went immediately to Summit to spend a few weeks with Uncle Harry and Aunt Patty. Surrounded by doting relatives Helen could, at least figuratively, live out the fantasy in which she indulged during times of harshest privation in France: "When I get home I'm going to practically live in a bathtub and wear nothing but silk for a year."

Big Helen was not present for her daughter's return. She was in San Diego with her sister-in-law, Alice Doane. Big Helen returned to Trenton in July, by way of Grand Rapids, visiting Tom and his family. She stopped also in Indianapolis to see Henry and Evelyn. Henry had returned from France in March, and he and Evelyn were enjoying their first experience of married life together since their wedding fifteen months earlier. Evelyn was already pregnant, expecting their first child in December.

The Helens were reunited on July 8. Joined by Donald Rice (one of Helen's Trenton beaux) and his mother, Helen met her mother's train in Trenton, and took her to the new apartment at 1320 W. State Street. The Westfield Apartments were familiar to Big Helen; it was where the Rices lived. Helen was back at the State Museum. The two women, Helen told her mother, were "together again, for all time." Life, it appeared, was back to normal.

But John Curtis was home from Ireland as well, in New York and embarking on a career as an interior designer. Helen's indecision regarding her future returned. It did not take her mother long to notice. John Curtis, she wrote, was "ubiquitous." He was not alone. "J[ohn] Wimmer on deck again," Big Helen wrote in her diary. And Donald Rice was a third man "in the race." Helen had regularly mentioned all three men in her letters home from France, indicating that she was corresponding with them all.

Helen's enjoyment of male companionship coincided with a marked reluctance to marry. She joked more than once about going into a convent. Involvement with more than one man forestalled a decision, which, she recognized, would mean an end to her professional career. But indecision was also stressful. "Helen very blue and forlorn abt. J.C.," her mother wrote in her diary in mid-July. "J.C. will not take no for an answer." A few days later Big Helen—perhaps recalling her own initial misgivings about marriage—sat her daughter down and "had [a] long talk with Helen abt. J.C. and her other beaux. She longs for him, but will not say the word."

On July 30, Helen abruptly accepted John's proposal. The two went for a walk, Big Helen wrote, "and returned engaged! I am glad for them, and sorry for myself." News of the engagement was kept within the family circle. Mrs. Rice and Donald continued to be regular visitors at the Perry apartment. It was only on October 13 that "Mrs. Rice came in and Helen told her of her eng[agement]. She [acted] awfully funny." Donald's reaction is not recorded.

Notice of Helen's engagement appeared in late October, under the headline "Curator of State Museum Engaged to Wed New Yorker": "The engagement of Miss Perry is one of the most interesting of the early fall season, as the bride-elect is very well known in this city." Even so, Helen demurred. "No date has been set for the wedding," the story continued, "which will not take place for some time."[1] Nevertheless, John gave Helen an engagement ring from Tiffany's, a small diamond set in platinum.

Aunt Patty was among the few told earlier of the engagement. On August 14 she sent John an extraordinary letter. "My dear John Curtis: Congratulations. You have been kind, persistent, faithful and patient. I don't mind telling you that I think my niece has been pretty hard on you, but you have won." Helen, she continued, "has [been] more like a daughter than a niece for many years. . . . Some day you may be willing for me to know you better too. Please give me that privilege."

Throughout the autumn, as the first anniversary of the Armistice approached, Helen was busy with speaking engagements, sharing the story of her YMCA experience with Rotary Clubs, business club events, women's lunches, and area schools. But in early December something happened that radically altered Helen's professional life. The New Jersey state legislature cut in half the space allocated to the museum. This was triggered by planned renovations to the capitol building. Space occupied by the museum was to be given over to legislative offices.

---

[1] "Curator of State Museum Engaged to Wed New Yorker," *Trenton Sunday Times-Advertiser*, October 26, 1919.

Helen was devastated. The reductions derailed plans for upcoming exhibits, and made impossible a hallmark of Helen's tenure: hands-on experiences for school children. Big Helen's diary chronicles Helen's reaction: "She is sick over it, & very disconsolate." "Helen telephoned [friends] all evening & was most awfully blue on curtailment. . . ." "She is forlorn and very discouraged." Stress took its toll. Helen lost weight. She was, on one occasion, "sick in bed all day, tonsillitis and heartbreak."

Helen could take comfort from the public outcry. "Spare Museum, Say Educators, Manufacturers," headlined the December 6, 1919 *Trenton Evening Times*. "The Museum is worth too much to the State's industrial and educational work. . . . It has received too much assistance from manufacturers and others to be set aside as a luxury at a time when it is filling an important mission, with greater things in sight." Letters to the editor further validated Helen's accomplishment in transforming the State Museum. The museum is "really the only show place in the capitol that carries a state-wide appeal," one reader argued. Others noted the economic benefit in "what's been done by Miss Helen C. Perry, the curator. . . . These exhibits have a decided state value from an advertising viewpoint . . . as well as educational worth." Inasmuch as students from the Normal School used the museum for internships, a petition signed by members of the State Board of Education, the head of the Normal School, and directors of public libraries begged the legislature to reconsider. Yet even as the outcry continued, even as some proposed alternatives (moving the museum or the legislative offices to an unused armory, for example), the partitioning of the museum space and dismantling of exhibits proceeded. On December 19, Helen submitted her letter of resignation.

Two family tragedies occurred that autumn and winter as well. In November, 1919, John's oldest sister Clintie died, a victim of the influenza pandemic. Grief at Clintie's death was compounded when John's second sister, Dorothy, died in February of meningitis. The blow struck John doubly hard. John had introduced Dorothy to Blaine Darrah, John's fraternity brother at Columbia. Blaine and Dorothy were married in June of 1917. At the time of Dorothy's death, the couple had a two-year-old son and Dorothy was pregnant with their second child.[2] The death

---

[2] Blaine's affection for John was evident in a letter he wrote in April of 1918 as he was being sent to France (John was already in Ireland). "John, our lives are what we make them. Ours must be such that those who love us may see in us virtue mixed with bravery. Mine will. John, I don't know where we are going, and don't suppose I will until we are on board a transport. We have lived full lives and hope we have lived only a short part. God bless you and bring you safely home in due time."

of John's two sisters, stark proof of the unpredictability and fragility of life, along with the upending of her museum career, convinced Helen to move ahead with plans for a wedding.

In light of the recent deaths, John and Helen planned a simple wedding. They were married on Wednesday, April 24, 1920, at the Twombly home. Sixteen people attended a luncheon at the house, followed by the ceremony at 3:00 p.m., in the presence of some forty guests. A friend of Helen's father officiated. Helen, in an antique gown of white organdie, once worn by a Doane great-aunt, was given in marriage by her mother. Blaine Darrah was John's best man. Helen had no attendants. Nor did she wear a veil. John had brought from Ireland a length of Irish lace for a veil, part of his campaign to persuade Helen to marry him, but in view of the scaled-back wedding, Helen decided to forego the veil. The Irish lace would have to await another Curtis bride.

"Helen's wedding day," her mother's diary noted. "Windy and sunny. . . . Very lovely and just what Helen needed."

Helen and John Curtis on their honeymoon; April, 1920.

Helen and John honeymooned at Skylands and Luray Caverns in Virginia. Upon their return, the couple took up residence in New York City, where John was establishing a clientele. John and Helen incorporated the decorating business under the name John Morrison Curtis, Inc. Cousin Edward Twombly was a third partner, responsible for the financial aspects of the business.

On February 11, 1921, ten months after the wedding, Helen gave birth to Jeanne Hathaway Curtis. Big Helen, in San Diego with her sister-in-law Alice, wrote in her diary: "A telegram from John, saying Helen's daughter arrived after a three hours journey Friday a.m. Both unusually well. Happy and so relieved."

Fourteen months later, on April 25, 1922, Helen gave birth to Polly Eldridge Curtis. It was the day after Helen and John's second anniversary. John and Helen were in the throes of relocating from New York to Summit. Helen was still in the hospital when John, assisted by Clara Sipprell and Jessica Beers, packed up the apartment and moved to Summit. (Jeanne later insisted that Polly arrived with the moving van.) Uncle Harry had purchased a house at 8 Franklin Place, not far from the Twombly home, signing the deed over to John and Helen and assuming their mortgage payments for a year. Harry also financed the relocation of the business to Summit where, away from the competitive scene of New York City and with the advantage of Twombly family connections, it stood a greater chance of success. If Harry and Patty had long regarded Helen as a daughter, Harry now assumed a paternal attitude toward John. He acknowledged as much, writing: "You have been very much like a son to me, and I have been very glad to have been a little help to you." Uncle Harry, not for the last time, threw John and Helen a lifeline.

The *Summit Herald* reported on the opening of the business, renamed The Band Box, and located in the renovated barn behind the house. Helen's role featured prominently in the story. "Mrs. Curtis (who is well-known as Helen Perry, a niece of Mrs. H.B. Twombly) has long been professionally interested in decorative art." The barn provided office space for meeting with clients, as well as a store selling antiques, furniture, glass, china, and needlework. John and Helen ran the business from Franklin Place until 1928, when the store moved downtown to the first of two locations. In late 1945 John brought the business back to Franklin Place. The Band Box name was dropped in the early 1940s; the business was henceforth known as John Morrison Curtis Interiors.

John's gallery regularly showcased the work of Clara Sipprell and

Jimmy Scott, friends from their days at Columbia and the Art Students League. John was listed, on business cards and advertisements, as agent for both. John sold a number of Jimmy's paintings to clients, and garnered commissions for Jimmy to do paintings and murals for clients which were integrated into John's designs. Jimmy, equally skilled as a silversmith, also made custom jewelry, assembling heirloom gems into rings, brooches, and necklaces for Band Box clients.[3]

From the beginning, John and Helen took an entrepreneurial approach to augmenting their income. John gave lectures on home decorating at women's clubs and art galleries in Summit, Trenton, and Princeton. These yielded modest honoraria and further opportunity to build a clientele. His most popular lecture was "Color in the Home," wherein he recommended reds to convey warmth; blue for a feeling of spaciousness; yellow to transform a dreary interior. Audiences appreciated his assurances that they should "do just as you please," regardless of current trends. John did provide a few caveats. Don't swaddle a simple country home in damask coverings and velvet draperies, nor, "unless you like a museum atmosphere in your home," create period rooms. Do not slavishly follow suggestions from decorating magazines, which "often go to extremes in publicizing wild ideas for people who want to be different. . . . Always be different, but never eccentric."

John developed several lecture series on the history of design, which he presented at the Metropolitan Museum of Art and the Brooklyn Academy of Fine Arts. The connection with the Metropolitan resulted in a commission to restore an historic colonial home in Portsmouth, New Hampshire. By 1946, indicative of his reputation as a decorator, John held a staff appointment as a set decorator at CBS, as the network made its initial foray into television.[4]

Helen showed an entrepreneurial streak as well. She embarked on a career as a freelance writer for *Women's Home Companion, Ladies Home Journal, House and Garden, Parents', American Home, Modern Priscilla, American Girl,* and *Vogue.* She collaborated occasionally with Clara Sipprell and John: photo spreads for which Helen and John wrote the text, or articles on design for which Clara supplied photos.[5] From the beginning Helen used her maiden name, signing her work "Helen

---

[3] James H. Scott, "James Scott, Artist," (2000), 4. James H. Scott is Jimmy Scott's son.
[4] *The Montclair* (NJ) *Times*: October 16, 1931; *Brooklyn* (NY) *Daily Eagle*: October 11, 1932; *Summit Herald and Record*, October 23, 1941; *The Chatham Press* (Chatham, NJ): December 6, 1946; *The Item* (Milburn and Short Hills, NJ): August 15, 1946.
[5] Clara E. Sipprell and John and Helen Curtis, "Winter Bouquets," *Delineator* 49 (December 1922):19; "The House in Good Taste: Candle-Lighting Time," *House Beautiful* 26 (December 1922): n.p.; Clara E. Sipprell and John Curtis, "For the Thanksgiving Festivities," *Women's Home Companion* 53, (November 1926): 148.

Perry Curtis." The articles drew on her Columbia arts training and life-long talent at sewing, along with her newer interests in homemaking and child rearing: "Three Dresses in Three Hours for $3.25;" "Simple Ways to Smarten Small Frocks;" "Equal Rights on the Clothes Question" (advocating "Dutchman's breeches" as suitable play clothes for girls); "Kitchen Parties;" "Indoor Treasure Hunt;" "Let's Eat Out of Doors;" "Garden Exchange;" "Luxuries You Can Make;" "Let's Sew." Helen published drawn-to-scale patterns for women and children's clothing, showing the influence of European-style peasant and folk costumes, reminiscent of exhibits from the Homelands Exhibits at Newark and Trenton (Helen in fact borrowed items from Newark's collection to use as prototypes.) She made children's clothing which she sold at The Band Box, the designs often displaying colorful embroidery.

Helen further mined her home and family for material. "A Decorator Lives in a Victorian House," an article written by Helen, ran in *The American Home* magazine. [6] It described renovation efforts and included photos of the Curtises' living room with its antique furniture and bookshelf-lined walls; the sideboard set with European pottery; the master bedroom with its canopied bed, colonial-style chairs, and dresser; Jeanne's bedroom tucked under the eaves.

Jeanne and Polly were often featured in Helen's articles. Clara Sipprell photographed the girls in clothes designed for them by Helen: European-inspired smocks and pinafores, richly embroidered. Clara captured the girls' childhoods in a series of portraits: the girls as infants in Helen's lap; as toddlers, seated on the porch or in the wing-backed chair in the living room; Jeanne standing behind John's chair, Polly in his lap, as he read to them. Clara trained an affectionate lens on Helen as a young mother, hair drawn back, a scarf loosely draped around her neck; or John, hands clasped around his knee, contemplating a portrait of his mother. Clara's portraits of Jeanne and Polly follow the girls into young adulthood. Taken together, they are one of only two long-term portrait series done by Clara. The other was of her goddaughter Nina Cekich, daughter of Irina Khrabroff and Feodor Cekich—all friends of John and Helen as well.

---

[6] Helen Perry Curtis, "A Decorator Lives in a Victorian House: The Summit, New Jersey, home of Mr. John Morrison Curtis," *The American Home* (January, 1939): 8-11.

Jeanne, John, and Polly Curtis, by Clara Sipprell.
Family collection

Later, following travels in Europe in the 1920s and 1930s, Helen wrote about holiday customs in Europe. She told the story of the Christmas crèche she and John bought in Germany in 1926. Helen recast that visit to the studio and purchase of the crèche as "The Tower of Rothenburg" chapter in *Jean & Company*. Other articles on holiday customs were rewritten as the "Christmas in Switzerland" chapter, wherein a merry group of visitors from France, Germany, and Italy spend the holiday together at an Alpine chalet.

Over the course of the 1920s and 1930s Helen published some seventy articles, including the eleven *American Girl* stories which were later reworked into *Jean & Company*. In 1929, she published *When Sally Sews: She Makes Fifty Things Any Girl Can Make*. The book brought together earlier published work along with new material.

A syndicated newspaper interview addressed Helen's strategy. The high cost of living, the article noted, has driven many women to look for ways to supplement the family income, only to despair that they had no way of making a contribution. "Helen Perry Curtis of New York (sic) was not one of these. . . . When she felt the need of augmenting the family income, like the prophet of biblical times, she asked herself the question, 'What hast thou in the house?'" Referring to Helen' work with the Homelands Exhibit, the article noted that "when the blaze on the family hearth grew somewhat dim, Mrs. Curtis harked back to these experiences. . . . From these she is picking up many little pot boilers that feed a constant, cheering, generous fire."[7]

Helen's role as a mother drew her into the Child Study Association, led by Sidonie Matsner Gruenberg.[8] Born in Vienna in 1881, Sidonie grew up in a secular Jewish household. The Matsners emigrated to the United States in 1895, where Sidonie's parents joined Felix Adler's Ethical Culture Society. (The young John Cotton Dana had once sought a position as a lecturer with Adler's school.) Adler's movement grew out of dissatisfaction with the ways in which traditional religion addressed contemporary social issues. The senior Matsners were instrumental in building the Ethical Culture Workingman's School and later the Ethical Culture Normal School. In 1923 Sidonie was named director of the Normal School's Child Study Association; a post she held until 1950. A dynamic administrator and prolific author, Sidonie published twenty-six books and numerous articles for *Child Study Magazine* and *Parents*. She subscribed to a progressive philosophy of childrearing, rooted in the behavioral science research of the day.[9] She also addressed the role of parents, especially mothers. Women, she wrote, need to prepare for a number of life stages. "We have to choose not once, but many times and at each stage with the same degree of uncertainty." It was advice that Helen would take to heart.[10]

The circle surrounding Sidonie Gruenberg intersected with that of Jessica Beers and Clara Sipprell. Jessica came to New York in 1915 when she was hired as principal of the Ethical Culture Normal School; Clara worked at the School as a contract photographer. Another intersection was *Parents'* magazine, for which Helen regularly wrote. Women's club connections also came into play. Summit's Fortnightly Club sponsored lectures on child rearing. The Band Box hosted Child Study Association speakers, and Gruenberg came to Summit for a series of talks. Sidonie Gruenberg's friends included Carl Van Doren, founder of the Junior Literary Guild; and Helen Ferris, editor of *American Girl* and subsequently editor-in-chief of the Junior Literary Guild. These connections would prove to be significant ones for Helen.

In September of 1926 Jeanne entered Miss Hood's Pre- and Primary

[7] Thompson Feature Service, Frances L. Garside, "Pot Boiler Becomes Big Business," December, 1922.
[8] While the correct German spelling is Matzner, the family Anglicized the name to Matsner. Sources, both in Sidonie's lifetime and afterwards, are inconsistent in the spelling.
[9] Sidonie Matsner Gruenberg, *We, The Parents: Our Relationship to Our Children and to the World Today* (New York: Harper and Brothers, 1939).
[10] Roberta Wollons, "Sidonie Matzner Gruenberg." *Jewish Women: A Comprehensive Historical Encyclopedia*. 27 February 2009. Jewish Women's Archive.

School in Summit, Polly following a year later. In 1928 the girls transferred to the Buxton School in neighboring Short Hills. Buxton, a newly founded country day school, was the work of Ellen Geer Sangster, a social worker influenced by the writings of John Dewey. Sangster created a school centered on experiential learning with an emphasis on the creative arts. Buxton attracted like-minded families from Summit, people who would become life-long friends of John and Helen, Jeanne and Polly.

Buxton drew Helen into yet another orbit, that of the Duncan School of Dance. Kathleen Hinni, the dance teacher at Buxton, was a pupil of Anita Zahn, who was in turn a student of Elizabeth Duncan, sister of the famous Isadora. Elizabeth, lame since childhood, taught at the school Isadora founded in the Berlin suburb of Gruenewald. In 1909, when Isadora moved to Paris, Elizabeth's partner Max Merz convinced Elizabeth to start her own school in Darmstadt. When World War I began, Elizabeth and a group of students, including Anita Zahn, came to the United States, settling in Tarrytown, along the Hudson River. After the war, they returned to Europe, where Elizabeth reestablished her school at Schloss Klessheim, a former palace on the outskirts of Salzburg.

In 1922, Anita returned to the United States, opening a Duncan School in New York City. By 1928 the Anita Zahn School of the Duncan Dance had branches in Trenton, Princeton, Short Hills, and Summit, where Kathleen Hinni's teaching of dance at Buxton drew the interest of artistically-minded, avant-garde parents to Anita's school.

The philosophy of Duncan Dance was that the body should express itself through motions most natural to it. "Let us first teach little children to breathe, to vibrate, to feel, and to become one with the general harmony and movement," Isadora wrote.[11] She rejected the formalism of ballet, finding inspiration instead in nature: wind in the branches, waves in the sea. Isadora was enamored of Ancient Greece, and her choreography incorporated poses found in the statuary of classical Greece. Training the body was as important as developing the mind. "Only that education is right which includes the dance." Elizabeth Duncan emphasized the simple motions of running, walking, and jumping as the starting point. "The aim is to lead the child to find itself, to liberate and increase its natural creative forces and to lead them to expression through the medium of a well-trained body."[12] Jeanne and Polly performed as "Little Duncan Dancers" with Anita's

---

[11] Isadora Duncan, *The Art of the Dance* (c. 1928, New York: Theater Arts Books, 1970), 77.
[12] "Elizabeth Duncan School, Schloss Klessheim, Salzburg" (New York: Elizabeth Duncan Association, Inc., 1925), Anita Zahn Archive, New York Public Library, Performing Arts Division.

school, and continued to dance with Anita through high school. Along with recitals in Summit, the girls danced at the Guild Theater on 52nd Street in New York and at a benefit concert at the Fifth Avenue mansion of philanthropist Adolph Lewisohn.

Anita and Helen became life-long friends. By 1935 Helen was the contact person for Anita's school in Summit.[13] The friendship with Anita put Helen at one remove from Elizabeth and Isadora Duncan (she later met Elizabeth), precisely the kind of connection Helen relished. It also introduced her to Leopold Stokowski, who conducted many of the Duncan recitals.

In the 1930s Anita Zahn conducted a summer school at Siasconset on Nantucket. Anita's school was part of the Sconset School of Opinion, founded in 1922 by Frederic C. Howe, a Progressive reformer, activist, author, administrator, and member of both the Wilson and Franklin Roosevelt administrations. Howe purchased property on the eastern end of Nantucket Island, converting an old barn into a gathering place he named "Tavern on the Moors."[14] His vision was of a place "where we would dine, talk, and have music and dances, intimately, informally, as if we were around a fireside. . . . We would invite people to share it with us who had something to say about the things we were interested in." The School drew speakers such Sinclair Lewis, Eugene O'Neill, Walter Lippmann, Arthur Schlesinger, Sr., perennial Socialist Party candidate Norman Thomas, and artists including African-American baritone Paul Robeson, himself a political activist. It was in this setting that Anita Zahn ran her school. Nantucket resident Edouard Stackpole recalled that "Anita used to conduct classes on the lawn of the School. . . . I can see them now in their little white gowns . . . going through the recital of the dance."[15]

Attendance at Siasconset determined Curtis family vacations for several years in the 1920s and early 1930s. Joining the Curtises were Jimmy Scott, now married to Danish-born Kirsten Olrik. Jimmy and Kirsten met at Elverhoj when Kirsten accompanied her father,

---

[13] The list of patrons for the school include the names Mr. and Mrs. John Morrison Curtis, along with the Scotts, the Gouchers, the Chalifs, and Angela Hagen, all but the Scotts parents of Buxton students. Miss Helen Mabie, Helen's friend from her 1908-1909 year in Summit, was another patron. So too was Susan Darrah, second wife of John's brother-in-law, testimony to the enduring closeness of the two couples after the death of John's sister Dorothy.

[14] Frederic Howe pursued graduate studies at Princeton, where (like Raymond Fosdick) he was inspired by Woodrow Wilson. In 1914 Howe was Commissioner of Immigration for the Port of New York in 1914, in which role he intervened on behalf of Elizabeth Duncan and her students, including Anita Zahn.

[15] Kenneth E. Miller, *From Progressive to New Dealer: Frederic C. Howe and American Liberalism* (University of Pennsylvania Press, 2010), 335-345; Lee Rand Burne, "The Sconset School of Opinion," *Historic Nantucket* (41:2, (Summer 1993): 27-29.

Denmark's Secretary of the Navy, on an official visit to the artist colony. The two married in 1925. Jimmy taught art classes at the summer school and Kirsten played piano for Anita's dance classes.

Prior to summers on Nantucket with the Siasconset School, the Curtises vacationed on Martha's Vineyard. It was the start of a family love affair with the island. There John and Helen spent time with Jack and Grace Rosé, neighbors from Franklin Place. The Rosés were part of another circle in which the Curtises were active, that of the Summit Playhouse Association. John and Helen shared a love of theater; during their courtship they regularly went to plays, sometimes twice a week, in New York. They now directed that passion to an organization close to home. While their major contribution was behind the scenes, John occasionally acted in a production, earning favorable reviews. [16]

John and Helen returned to Europe in 1926 and 1930. Both were in part buying trips: acquiring antiques, furniture, and paintings for the business. Uncle Harry accompanied Helen and John in 1930. The trips were opportunities to revisit places and people John and Helen knew during the war.

The 1926 trip, ten weeks in duration, took John and Helen through France, Italy, Yugoslavia, and then to Austria, Germany, and England. Jeanne and Polly were left in Summit with a nanny, Miss Foote. The girls, four and five years old, joined the delegation seeing John and Helen off at the boat. Jeanne and Polly, Helen wrote, "were thrilled over seeing the boat, and perfectly happy to go back with Ellen and Sophie and Miss Foote. Happier than we were to leave them!"

In contrast to their recent voyages on troop ships, John and Helen luxuriated in the opportunity to relax, sleep, eat, and read in deck chairs. Both indulged in the snobbery of the sophisticated traveler encountering those less favored. John wrote to Clara and Jessica that there were a large number of Americans on board, who "drank up the liquor supply before we got to France." (He would later complain of having to endure the presence of two American women at the next table in a Parisian café, loudly discussing their divorce proceedings and gambling losses.) Helen had her own complaints. "I was reading *The Private Life of Helen of Troy* the other day, when I heard the woman

---

[16] *Summit Herald*, December 7, 1928.

sitting next to me say to her companion, 'Who is this Helen of Troy, anyway? Is she an American girl?'" A happy acquaintance on shipboard was the artist Georges Plasse. Helen's editor at *Modern Priscilla* had told her about Plasse, who was returning from an extended stay in the United States.

John and Helen arrived in Paris on April 24, their sixth wedding anniversary. The two had known Paris only in wartime. Now, even the rain could not dampen their mood. Their hotel, the Le Bon, was three metro stops from the Arc de Triomphe and a ten-minute walk to the Bois de Boulogne, and offered a view "worth the trip to Europe." Helen, usually the more enthusiastic of the two, expressed one reservation concerning the hotel. "Green and orange wall-paper in stripes about two inches wide, exploding into bunches of green and orange and pink flowers at the top. A turkey red carpet, magenta velvet curtains, purple and yellow striped satin on the furniture, and a rose-colored quilt on the bed. We thought at first we must have been drinking, but we're a little hardened to it now."

Not that John and Helen spent much time in their room. They wandered the bookstalls on the Left Bank, and lunched at sidewalk cafés. The first evening they went to a performance—appropriate for their anniversary, Helen noted—of "The Marriage of Figaro." They visited the Louvre, Notre Dame, and made excursions to the artist colony at Barbizon, to Fontainebleau, and Versailles.

True to plans made on shipboard, Georges Plasse hosted John and Helen at his apartment and studio in Montmartre. "Rosy-faced, Van Dyke bearded," the artist greeted his guests wearing an old brown monk's robe and a skull cap, defense against the lack of heat in the apartment. Plasse showed them around: a salon, a tiny bedroom, and even smaller kitchen. Disappearing briefly, he returned with a half-dozen bottles of wine. A servant set up a card table in the salon and served dinner. "We became friends for life during that meal," John wrote. The next day Plasse called for Helen and John, taking them to meet the artist Octave Denis Victor Guillonnet, who had recently completed a commission doing the murals on the walls of the Hotel de Ville, Paris's city hall. The four spent a long afternoon examining dozens of canvases, charcoal sketches, and cartoons for murals. "My brain reeled, drunk, completely over-stimulated with the wonderful beauty with which we were surrounded," John wrote to Clara Sipprell. Guillonnet invited his guests to tea, served, according to Helen, "in one of the most beautiful rooms I have ever seen, all soft blues and greens and lavenders," a description that aptly characterized the palette in which Guillonnet worked. Neither Guillonnet nor his wife spoke English, and Helen wrote that their French was inadequate to what they wanted to say "when we talked of the war, so we all shook hands several times, and wept together, and shook hands some more, and now we are fast friends."

Memories of the war were ever-present. Helen and John called at the pension where she and her mother stayed in 1914, still maintained by Miss McTavish and Miss Galloway. "Very Dickensian English maiden ladies," John described them, "too good to be true." John and Helen called on Henri Lacour, a young art student John picked up in his ambulance in 1917. Lacour took them to "a swank café" on the Champs Élysées, where "we spent an hour and a half over a thimbleful of some kind of aperitif." John, in his wartime letters to Helen, had shared the story of Lacour, a twenty-year-old student whose plans to attend the École des Beaux Arts were upended by the war. Lacour in turn wrote to Helen, thanking her for the sketch block and pencils she sent him, noting that "Mr. Curtis is veritably kindly to tell you so much about me." The visit with Henri Lacour was, in a way, a first meeting for John as well. During the entire time John knew him in 1917, Lacour was heavily bandaged. "John had never seen his face."

From Paris John and Helen went by train through the Rhône River Valley to Avignon and environs. "It is impossible," Helen wrote, "to believe that [what] we saw could be real, it seemed like the illustration for a fairytale, and we momentarily expected the princess or the knight in armor to appear." From the train they could see "hill after hill crowned with battlements and towers and the slopes below them stretching down to the plains like a huge checker-board of gardens and vineyards."

From Avignon they made day trips to Nîmes and the Pont du Gard, to Uzès and to the walled city of Carcassonne. In Villeneuve-lès-Avignon they climbed to the fortress and looked out at the old city across the Rhône. They listened to the singing of the nightingales "while we lay on the ground and dreamed of all we had seen...and tried to think of it as being really true." In Montpelier John purchased a set of Louis XVI furniture: sofa and six chairs. John was ever-alert to issues of provenance, buying where possible directly from families, many of whom were closing and selling ancestral homes. This was but one sign of the change underway in the French countryside, as France's population was inexorably shifting from rural to urban.

From Avignon to Marseilles, and then along the Riviera, "flashing in and out of tunnels all day, but having gorgeous glimpses of blue sky and blue sea, and white villages with red roofs all along the way." A night in Genoa, and then on to Rome, where to their surprise they discovered that Rose Morrow Previtali, Helen's friend from 1915, was staying at the Park Hotel, in the room just above theirs. Rome offered opportunities for buying antiques and other wares for the business. Helen and John went to the Rag Market, held once a week, where merchants sold their wares at canopied tables in a public square. It was "colorful, gay, and lots of fun."

As in Paris, they spent time with artists. One afternoon it was Pietro D'Achiardi, a friend of Clara Sipprell. They found him at his studio, at work on a commission: mosaics for the dome of the Church of All Nations on the Mount of Olives in Jerusalem. "It is thrilling," Helen wrote, "to see anybody at work on such a big scale, doing for this century what other great artists have done for their time, and to think that these mosaics may live as long again as the Roman mosaics." D'Achiardi invited the Curtises to his country home, its terrace overlooking the ruined Baths of Caracalla, its gardens filled with ancient cypress and sycamore trees. There they looked over hundreds of paintings, drawings, and etchings, two of which John purchased. "We are having so many wonderful experiences of this sort, meeting really great artists, and seeing them at work."

Conversant though John and Helen were with the artistic world, when it came to politics they were woefully naïve. "Rose is an ardent *fascisti* and she has filled us full of it." Italians, Helen claimed, were supportive of Mussolini's "government of law and order," and were indignant at the coverage of Mussolini in the American press. "We are so glad to be learning something about it first-hand." John was equally gullible. "Something must be done to counteract the dreadful untruths about Mussolini and Fascism with which we are fed by our ignorant as well as intellectual press. *Atlantic Monthly, Outlook,* [and] *Literary Digest* offend the Italians as keenly as any Hearst newspapers. . . . We have been given entirely the wrong ideas about him in America." Helen concurred. Coverage of the Matteotti case in the American press, she opined, amounted to "plain lies." Two years earlier, in May of 1924, Giacomo Matteotti, a socialist member of parliament, denounced the ruling Fascists for the violence, intimidation, and fraud which marked the elections. Eleven days later Matteotti was murdered.

Historians agree that Mussolini was, at a minimum, aware of plans to kill Matteotti and did nothing to stop it. The murder, and the king's refusal to remove Mussolini as prime minister, signaled the death of democracy in Italy. By 1925 all political opposition was silenced and Italy was a one-party state.

How did Helen and John get it so wrong? Sadly, they were not alone. Many Americans embraced fascism's opposition to Bolshevism (this was, after all, the era of the Red Scare) while others fell for the simplistic platitudes that Mussolini made Italy's trains run on time and restored crucifixes to the classroom. John and Helen, like many intellectuals, responded to the claim that fascism marked a restoration of social harmony. Helen, attracted to the work of William Morris, John Ruskin, and the Arts and Crafts movement, was susceptible to the strain of Romanticism that informed their work. The yearning for the restoration of an organic, pre-industrial community, driven by revulsion at the exploitation of labor under modern capitalism, was appropriated by conservative movements in the late nineteenth century and cynically exploited by fascism in the twentieth. Helen's idealized view of pre-modern society led her, and others, to see in fascism the restoration of the traditional folk community.

From Rome, Helen and John went to Ravello, on the Amalfi Coast. Helen was there in 1915, but now the two were so enamored of the place that they skipped Siena in order to stay longer. Helen described Ravello as "the most heavenly spot that I have ever seen. . . . It is everything that is beautiful in Italy, concentrated into one spot." Writing to Aunt Patty, Helen tried to convince the Twomblys to change their plans for England later that summer and come instead to Ravello, where

> you could have rooms in this quaint old palace with a wide
> balcony looking down hundreds of feet to the sea, you could
> walk in the so-called "enchanted garden" which belongs to
> the palace. . . . You could see Pompeii . . . take lovely little
> trips up and down the shore in a little steamboat, motor in
> every direction, and Uncle Harry could climb mountains to
> his heart's content."

John and Helen's time in Ravello coincided with the visit of Crown Prince Umberto, and Helen and John's romanticism and political naïveté were again in evidence. Helen described banner-draped balconies, carpets spread on the street, and garlands of flowers everywhere. Posters announced the visit of "the most beautiful flower of Italy, coming to this village of flowers." (Helen took a poster as a souvenir.) The prince, whom they saw at their hotel, she described as young, fine-looking, gentle, and modest of manner, wearing a plain dark suit, hat in hand, smiling at everyone. "No royal pomp, just the village people giving their best to their prince. It was just like a medieval town, the quaint old houses all hung with gay colors and many of the people in peasant costume." [17]

From Ravello Helen and John went to Assisi, Perugia, and Florence. They arrived in time for Decoration Day, May 24, the anniversary of Italy's entry in the First World War. Helen described "the most beautiful sight I have ever seen, the Palazzo Vecchio . . . with its castellated walls and tower outlined with lights . . . little oil lamps that flicker in the wind, like candles." They saw a torchlight parade; earlier in the day the Fascist youth organizations marched past.

> They are dressed all in white, with sweaters and tam-o-shanters in various colors, here a squad of red, here green, here blue . . . each with its own small band of trumpets and drums, some of the children no bigger than Jeanne and Polly, proud little figures with many badges showing their rank. It was a beautiful sight to see, so beautiful the tears came.

John and Helen's accounts of their ten-weeks in Europe tilt towards the first month of the trip, the time in France and Italy. With the exception of one diary entry written by Helen in Rothenburg, there is no other written record of the final weeks of the trip. Helen admitted as much. "We haven't written about our trip to Jugo-Slavia, but will write another time." She never did. Their itinerary, however, can be reconstructed from photo albums. From Ravello, John and Helen went to Venice, and then to Yugoslavia. A decade later, Helen wrote an *American Girl* story set in Yugoslavia; slightly revised, it is "The Strange Land of Yugoslavia" chapter in *Jean & Company*. Those accounts take the reader from Venice, along the Dalmatian coast to Spoleto, Dubrovnik, Sarajevo, and Zagreb. Photos of these locales are in Helen's 1926 photo album. The mother of

---

[17]Already, but evidently unknown to Helen, there were stories of promiscuous sexual behavior by the prince, including pursuit of young army officers. Umberto was destined to be the last king of Italy. Known to history as the "May King," he ruled from May 9 to June 12, 1946, following the abdication of his father at the end of the Second World War. A referendum on June 2, 1946, abolished the monarchy.

Clara Sipprell's friend, Feodor Cekich, lived in Zagreb. In the sole case in which Helen used a surname in *Jean & Company*, she has Jean and her mother staying in Zagreb with a Madame Cekic (sic) and her daughter Jovanka.

From Yugoslavia the two went to Vienna, Nuremberg, Rothenburg, Amsterdam, and finally to England, sailing from Southampton to New York on the 26th of June. For Helen, the time in Germany summoned up associations with the war. "They have been very nice to us, and we have nothing against them as individuals, but it is difficult for us to get over a sort of general

Helen in Venice, 1926

repugnance, especially when a fully equipped army marches by." Military displays in Italy did not trigger revulsion. The same kind of display in Germany did. "They said it was just a special parade, but it made us almost ill to see it."

Helen and John returned to Europe in 1930, with Uncle Harry. It was the start of a custom Harry carried out over the coming decade: taking a family member on a trip nearly every summer. For each of these trips, Uncle Harry kept a diary. Afterwards, he had these transcribed and, along with appropriate photos, bound in gold-stamped, green leather bindings. Because none of Helen and John's letters from 1930 have survived, Uncle Harry's travel diary is invaluable. His accounts are witty and engaging; moreover, Harry proved to be a perceptive observer of the European political scene.

The two Curtises and Uncle Harry sailed for Europe on March 28, 1930. Their first destination was Paris; from there south through the Gallic region and the Midi, which John and Helen had visited four years earlier. In Paris they again visited Georges Plasse at his studio. And Harry had his own annoying encounter with American tourists: "One man thinks Marie Antoinette was burned at the stake and that this all happened in 1500."

From France the three went to Spain, traveling by chauffeured car through Barcelona, Valencia, Alicante ("said to be the most African of all the Spanish cities"), Ronda, Seville, Cordoba, Toledo, and Madrid. There they saw the Escorial Palace, and heard the account, eerily prophetic, concerning the number of niches remaining in the royal burial vault. [18] From there it was on to Avila, Segovia, Burgos, Santander, and San Sebastian in the Basque region, before returning to France.

The 1930 trip was Helen's only visit to Spain. Lacking a first-hand account, it is difficult to gauge her reaction, but it is revealing that she never wrote an *American Girl* story or *Jean* chapter set in that country. Spain in 1930 was one of the most backward countries in Europe. Since 1923, a military dictator ruled alongside the monarch. Spain was, in fact, poised on the brink of a decade of upheaval: revolution, abolition of the monarchy, civil war, and the establishment of the dictatorship of Francisco Franco. Harry wrote that "ignorance seems the curse of Spain, nobody outside the Intelligentsia seems to know or care much who governs." He noted, while driving from Toledo to Madrid, that the peasants were using only oxen and donkeys in the fields, too poor either to own or maintain machinery.

Spain's historic monuments and sites were, however, impressive. The Alhambra "is all it is cracked up to be." Harry was equally dazzled by the mosque at Cordoba, but claimed that "the Christians spoiled it all" by transforming it into a cathedral. In Seville John, Helen, and Uncle Harry went to a bullfight, "but [it was] brutal in our eyes, and we didn't stay long." And Harry had a poignant encounter at the cathedral in Seville. "While in the garden, the Princess [Beatriz] came out for a walk . . . and, in response to my lifted hat, bowed graciously." Eleven months later the monarchy was overthrown and Spain declared a republic. The Infanta Beatriz followed her family into exile.

There were lighthearted moments. Harry affectionately teased his niece and her husband in a diary entry, capturing at the same time

---

[18] The Escorial's burial vault was built by Phillip II (1556-1598). In 1930, there were niches designated for the ruling king, Alfonso XIII, and his wife and mother. There remained then only two more niches. The monarchy was overthrown in 1931. It was restored with the death of Generalissimo Francisco Franco, who ruled Spain from the end of the Civil War in 1939 until 1975. Since then, two kings have ruled Spain: King Juan Carlos from 1975 to 2014, and the current king, Felipe VI. "Heaven only knows," Uncle Harry quoted the guide.

the personality of each. "Rained hard. John said, 'I wish we could see the sun.' Helen said, 'How green this rain will make the fields and the flowers!' I said, 'We're having a bang-up time and I don't give a damn for the rain.'"

From Basque country, Harry and the Curtises returned to France. Their route took them to Biarritz, Tarbes, Toulouse, and Carcassonne, exploring again a town John and Helen remembered fondly from 1926. From there to Nîmes, Avignon, then south to Aix-en-Provence and the Riviera: Cannes, Nice, and Monaco. In Monte Carlo they watched the gambling in the casino. "It seemed very tawdry to me," Harry wrote.

Before leaving France there was another departure from the 1926 itinerary. Harry, John, and Helen went to the tiny village of Roquebrune-Cap-Martin, high above the Mediterranean near the Italian border, to visit the grave of Helen's brother Carl.

Things had not gone well for Carl since the two Helens were with him in Turin. In November of 1915 Carl was recalled to Washington. Big Helen was in Grand Rapids visiting Tom's family when she received a letter from a Mr. Wilbur Carr at the State Department, "saying Carl is in bad repute and is likely to lose his place." Tom went to New York to meet Carl's boat; a month later Carl came with Helen to Grand Rapids for Christmas.

Back in New York, it became increasingly clear that Carl was in financial trouble. Upon his return from Europe, Carl asked Tom to guarantee a loan for $3,000, a request Tom was unable to fulfill. In early January, 1916, Tom alerted his mother that Carl was again asking for money. Big Helen turned to Uncle Harry, who stepped into the breach. Big Helen paid $154 to cover Carl's expenses at a club in New York. Carl lived for a time with his mother and sister. It was a repeat of Turin. "Carl out nearly all night and I didn't sleep." "Carl out all night." "Carl out very late and I had bad night." Helen's patience with her brother was wearing thin. "I can't discuss Carl with Helen," her mother confided to her diary.

Carl was officially dismissed by the State Department in April, 1916. In May he went to Toledo, Ohio, on unspecified business. His mother was encouraged. "Good opening there . . . and we are very happy. . . . I feel sure Carl will make good." Nothing came of it. Instead, by October,

Carl was packing for Calcutta, where he had once held a diplomatic post, and now had a job representing a New York bank. His departure was chaotic. Carl frequently failed to show up in Summit, where his belongings were stored, to help his mother sort and pack his things.

In February of 1918 Carl surfaced in England, where he applied for a civilian US passport (he had been using diplomatic papers), declaring his intention to go into business there. The application states that he had been in England since the previous October. Carl's family was largely in the dark regarding these developments.

In October, 1918, Carl married Mary Jane Kathleen (Mai-Mai) Wilson in the registry office in St. George Hanover Square, London. Four months later a son, Carlo, was born, followed a year later by a daughter, Barbara. Mai-Mai, herself orphaned at a young age, was already raising a six-year-old nephew, Horace. The boy's father was killed early in World War I; his mother died shortly thereafter.

Carl did not inform his family of his marriage. Helen discovered it in March of 1919, when she spent ten days in England prior to returning home from her YMCA work. "A letter from Helen," her mother wrote in her diary, "telling of Carl's wife and baby. Charles B., Jr. Had known nothing of this, and it broke me all up."

Carl and Mai-Mai Perry, with Carlo and Barbara; London, 1921.

Helen and John saw Carl in England at the end of their 1926 trip. Two months later Harry and Frances took a long-planned trip to England, and Frances, upon her return, wrote to her sister in San

Diego confirming Helen's suspicion that Carl had tuberculosis. "Long letter from Frances, says Carl must go to sanitarium, both lungs badly affected, may not, probably will not be able to do a man's work again. Very tragic + heartbreaking." Within weeks Carl and his family were in Davos, Switzerland. Worries continued. "Carl hasn't paid any or much of his sanitarium bill," Big Helen wrote in her diary on March 10, 1927, "and they have wired Tom about it. I am heartsick." Three days later she wrote: "Very bad news abt. Carl + his debts."

Carl did not improve. The doctors recommended the south of France. In March of 1928 Carl's family moved to Roquebrune, into a rented flat, one of four apartments in a converted farmhouse. The tall French doors in Carl's bedroom admitted maximum sunlight and fresh air. Big Helen sent a check, which Mai-Mai promised to spend only in an emergency. Late in April, Carl, too weak to hold a pen, dictated a letter expressing his gratitude. "We really think we have a wonderful family. First Aunt Patty who steps into the breach when it doesn't seem as if we could go on. Then Evelyn with a cheque. Helen with clothes and yet more clothes. Tom with books. Something unexpected keeps turning up." At the same time, Carl revealed how ill he truly was. "The jumping muscles of which I was so proud, vanished; and only a handful of skin and bones left. I think I may weigh about 110 pounds, against 168 stripped in my football days, so it is going to a long hard pull to come back."

Any belief Carl held that he might recover was unfounded. Mai-Mai sought the advice of Dr. Brett, an English expatriate and neighbor. The doctor assured Carl that he and Mai-Mai were doing all that they could, words which Carl took to mean that "we are going in the right direction." The next morning, Mai-Mai brought him his breakfast tray. The mail arrived with a letter from brother Henry, much to Carl's delight. At noon the children returned from school. From the kitchen Mai-Mai heard Carl trying to get out of bed. Entering his room, she found Carl sitting up, trying to cough. "He looked awful, made a strange noise and fell backwards across the bed. I pushed some pillows under his head and then I think I became insane. I pounded on the door of the flat opposite; almost broke it down. There is an old lady there, she came in and she said he was dead, she had seen many people die. . . ."

The woman sent her little granddaughter for Dr. Brett, who pronounced Carl dead. "I realize," Mai-Mai wrote to Carl's family, "that it was the kind of death he would have liked, to know nothing at all about it. But I feel such a fool not to have known how near the end was." Dr. Brett told her now that when he saw Carl earlier, he knew that there was no chance he would recover, but he thought that Carl would linger for months. He asked Mai-Mai if she would prefer he went as he did, "and I had to answer yes." Mai-Mai told the children that their father "is now in Heaven and happier, which I firmly believe. I know God wanted him for some reason and I am not frightened for him going. He had no sins," she continued, "he was too good. That he was foolish about money was the *only* fault he had. . . . Often when one of your letters came, I would say to him 'You are loved a lot,' and he used to say 'More than I deserve.'"

Mai-Mai wanted to have Carl's body cremated, so that his ashes could be returned home. The cost was prohibitive. Mai-Mai decided to bury him in Roquebrune.

> I do hope that I have done as you would have wished. He had
> an oak coffin with a brass plate and his name and age on top.
> The Doctor chose it all. I don't know much about funerals but
> it seemed to me very quiet and everything that one could wish.
> A horse hearse; and the clergyman and I rode in a carriage
> behind. The cemetery at Roquebrune is very beautiful. Perched
> upon on a high hill overlooking Cap Martin and the sea. I
> threw a big bunch of roses on to the coffin. He always had
> roses in his room and used to say how lovely they looked when
> the early morning sun shone on them. [19]

Now, two years later, Helen, John, and Uncle Harry stood at Carl's grave. "High up on a mountain top overlooking the sea," Harry wrote, "a most beautiful resting place."

Crossing the French Alps, the three went to Turin. "Helen," Uncle Harry noted, "has a strong bias for Mussolini and everything Italian." He quoted Helen's claim that Italy is the only country in the world with no unemployment, adding cynically, "in spite of the lot of men I saw sitting around in the Italian villages apparently doing nothing but sitting and

---

[19] All of the events described in Mai-Mai's letter occurred on the same day, May 14, 1928. The Mediterranean heat dictated that burial must occur immediately. Mai-Mai wrote to Carl's family that evening: "While it is fresh in my mind, I want to tell you all about today."

drinking." In Turin, John, Helen, and Harry visited a Mr. Gianolio, who served with Carl in the American consulate. "Of course, we discussed Mussolini. Gianolio is all for him; thinks he saved Italy from Communism and is now trying to solve the problem of labor and capital." But Harry encountered a different view from a taxi driver, "who freely said that the number of the unemployed was underestimated and that there was great unrest in Italy; that the next war in Italy would be a revolution."

Harry noted warily the evidence of military preparation.

> Turin was full of soldiers. . . . We saw a regiment of black-shirted Fascist soldiers *en marche*, and in a small town outside of Turin the Fascists were training in considerable numbers in the Town Square, and up the street came a company of small boys of about 12 years of age, clad in black shirts and hats, marching to the time of three drummer boys. Soldiers and Blackshirts are in every town.

Whereas a parade of the fascist youth four years earlier moved Helen to tears, Harry had a different reaction. "Mussolini intends to be prepared to try to make good his bombastic threats should occasion arise. . . . Mussolini sounds like Napoleon in his high-sounding phrases and threatening warnings to the rest of Europe." In Rome, Harry's negative impressions were strengthened. He wrote about the vast archeological projects underway at the Roman Forum, part of Mussolini's zeal to restore the Roman ruins as a symbol of the restoration of Italian greatness. "All central Rome is in daily terror of losing their homes to uncover other temples and stadia ruins." Harry cited other reasons for the projects: "Mussolini is of the opinion that ruins bring tourists, and tourists spend money, and money is what Italy needs." While John and Helen prowled the antique shops and markets on buying errands, Harry sat in on a session of the Italian Senate. "The Senators spoke mostly from manuscripts, with many and vigorous gestures of all sorts." Harry noted that while there was some bickering, most of the discussion was amicable, with much applause. He did not state the obvious: every senator was a member of the Fascist Party, Mussolini having abolished all political opposition parties six years earlier. Harry saw Mussolini. "[He] spoke briefly, but what he said was received with much applause. . . . He evidently feels sure of his position and influence."

As a final commentary, Henry included in his diary a picture postcard of Mussolini in full military uniform. "Mussolini in War Paint," Harry wrote.

From Rome the three wound their way through the smaller towns, villages, and cities. The latter included Florence. There they had rooms at the pension where John and Helen stayed in 1926; John and Helen securing their old room. Helen had described the place in 1926 as

> near the center of things, and our window overlooks the Arno, the Ponte Vecchio, and the villas and hills across the river. . . . Women are washing at the steps just below the window, and men are sand fishing in the river, digging up sand with long shovels and filling their flat-bottomed boats, and processions of school children and nuns and soldiers are constantly passing by. At night there are lights across the river and the moon reflected in the water. It is enchanting.

From Florence they went to the Tuscan hill towns: Siena, Perugia, and Assisi. There Harry, son of a Congregational minister, was deeply moved by the Franciscan church of San Domiano. "It was all full of a silent, mystic atmosphere of deep reverence, added to by a beautiful chant of the monks at the service filling the place with a strange melody. Our little monk was so dear and unaffected that no one could help being deeply affected by his earnestness and sweetness."

The time in Italy was bookended by two special visits. One was to Bergamo, in Lombardy, to the estate of Rose Previtali and her Italian doctor-husband. Uncle Harry described the house, a former monastery, as a "most delightful home . . . on the side of a high hill, overlooking the vast Lombardy plain stretching out for miles in front and dotted with chateaux and peasant villages. . . . It is a remarkable life Rose is living as the Senora Padrona of her large estate." Harry contrasted Rose's estate, where he credited her with some significant reforms, with the condition of the peasantry in neighboring villages:

> None of the peasants own any land or their own houses, which are all owned by the Padrone who has been accustomed to get the last cent out of the peasants, with no regard to their comfort, health or well-being. In one

village of less than 1,000 people, between January and
May 1930, 73 babies died from lack of food and proper
care. The peasants have their miserable hovels rent-free
. . . the Padrone furnishes the land, seed, manure, horses
and implements, and the peasants do all the work on
a 50-50 basis. If the crop is a failure, the peasant gets
nothing. . . . Their houses have no running water or sanitary
conveniences, and are filthy dirty. . . . The Padrone treats
them like animals.

The peasants on the Previtali estate were still tenant farmers,
but Rose had seen to the renovation of the living quarters, including
running water supplied by a hillside reservoir. Despite this, or perhaps
on account of it, Rose commanded a level of deference.

They treat her with the greatest respect as the "Senora
Padrona." When she comes home from town, her three
maids, clad in clean dresses and white aprons, line up to
meet her, greet her with a smile and kiss her hand with
real affection. . . . She treats her peasants a good deal like
children; she reproves them and orders them around; and
they like it and her. . . . They follow her around like faithful
dogs, and her word is law; it is feudal indeed.

Harry found Rose's faith in Mussolini undimmed. She excused his
"bombastic speeches" as intended merely for domestic consumption,
necessary to redress the long-held Italian inferiority complex. Fascism,
Rose argued, was a defense against Communism; it gave the common
people a feeling that they were a part of the resurgent greatness of Italy.

Agreeing to disagree, the group spent a last night together. "We sat
out in the starlight in the evening and watched the lights twinkle in the
valley below. The peasants . . . sang some of the harvest songs of Italy,
while the bells in the towers of the many churches in the valley chimed
in the distance.[20]

No trip to Italy, indeed almost no trip to Europe would, for Helen,
be complete without Venice. It was the place she was most eager to

---

[20] John and Helen changed their views on fascism by the time of the Second World War, as their work on
behalf of the war effort showed. Still, there is a jarring reference in *Jean & Company,* published in late
1937, when the girls at the convent, including the Italian Giovanna, first introduce themselves: "'Viva
l'Italia!' laughed the others, jumping to their feet and giving the Fascist salute."

see on her first trip in 1914-1915; she returned there in 1926 and 1930, and would visit again in 1933 and 1937. As the place to which Helen returned most often, it is no surprise that it was the Italian city she chose to fictionalize in *Jean & Company*.

For Harry, the highlight of Venice was a visit, thanks to an introduction provided by Rose Previtali, to the home of the artist Gennaro Favai, located on the Zattere on Venice's Grand Canal. Together Helen and Uncle Harry explored Pauly & Cie, the company that oversaw the manufacture and distribution of Murano glassware. On the final night in Venice they heard the singing boats, a scene Helen would write into *Jean & Company*. "We listened. . . by the light of the moon—truly a romantic sight."

From Venice, Helen and Harry went by train, John by plane, to Trieste. There they boarded the *Saturnalia*, bound for New York, but not before squeezing every last ounce from the trip. The boat called at Patras in Greece and again at Naples, allowing for shore excursions; and then called again at Gibralter and Lisbon. On June 28, exactly three months to the day after they left, they returned to New York.

The 1930 trip proved to be a brief interlude before the full realization of the significance of recent events sank in. The stock market crash of October, 1929, signaled the onset of the Great Depression. For John and Helen, the crash was a disaster. They lost $14,000, money that cousin Edward had invested for them. The loss represented the work and profits of a decade.

By 1932 it was clear that the Depression was not only lingering, it was deepening. It was one thing to lose past gains; it was another to face the reality that the opportunity to rebuild was elusive. Even the well-to-do families who made up the Band Box's clientele were not likely to redecorate or buy antiques for some time to come.

It was now that Helen came up with a dazzling idea. She would take Jeanne and Polly and go to Europe for a year. One of her editors, a Mrs. Cousins, owned a villa in Provence, just outside of the town of Grasse, some twenty kilometers from Cannes on the French Riviera. A town long renowned as a center of the perfume trade, Grasse was increasingly a destination for artists, tourists, and expatriates. There the girls would attend school, freeing Helen to travel and write the kinds of articles her editors had come to expect: home décor, arts and crafts, gardening, food, child rearing, and fashion. The European setting would give her topics a kind of cachet that would appeal to readers. Arguing that she and the girls would be able to live more cheaply in Europe than they could at home, she further pointed out that they could rent out the house at 8 Franklin Place, bringing in additional income. John would stay in Summit, keeping the business afloat as best he could.

John agreed. And thus Helen, Jeanne, and Polly embarked on a year-long adventure, one that led to the writing of *Jean & Company, Unlimited.*

Chapter 8
" . . . under eighty cents a day per person"

Years later, what Helen's nephew Henry Perry remembered about that day in early September, 1932, was the stunned look on the faces of the two fathers, watching from the Hoboken pier as the boat carrying their wives and children slowly moved away from the dock. On board the *Vulcania*, Helen, her sister-in-law Evelyn, and their collective six children, were bound for the south of France.

Evelyn Perry decided to join Helen because, as she told friends, she "had no intention of turning forty in Peoria." While Henry's business did not escape the effects of the Depression, the Perrys were in a stronger financial position than were the Curtises. Evelyn had a sizeable inheritance from her father, and her brother John had the foresight to take her money out of the stock market before the October 1929 crash. Helen acknowledged the difference when, explaining some of Evelyn's expenditures while in France, she wrote: "Neither did she come over here, as I did, just to economize."

Henry was in full agreement with Evelyn's plan to join Helen, Jeanne, and Polly on the European adventure. He accompanied Evelyn, along with twelve-year-old Phebe, eleven-year-old Henry, nine-year-old Howard, and little Evie, not yet three, to New Jersey. There he purchased a car for his wife, a wood-paneled Ford station wagon that, along with nineteen pieces of hand luggage and five trunks, made the trip to France. Helen and her daughters added another eight pieces of luggage and trunks to the inventory. Additionally, the group was loaded down with the by-now familiar departure gifts from family and well-wishers: bouquets of flowers, baskets of fruit, boxes of candy, books, and games for the children.

John and Henry, accompanied by Big Helen, came to the dock at Hoboken to see the travelers off. Things did not go well.

> By the time we were securely packed into our four
> respective staterooms . . . Polly was in tears, Henry was

furiously kicking at a refractory suitcase, Evie was sleeping in a discouraged heap on the bunk between two piles of dresses, our husbands were mopping fevered brows, and Evelyn and I were ready to drown the whole outfit, including ourselves.

But once at sea, matters improved. A good dinner, a long nap, and the salty sea air returned curiosity and excitement to the fore. The children explored the ship; discovering the gymnasium, swimming pool, dog kennels, pastry kitchen, even the engine room and navigation instruments. Access to the latter was permitted because the captain, it turned out, was the friend of another captain whose acquaintance Helen—open as always to meeting potentially helpful people—had made on one of her earlier crossings. Late summer travel meant a less crowded boat, so the newly befriended captain assigned Helen's party two extra staterooms and a private dining room at no additional charge. "We have lots of room to spread out in," Helen wrote to her mother from shipboard. "They gave us another room for the boys, and a crib has been put in Evelyn's room in place of the double bunk. Each little girl has a room to herself, and so have I." In contrast to her earlier sarcastic observations about American tourists, Helen reported that there were nice-looking people on board, including a family with three children accompanied by a governess and a maid. "We feel very slummy in comparison." The ship's doctor and nurse were attentive when Howard suffered a severe bout of sea sickness. Four days out they celebrated Evie's third birthday with ice cream for all the children on board, "a mountain of a cake borne in proudly by the chief steward," a sailor doll from the captain, and "boxes of candy and strings of near-pearls from susceptible elderly gentlemen." Another night saw a children's party, with games and prizes.

Five days into the voyage the ship passed the Azores, "lovely rocky islands rising right out of the sea, with the mountain-tops veiled in clouds. We are near enough to see the little white villages and checker-board fields and vineyards." Three days later they reached Gibraltar. Helen took the four older children ashore; Evelyn stayed aboard ship with Howard and Evie. In a rainy ride in a leaky-curtained, squeaky-wheeled carriage, Helen and the children passed British soldiers and fortifications, beautiful parks, Spanish antique shops, and gypsies peddling brightly embroidered wares. They arrived back at the boat "thoroughly soaked and utterly happy. It was our first adventure."

Two days later the ship docked at Cannes. There were the rituals of arrival, including a long wait in line with their passports. At customs, Helen and Evelyn shuddered at the prospect of opening thirty-some bags and trunks for inspection. A customs officer, however, took one look at the "assorted collection of children, tennis racquets, thermos bottles, roller skates, and handbags, and then at the pile of luggage." Pointing a finger at one small bag, he asked Helen to open it. Rifling through an eclectic mix of a hot water bottle, game of dominoes, a baseball cap, and an evening slipper, he asked if all the bags contained the same. He then marked the remaining luggage with chalk and waved them through.

They were met by a young Englishman from the Thomas Cook agency. By this time, the station wagon had been unloaded onto the docks, drawing "bug-eyed stares" from the longshoremen. A friend of Helen's editor, Mrs. Burke, arrived; along with a hired truck for the baggage. With the Thomas Cook man at the wheel of the station wagon, and Mrs. Burke driving her own car, the group left Cannes, traveling winding roads lined with olive and fig trees, terraced vineyards on either side. They arrived at the villa at Tourlaque, two miles outside of Grasse, where they found themselves "on top of the world, with Grasse in full view on one side and a vineyard-clad hillside all around."

The villa was a three-story (ground, first, and second floors) stone farmhouse. Its thick walls, narrow windows, and windowless southern façade kept it cool in the Provençal summers. The house had several open fireplaces: a source of light for reading at night and of heat in the colder months to come. A kitchen and shared living space occupied the ground floor. Evelyn claimed the master bedroom on the first floor. Evie slept in the same room as her mother; Henry and Howard in the other first floor bedroom. Helen took the studio on the second floor, with its "marvelous views from tremendous windows." She intended it as both a bedroom and an office for writing. Jeanne slept in the room with her mother, Polly and Phebe in an adjoining room.

Helen provided a vivid description of the house:

There are pots of red geraniums in the casement windows,
piles of fagots by the hooded, high-hearthed fireplaces,
ancient Provençal furniture, kerosene lamps downstairs,

and a shelf full of candles on the stair landing. There are balconies opening off long French windows in the bedrooms, checked gingham curtains, great carved wooden chests and wardrobes, views of silver-green olive groves, tall black-green cypress trees and pink-roofed farmhouses. It is altogether enchanting. Even the hot water runs!

The villa was furnished with heavy pieces of polished oak, carved in the Provençal style. Breakfast was cooked outdoors over an open fire; lunch and dinner in a kitchen that was "primitive in the extreme:" a tiny icebox, a large coal stove, and a small iron sink with hot water tank suspended above it. Meals were eaten at a long table under a grove of trees, "with a most enchanting view down the valley in front, and a view up to the very mountain tops behind. Our land is all terraced, and today we have watched it being plowed by cream-colored oxen." Vineyards and jasmine fields fanned out below, and olive and fig trees grew on the property. The villa, in short, had "all the comforts we can possibly need." Only much later did Helen acknowledge what was implicit in the references to candles, kerosene, and reading by firelight: the house had no electricity.

At the behest of Mrs. Cousins, Mrs. Burke engaged two maids from neighboring houses. Seventeen-year-old Fifi did the cooking, and Cecile, twenty-one, cleaned the house. Helen paid the two maids a total of thirty dollars a month. Additionally, and for another eight dollars, Fifi's mother did the laundry "in a great stone tub covered with climbing geraniums." Ice was delivered, "when he remembered it," by a "stalwart small boy who carried it up the hill on his shoulder." Reinforcing the point that coming to Europe was a way to economize, Helen wrote that fruit and vegetables for the first week amounted to less than ten dollars. Meat, delivered daily by a butcher from the village, cost five dollars. "It's just unbelievable, how little things cost . . . under eighty cents a day per person."

The two sisters-in-law divided expenses equitably. Whenever the family purse ran low, Helen added three hundred francs and Evelyn five hundred, representing the respective size of each family. Helen spent a half hour or so each morning planning the day's meals. "The maids get all the fruit and vegetables, chickens, eggs, milk, etc. from the neighbors and expect to do every single thing about the house. I have never done so little housekeeping in my life." Evelyn's job was to be the chauffeur (Helen did not drive), doing whatever special marketing was needed, and, once the children started school, taxiing them to and fro.

The presence of two American women and six children at Tourlaque attracted attention. "I think our neighbors think that we are running an orphan asylum, and the butcher inquired the other day about our boarders." The American station wagon, dubbed by Polly "the Woody Wagon," was an object of curiosity as well. "Whenever we leave it, we find an interested crowd around it when we reappear."

Once settled in the house, the next order of business was finding schools for the children in time for the start of the term on October 1. The public schools were out of the question, Helen wrote, "as the local French is very bad." The two women turned their attention to the "several good convent schools, and a beautiful Chateau School, where boys and girls can go together." The latter came at the recommendation of a Peoria friend of Evelyn's. For all that living in Europe was to be a means of economizing, when it came to choosing schools Helen turned to the familiar. Jeanne and Polly, after all, attended private school at home.

The school the mothers chose for the three older girls was a Dominican convent boarding school in Grasse. Jeanne, Polly, and Phebe attended as day students. Helen never mentioned the name of the school, but it was in fact the École Ste. Marthe. With a commanding view over the town of Grasse and surrounding mountains, the school was housed in a seventeenth-century building, recently renovated to include new classrooms and an auditorium with a well-equipped stage. The school was set in an ancient garden surrounded by tennis courts and basketball fields, and encircled by a stone wall. Helen and Evelyn spoke with the "tall and gracious Mother Superior, in her white Dominican robes," and were assured that it did not matter that the girls were not Catholic. They could go to services with the other students if they wished, but it was not compulsory. Helen was amused at the apology offered by the Mother Superior concerning the semester's fees. The tuition for day pupils was more than she liked to ask, the Mother Superior said, but it did include art supplies, copybooks, and the tutoring in French that Jeanne, Polly, and Phebe would need. Would eight dollars per girl, per term, be too much?

Evelyn enrolled Howard and Henry as day students at "the Chateau School," in reality the Riviera School in Mouans-Sartoux, between Cannes and Grasse, ten kilometers from Tourlaque. Housed in a fifteenth-century chateau, Riviera was an international school; the teachers were French, English, and American. Instruction was in both English and French. There was a nursery school that Evie could attend. Based on the English public (i.e. private) school model, the Riviera School had servants to wait on the boarders, and a formal dining hall with elaborate menus. Even so, Helen noted, it was considerably less expensive than an American private school. Moreover, Evelyn had at her disposal a bequest from her mother intended for the children's education. "[Evelyn] is so thrilled to give them one year of a really lovely school, after all this time at public schools in industrial towns."

The choice of private schools reveals something of the ambivalent character of Helen and Evelyn's time in Provence. On the one hand, Helen reveled in what she saw as an experience of an authentic, timeless Europe.

We . . . carefully avoided the tourist element of the Riviera, and our villa was set in the heart of the perfume country, surrounded by fields of jasmine, roses and violets, wide vineyards, old stucco houses with pink-tiled roofs built around courtyards teeming with chickens, rabbits, donkeys, children, and women energetically slapping their washing on the edges of the great washing tanks.

She loved to watch from her window in the mornings as Fifi, "in a scarlet blouse and blue kerchief" ran barefoot through the vineyards, carrying "across her hip a great flat basket which she filled with white and purple grapes, and purple figs still wet with dew, which we would eat for breakfast." It was grape picking season, "and the vineyards are full of people singing as they picked."

But Helen and Evelyn's interactions with the villagers were that of employer and employee, observer rather than participant. There is a dismissive tone in Helen's remark about the local schools with their "bad French;" a hint of paternalism in the relationship with the servants, reminiscent of Rose Previtali on her estate at Bergamo. "Our little maids are all broken in," Helen reported after the first month in Tourlaque. They had "no qualifications whatsoever except the very French ones of making everything, from a wild salad picked on the lawn, to a soup made with one bone and bunch of herbs, taste like ambrosia and nectar." No job was too small: the maids served breakfast in bed, shined the shoes, weeded the garden, and ran errands. Fifi "follows me around like a little puppy-dog.. . . . I am teaching her how to make her own dresses, which thrills her."

Helen and Evelyn's social life revolved around the community of American and English expatriates living in and near Grasse. Helen was surprised, despite living in a home owned by an American, and the list of contacts she had been provided, to learn just "how many charming people have settled down here near Grasse, not the sporty variety who have villas on the shore in resort places, but people who have come to rest or visit here for a few months and have liked it so much that they have just settled down here." It was a distinction Helen would often make: expatriate versus tourist, counting herself among the former. "We might have rented a more expensive villa in the tourist-ridden part of the Riviera, we might have hired more efficient and less picturesque maids . . . we might have eaten extravagant imported American and English foods, but we had no desire to." Nor were all expatriates equal. She and Evelyn had lunch at the home of a Mr. and Mrs. Scully, cousins of the friend from Peoria who had recommended the Riviera School to Evelyn. "But their home was so huge and the whole place so new and shining that we were perfectly delighted to get home again to our funny little intimate home, so nice and mellow with age."

In addition to the network of people to whom they had entrée through Mrs. Cousins, there were individuals with connections to Summit, or to Henry and Evelyn in Cincinnati or Peoria. "People we know keep turning up." Helen and Evelyn, joined by the children, had tea with a family consisting of an American man and his French wife and their children. The husband's brother lived in Short Hills, and knew the Twomblys. Five or six of Evelyn's longtime friends were traveling through or living in France, and came to Tourlaque for a visit.

There were, admittedly, exceptions. A local family was arranging a charity performance to be given at Christmastime in Cannes. Jeanne and Polly, along with Phebe, joined in, performing dances they had learned from Anita Zahn. Rehearsals were "in a charming French house owned by the patron of the largest perfume factory here, a direct descendent of the painter Fragonard." Four generations of the family lived in the house, Helen reported, and all were musical. The daughter accompanied the dancers on the piano, "and everyone who doesn't dance sits around and looks on, as we do at home." Afterwards, the visitors joined the family for tea. "It is a beautiful experience for [the children] to have this delightful friendship with such an interesting French family."

If Helen's magazine account of the time in Provence is to be fully believed, it was the children who got to know the locals.

> They were soon chattering in French with the farmer
> neighbors, who enjoyed the novelty of having them around.
> They were helping to prune and spray the vineyards, pack
> the olives and take them to the press, gather jasmine flowers
> for the perfume factory and watch them being turned into
> priceless perfumes, feed the rabbits and chickens, go to
> market in the donkey cart astride a heap of carrots, attend
> the little chapel of St. Matthieu on fête days, ride the merry-
> go-round at the carnival, swim in the warm Mediterranean,
> picnic on the mountain top. Aside from a few courageous
> American friends who hunted us out on our isolated hilltop,
> they saw only French people. [1]

Almost none of this is contained in Helen's letters to her mother. Given Big Helen's concerns about the wisdom of this whole venture, it is understandable that Helen would not write to her mother that the children were spraying vineyards or riding in an open donkey cart. Nor is it true that only a "few" American friends found their way to the door of the villa at Tourlaque. Apart from telling her mother about the dance rehearsals ahead of the Christmas gala and the performance itself, Helen's reports concerning the children's activities outside of school are confined to cozy domestic news. Two Siamese kittens, Mignon and Coquette, join the household. Polly and Phebe rig up a basket and a rope with which to pull the kittens into the tree house. A neighbor's dog comes daily to play. Jeanne has a perch in one of the trees where she reads for hours. Henry compiles statistics about the cities in the region and is thrilled with the places of geographical interest that he sees. Howard draws castles and towns and makes paper models of them. Polly and Phebe stage a show, with a green bedspread for a curtain and the Siamese kittens as the performers, leaping over bars and being decked with ribbons for prizes. On nice days they all take a picnic basket and go for lunch at the beach or in the mountains.

---

[1] "Europe First-Hand for Your Children." Portions of this manuscript were subsequently published by *Parent's Magazine* under the title "Travel is a Liberal Education," (April 1938): 20-21 + 90-91.

Helen was walking a line: writing to her mother about the most benign of activities, while striving, for her magazine audiences, to paint a tantalizing picture of the adventurous possibilities inherent in European travel. She was, in other words, already moving in the direction of fictionalizing her daughters' experiences in Europe.

Helen and Evelyn's busy social lives contrasted with the leisure time they enjoyed at Tourlaque. "No noise, no interruptions, no telephone, long days to ourselves. Could anything be nicer?" They went for long walks, and Helen worked in the garden, reveling in the prospect of a winter garden, flowers blooming in February. Helen looked over both their wardrobes and altered or refashioned dresses and remade hats, delighted that no money needed to be spent on new clothes. She bought material with which to make capes for the three girls to wear with their school uniforms.

Exploring the ruins in the Riviera town of Èze: Howard and Phebe Perry; Polly, Helen, Jeanne Curtis; and Henry Perry, 1932.

But Helen had come to Europe to write. "I am working at some more articles and have some new work in sight. Several of my things have been published in the *Women's Home Companion* lately, and I am constantly busy for the *American Girl*, *Parents'*, and the *Girl Scout Leader*. Now I am starting work for *Child Life*." The element of hustle, or keeping the pot at the boil, is evident as she reports that she is writing to editors about material that she is finding, gauging their interest, hoping these initiatives will result in more jobs. In December she reported that "I have finished another job today. . . . That makes six articles in ten weeks."

In continually referencing her work, Helen was addressing her mother's ongoing skepticism. She writes that "we are doing what we are doing with the full sympathy and enthusiasm of our husbands . . . so please don't disapprove." She repeatedly makes the point that she is earning their way, an article at a time. The sale of an article pays the rent for a month; another the school fees for the term. And Helen insisted that the experience she was providing for Jeanne and Polly was worth it.

Big Helen was unconvinced. In a letter to the Twomblys, Helen wrote that her mother had forwarded an article from the *Saturday Evening Post* about casino life on the Riviera, with its cocktail parties and men in pink and blue pajamas. "Mother evidently thinks we move in those circles." As late as March, six months after arriving in Provence, Helen wrote her mother a sharp and pointed letter:

> You keep saying we ought to come home to economize.
> That's exactly the reason that we are staying here. . . . If we
> saved, which would be grand if we had anything to save,
> would we put it into the bank (which has been known to
> close) and into investments (in which we lost $14,000 by
> investing through Edward two years ago) or what? . . . It
> seems wisest to us to put what little we have into the finest
> experiences and education that we can give our daughters
> and continue to do our best to earn more! Please stop
> worrying about and making us feel that you disapprove
> of everything we do, regardless, because we are doing our
> "durndest." To us money isn't important as money, but
> for the permanent satisfactions in life it can bring as we
> go along. Those who have done nothing in this world but
> earn money for an uncertain future have mostly lost it,
> and we have tried to spend the very little we have on living
> as beautifully as possible. . . . Do you think it has all been
> wrong? I should so like to have you feel that we are at least
> doing the best we know how. I don't know anyone we would
> like to please more than you and [Aunt] Patty, but you are
> the two last people to want us to shape our lives according
> to someone else's ideas. We were brought up to stand on our

own feet, and you want us to stand there, don't you? . . . I
may not be a very satisfactory daughter, but I love you very
much, nevertheless and notwithstanding!

At least one aspect of Big Helen's objections—leaving the husbands
at home—was partly mollified when Helen wrote that John would be
joining them at Tourlaque for Christmas. "Isn't it wonderful that he has
just sold those chairs when he did, and that alone will give him his trip
over here. I suppose some of you think it is reckless for him to come,
and perhaps it is, but just being together again will be worth it." "He
deserves this trip," she reasoned, "after all his anxiety of the past two
years." She added her usual justification: that she was "working hard
to get more jobs, and we are saving tremendously by living over here."

John arrived on December 15, phoning the convent (given the
absence of a telephone at Tourlaque) from Paris to notify them of his
arrival. Helen, Evelyn, and the children drove to Cannes to meet his
train. No letter describes John and Helen's reunion after three months
apart, but Helen wrote to her mother the day before that she was
"much too excited to write;" John would be arriving at midnight. Helen
fictionalized this Christmas reunion in *Jean & Company*, when Jean,
emerging from Midnight Mass at the tiny church in the Swiss village,
sees both her parents waiting for her.

> "O Mums!" she cried, "Did you know Daddy was coming?"
> Her mother's eyes shone with happiness. "I wasn't *quite*
> sure," she said, "so I didn't tell you for fear he might not be
> able to get here." It was a very radiant Jean who rode back
> up the mountain in the painted sleigh, squeezed tightly in
> between her father and mother.

The following night was the dance performance in Cannes, held
in a ballroom of white and rose-colored marble, making, as Helen
described it, a lovely background for the Duncan costumes Jeanne,
Polly, and Phebe wore, along with the Russian peasant costumes of
the others in the ensemble. "Everyone was in evening dress and it was
really a lovely evening for the girls to remember."

The families celebrated Christmas with a mixture of traditional
French and American customs. The children assembled a crèche and
put their shoes out on the hearth rather than hanging stockings. Holly

and mistletoe took the place of a Christmas tree. Helen made warm blue wrappers for each of the girls and gave books to the boys. The American element took the form of "a trunk-load of toys" from Henry. Big Helen and Aunt Patty sent money for the children, each receiving four dollars to "spend for their hearts' desires." What made the greatest impression was a phonograph record with a Christmas message from Henry for the children, his voice "so realistic it was almost spooky." The Perry children played it over and over again to hear their father's voice.

Immediately after Christmas, the two families crowded into the Woody Wagon for a trip to Villeneuve-lès-Avignon, which John and Helen had visited in 1926 and 1930. Staying in a converted monastery, they spent three days exploring the walled medieval towns of the region. They took the children to the Coliseum at Arles, the Roman Baths at Nîmes, walked across the Pont du Gard, and daily visited the Christmas crèche in a small church near Avignon. They packed baskets every day for lunch, marveling at the ability to picnic in December.

John's three-week visit passed quickly. Not only did he have the business to attend to, but he was scheduled for a series of lectures at the Metropolitan Museum of Art in New York. Evelyn wrote to her mother-in-law that they had all had a lovely time with John and hated to see him leave. "The children adore him. He understands children very well and knows how to listen to them."

The tempo of the stay at Tourlaque accelerated after Christmas. The first big change was a new school for Jeanne, Polly, and Phebe. Helen and Evelyn withdrew the girls from the École Ste. Marthe and sent them instead to the Cours Maintenon, a progressive boarding and day school in Cannes. Helen and Evelyn had insisted in their letters that the girls loved the convent, but Helen had expressed one reservation: the strict discipline at the École Ste. Marthe decreed no talking during the noon meal. As day students, this would have been the best opportunity for the girls to engage in conversational French.

Given the distance between Tourlaque and Cannes, and the desire to expose the girls to as much French as possible, Jeanne, Polly, and Phebe boarded at the Cours Maintenon. Helen reported that the new school was "working beautifully" for the girls; they were already beginning to chatter in French. Jeanne especially appeared to benefit from the more rigorous atmosphere of the Cours Maintenon. The head mistress told Helen that Jeanne had a "fine mind;" a few weeks later she was advanced to the next grade. The girls' school holidays were on

Thursdays, so Evelyn either drove to Cannes to bring them home for the day, or Helen and Evelyn collected the girls from school and took them for an outing. Jeanne, Polly, and Phebe came home on Saturday evenings, staying until Sunday night.

With the girls in boarding school, Helen and Evelyn began to take longer trips throughout the region, boarding the boys and Evie at the Riviera School as needed. For these drives through unfamiliar territory, Helen and Evelyn hired a chauffeur, Pierre, for two dollars a week. Pierre took on various tasks around the house as well, including tending the garden.

Late in March Helen and Evelyn took the most ambitious of these excursions, a five-day trip to Nice on the Franco-Italian border. At Roquebrune-sur-Menton they visited Carl's grave, Helen for the second time. Helen wrote to her mother that they brought bouquets of spring flowers: tulips and daffodils and anemones on behalf of Big Helen; violets and forget-me-nots for Mai-Mai and the children. They called on the English Dr. Brett, who had been so kind to Mai-Mai at the end. In Nice they attended a folk festival, where hundreds of young people in national costume performed. "It was a great experience and has given me material for an article."

The most significant change that spring was that Evelyn rented a separate house for herself and her children. Henry was coming from Cincinnati in April, planning to spend a few weeks with his family before taking them home. With Henry there, Evelyn felt, the villa would be too crowded. It is more likely that Evelyn doubted that Henry would appreciate the rustic conditions at Tourlaque. Perhaps she too had tired of living in a house lacking electricity.

The house Evelyn rented was owned by another member of the expatriate community, Stella Cobden-Sanderson. Helen described the house, a five-minute walk from the villa, as "simply enchanting . . . exquisitely furnished . . . one of the loveliest houses I have ever seen." A garden provided spring vegetables for the household, and there were enough flowers to fill vases throughout the house.

The friendship that Helen struck up with Stella Cobden-Sanderson proved advantageous on several levels. Stella was among the most interesting and well-connected of the individuals Helen was adept at befriending. Stella's grandfather was Richard Cobden, a wealthy Manchester textile manufacturer and one of the most famous names in nineteenth century British politics. Along with John Bright,

Cobden headed the Anti-Corn Law League in the 1840s, advocating free trade on the grounds that tariffs, designed to protect aristocratic and landed interests, hurt the urban working classes by driving up the price of basic foodstuffs. Cobden's daughter Anne (Stella's mother) adopted her father's liberal, eventually radical, political outlook. She became a socialist and advocate of women's suffrage. In 1907 Anne Cobden joined the Women's Social and Political Union, the WSPU, the organization led by Mrs. Emmeline Pankhurst. Along with others, however, Anne Cobden grew disillusioned with the authoritarian leadership of Mrs. Pankhurst and her daughter Christabel, and with the WSPU's emphasis on granting the vote to women of property to the exclusion of working-class women. In 1909 Anne Cobden left the WSPU and joined the Women's Freedom League (WFL). She was arrested in August, 1909 for picketing the prime minister's residence at Number 10 Downing Street, and served two months in the infamous Holloway prison.

In 1882 Anne Cobden married Thomas James Sanderson, a barrister who shared her political views. Signaling their advanced attitude towards marriage and the status of women, Thomas and Anne combined their last names; both of them henceforth used the hyphenated Cobden-Sanderson surname. The couple had two children: Richard, born in 1884, and Stella in 1886. Anne and Thomas moved in circles which included the economic thinker Henry George, whose book *Progress and Poverty* highlighted economic inequality, and William Morris, the artist and social critic. In 1893 Thomas Cobden-Sanderson founded the Doves Press in order to popularize the ideas of William Morris. Cobden-Sanderson is credited by many with coining the term "Arts and Crafts Movement."

Given this background and pedigree, it was only natural that Helen would be drawn to Stella. Stella's connection, through her mother, to key figures in the English women's suffrage movement would have recalled for Helen the stimulating dinner table conversations with Mary White in Summit in 1908. Helen, of course, encountered the Arts and Crafts designs, along with Morris's idealization of pre-industrial society, in her work at the Herter Looms. The friendship with Stella, the daughter of the founder of the Doves Press and proponent of the ideas of William Morris, was one that Helen relished.

Evelyn moved into the Cobden-Sanderson villa in early March. Helen and Evelyn met daily, however, for lunch at one or the other of their two houses. But "I come back always happily. . . to my simple farmhouse, with its quaint country air, and am quite content."

Helen wrapped up her time at Tourlaque in mid-April. She decided to take the girls out of school early, reasoning that they would benefit as much from extended travel as from school. Their destination was Italy, where Helen would search out new material. The friendship with Stella Cobden-Sanderson came into play, as Stella owned an apartment in an old palace in Venice which she was willing to rent to Helen. Located on a side canal in the shadow of the church of Santa Maria Della Salute, the apartment had, according to Helen, a gas stove, electricity (not to be taken for granted after Tourlaque), hot water, "and all the trimmings." By taking the girls out of school at the Easter holiday, Helen took advantage of a seventy percent discount on train travel from Cannes to Venice, with stayovers in Siena, Rome, Assisi, and Florence along the way. The whole trip, she reported triumphantly, would cost them only eight dollars apiece, "which is extraordinary." She and the girls would miss Henry's arrival, but the cost savings on travel in mid-April was something Helen could not afford to pass up.

Before leaving, Helen and Evelyn "invited everyone we know, French, English, and American, to a big tea at Evelyn's house and an exhibition of paintings by our friend Sidney Thompson. This will finish up our social career before I leave for parts unknown!"[2]

Helen and the girls went first to Siena, where they spent a week, followed by ten days in Rome, five days in Assisi, and another ten in Florence.

> We stayed in comfortable *pensions* where we had delicious
> food, for an average of a dollar and a quarter a day. . . . In
> all those places we had personal friends, or introductions to
> friends of friends. . . . We browsed in a leisurely way through
> churches and museums, taking them in very small doses,
> and added a large intermixture of zoos, horse races, outdoor
> theaters, special festivals (such as the Calcio or medieval
> football games), historical pageants, visits to private villas
> and castles, and while we rested we read children's books on
> early Roman and Florentine history.[3]

---

[2] Sidney Thompson was a New Zealand-born artist who studied in London and Paris before the war. He divided his time between his native country and homes in Concarneau in Brittany and in Grasse. Thompson's paintings captured the work of farmers and fishermen, and the sun-drenched, lavender-hued fields of the Provençal countryside.

[3] "Europe First Hand for Your Children."

Polly and Jeanne with their mother in Florence; 1933.

Arriving in Venice, the three moved into Stella Cobden-Sanderson's apartment. Together mother and daughters explored the back alleys and canals, on foot and in rented gondolas. They fed the pigeons in St. Mark's Square. They went to the island of Burano, where they saw women making lace; and Murano, to see the glass-blowing factories. They swam at the Lido, going out to the rocks to watch the fishermen pull in their nets. Evenings they picnicked on the lagoon, watching as the fleet, with its orange and yellow sails unfurled, returned to harbor with the day's catch on board. Helen took the girls to hear the singing boats, decked with colored lanterns, where choirs took turns performing for those floating in gondolas or strolling the promenade alongside the Grand Canal.

But it was not all play. Helen found a governess who, for fifty cents a lesson, tutored the girls two hours a day in Italian. And Helen, of course, had her work. Afternoons while she wrote Jeanne went to the market, practicing her newly-acquired Italian with the assistance of her tiny Italian dictionary. Polly was responsible for the housekeeping. [4]

There is another source for the time in Venice: the chapter Helen wrote for *Jean & Company*. Helen's evocative writing captures the first sights of the city:

> The late afternoon sky made an opalescent background for
> the pink houses bordering the canal, and Jean could catch

---

[4] Polly wrote to Big Helen, her grandmother, "We were in Venice for a month and we had a little house, and Jeanne was the cook, and I the house maid so that Mummy could do her work."

occasional glimpses of vines and flowers climbing over garden walls. . . . Past stately palaces they went, their front steps leading down into the water, with lacelike balconies against walls of pale pink and yellow and ivory. They slid into the blue shadows beneath the Rialto bridge; they glided noiselessly by another gondola coming around the bend, missing it by a hair's breadth as the gondoliers called musical but unintelligible things to one another. . . . At last the gondola drew up to the steps of an ivory-colored palace, between tall boat posts with spiral stripes like peppermint sticks.

Helen's description of the singing boats is likewise fleshed out in the pages of *Jean*. "They watched as the great red moon came up, seemingly right out of the central dome of the church of Santa Maria della Salute. . . . It was lovely to see the dark shadows of other gondolas slipping past silently and wonder where they were going, and to watch the myriad, flickering lights reflected in the mysterious waters." Even the governess who tutored Jeanne and Polly in Italian makes an appearance in *Jean & Company*, in the form of the governess who accompanies Jean and her Italian friend Giovanna around the city.

Following the month's stay in Venice Helen, Jeanne, and Polly went to Salzburg. There Helen enrolled the girls in the summer school program at the Elizabeth Duncan School at Schloss Klessheim, a baroque palace built in the early eighteenth century as a summer residence for the prince-archbishops of Salzburg. Surrounded by an English-style landscaped garden, the school contained classrooms, dance and music studios, a dining hall, and dormitory rooms. The summer school enrolled forty students from twelve countries. The ceiling of the dormitory room where Jeanne and Polly slept was painted dark blue, decked with silver stars and moons.

Helen knew about the summer school program through Anita Zahn. The promotional literature described the program as an opportunity for children, young girls, and women to recreate and study, to integrate mind and body. There were daily lessons in gymnastics, dancing, singing, music, drawing, and painting. The spacious grounds included a swimming pool. Participants studied folksongs and languages: English, French, and German. An advanced course offered certification to teachers in the techniques of Duncan Dance.

Having enrolled her daughters at the school, Helen stayed with a friend from Summit, Angela Hagen. Angela was born in Vienna, and met her American husband there. She had rented an apartment and was spending the summer in Salzburg. With Helen's arrival, Angela too enrolled her daughter Phyllis in the Duncan School, along with Jeanne and Polly. The two women moved to "a little country tavern nearby, where we can go to the lovely little river and meadow, and we have most of our meals out of doors." Helen wrote the country tavern into both her *American Girl* story and the chapter in *Jean & Company*, wherein Sue/ Jean, along with her mother, upon first arriving in Salzburg,

> sat at a little table under a tree outside an old tavern in Salzburg where they had an omelet so fluffy and light that one hardly knew it was an omelet and not a puff of down. They ate dainty fried cakes, too, that her mother told her were flat elderberry blossoms dipped in batter and browned. They ended up with crisp cornucopias of pastry as thin as paper, filled with whipped cream and tiny, wild, red strawberries.

Helen wrote only one letter to her mother from Salzburg. The descriptions in the *American Girl* story and the chapter in *Jean & Company* fill the gap. A highlight of both accounts was the visit to the Hellbrunn Gardens, with their trick fountains: the stone table and benches where water unexpectedly shot up from the seats; the golden crown held aloft in the air by a single spout of water; the grotto of mechanical birds which burst into song; and the tableau of miniature houses and hundreds of small figures walking, bowing, dancing, plying their trades, all powered by water. "Most exciting of all was when spouts of water sprayed up from the sidewalks or steps at unexpected moments as they walked along. The guide was careful not to let the girls really get wet, but he gave them all the surprises he could."

Schloss Klessheim appears only briefly, in the form of a day's visit, in the fictionalized accounts of Salzburg. Both note that Sue/Jean "had danced with the Duncan School in America and this was one of the places that she most wished to visit."

> They drove in through a high iron grilled gate, pushed open by a sturdy, small boy at the lodge, up the tree-shaded avenue with a glimpse of three tall girls in long, straight,

Greek costumes, walking arm in arm over the lawn like the Three Graces themselves. They were greeted at the summer palace by Elizabeth, sister of the great Isadora, looking very tiny as she stood in the high doorway. This was the school where for many years she had taught children and young people to dance and think and live beautifully. No wonder, thought Jean. In such a setting one could live only in beauty.

Both fictional accounts describe an outdoor performance of *A Midsummer Night's Dream,* staged by the Austrian director Max Reinhardt, utilizing Elizabeth's students as Titania's fairies. "Instead of having a stage and changing the setting for each act, pages with banners and torches led the audience from place to place for the different scenes," one act given on the lawn, another in the forest, another on the steps of the palace, another in the ballroom.

Helen wrote to her mother that John would be joining them for the final weeks of their stay in Europe, and they would all return home together. John would arrive in Bremen, and go first to Berlin and Dresden, "and I shall meet him in Prague." There is no letter from Prague, but all indications are that Helen did indeed go there. She wrote to her mother that "my trip will pay for itself . . . as it will give me material for a story about another country." [5]

John and Helen returned to Salzburg to collect the girls. From there the family went to Paris. "By this time, we were so reduced in funds that we travelled third-class, making a great lark of it and deciding that the wooden seats were much cooler and cleaner anyway than the thick upholstered ones of the first- and second-class carriages." In Paris they stayed at a tiny hotel on the Left Bank, costing fifty cents per person per night. And "after a serious financial conference, we decided to have one last European splurge and fly to London, the first flight for the girls. It was worth it, for they looked down on the cathedrals of Normandy, the English Channel, and the great estates and castles of England." In London, they explored the city, toured abbey country—as Helen and her mother had done nearly twenty years earlier—in a Thames river boat, and went to Oxford and Stratford. "In two weeks in England the girls learned more English history than in two years at home."

---

[5] *American Girl* published "Sue Goes to Prague" in June 1936, two months before Helen took Jeanne and Polly there. The story, therefore, is based on Helen's 1933 visit to the city with John.

In early August the Curtises sailed from Southampton aboard the *Minnetonka*, arriving in New York nine days later, bringing to an end a remarkable year for Helen and her daughters.

Just when Helen arrived at the idea of writing a series of stories about an American girl in Europe, and then just when she decided to turn those stories into a book, is hard to say. Her first reference to fictionalizing the European adventure is a letter written in early February, 1933. "I have just finished a long article for the *American Girl* about an American girl in France." By the time she was preparing to leave for Italy in April the article had been accepted. Helen wrote that "The *American Girl* magazine likes my international series of articles about girls so well that they want me to do Italy, Austria, and Germany as well, and I may go to Salzburg after Venice."

That first *American Girl* story, published in November 1933, was "A Day with Suzanne." An American girl, Sue, spends a weekend at the home of a convent school classmate. The story would become the "Old Provence" chapter in *Jean & Company*. In the book, Jean spends a weekend at the family villa of her classmate Jeanette. Except for the girls' names, the two versions, article and book chapter, are almost identical.

Descriptions of Suzanne's/Jeanette's house walk right off the pages of Helen's letters. Helen described to Aunt Patty a house she and Evelyn visited: "great cypresses, avenues of old sycamores, flagstone paths running between beautiful flower-beds, one garden after another laid out in terraces, and such view—the lovely valley with mountains on either side, the shoreline and the sea beyond." By comparison, when Suzanne opens the long, arched French windows, "Sue looked out on a most enchanting garden, with terrace after terrace of lawn and flowers, olive trees and vineyards, and far below in the distance the blue Mediterranean."

Nor does Helen ignore her house at Tourlaque. In a letter she described seeing the fields below the house being plowed by cream-colored oxen. Now Sue and Suzanne/Jean and Jeanette "climb the hill again on foot, stopping a moment to watch a pair of cream-colored oxen plowing in the upper field." Helen described the villa at Tourlaque as a "funny little intimate home, so nice and mellow with age, and being lived in." Suzanne's /Jeanette's house has been maintained in its original form. "Aside from adding a bathroom or two and a kitchen stove, no changes had been made to it." Like Tourlaque, the "mellow walls" of the fictionalized house were finished in rough plaster and whitewashed, the furniture was heavy and carved from wood, and every mantelpiece held lovely pewter candlesticks or bowls with wicks for burning olive oil. "How much more thrilling it was to use candles than pushing a button and getting a glare of electric light." Even the servants at Tourlaque find their way into the fictional accounts: Cecile, Fifi, and Pierre all make an appearance as tenants on Suzanne's/Jeanette's family estate.

Between November, 1933 and November, 1937 *American Girl* published eleven Sue stories, set in Austria, Yugoslavia, Sweden, the Netherlands, Czechoslovakia, England, Iceland, Switzerland, and Hungary. A final story, appearing the same month as the publication of *Jean & Company*, describes the shipboard journey back to America. Helen would have written the bulk of those stories between early 1934 and the spring of 1937. The magazine stories are nearly identical to what would appear in *Jean & Company, Unlimited*.

But not quite. In the magazine stories, Helen continued to call the girl Sue. But with the exception of the name Suzanne for the European friend in the first article, the rest of the stories already feature a girl whose name is the equivalent of Jean: Giovanna from Italy, Jovanka in Yugoslavia, Hannah from Salzburg, Janesika in Prague, Jenny from Norway. Helen evidently early on hit upon a unifying theme for a book: an international group of girls whose names were the cognate of a common American name, yet different enough one from the next to work across a spectrum of languages and countries. The name Sue or Susan would not work. The name Jean would. And "Jean" had the additional advantage, albeit with simplified spelling, of being the name of one of Helen's daughters.

If Helen were to turn the *American Girl* stories into a book, she needed a framing device. For that she returned to the months in Grasse and the École Ste. Marthe, as well as to her enduring fascination with folk costumes and customs. The first chapter of *Jean & Company*, "Ship Ahoy," explains that

[Jean's] mother, who had always been interested in
European folklore, had decided that this was a good time to
travel and collect material for the book she was writing. And
while her mother was studying folk music and folk costume,
Jean would go to an enchanting school in southern France,

a convent kept by Dominican sisters. . . . She would make friends not only among French girls but among girls from other countries as well. . . . For some weekends she would be invited to visit her new friends. She could spend her longer holidays traveling with her mother.

Descriptions of the convent in *Jean & Company* come directly from the pages of Helen's letters. The "tall and gracious Mother Superior, in her white Dominican robes," who welcomed Helen and Evelyn at the École Ste. Marthe, becomes the "grave and stately Mother Superior" who greets Jean and her mother. The fictional portress, Sister Irmengarde, dressed in the "white robe and black cape of the Dominican nuns," takes charge of Jean and shows her through the "garden . . . enclosed [on one side] by the convent building, mossy and old, on the other by a high plaster wall covered with heliotrope and climbing roses." Passing through a cool archway and into the auditorium and gymnasium, Jean sees the stage where older girls are working busily on a setting. Helen wrote to her mother about the École Ste. Marthe's new auditorium and stage, and the garden surrounded by tennis courts and basketball fields, encircled by a stone wall. Upstairs in the dormitory, Sister Irmengarde brings Jean her school uniform: a blue serge dress with white collar and cuffs, a blue jacket, a beret, and a black pinafore to wear over the dress during school hours. Helen's letters described Jeanne, Polly, and Phebe wearing black pinafores over their dresses, and carrying school bags slung over their shoulders, looking "like any other school-child in France."

Using the convent as her connecting link, rather than the Cours Maintenon or even the Duncan School in Salzburg, is interesting in that it reveals Helen's changing attitude toward Catholicism. She was earlier repelled by aspects of Catholicism: the gloomy churches and relics of saints she encountered in Paris and Italy in 1914 and 1915. She dismissed the Catholic wedding she attended in Summit in 1909 as "just a monotonous Latin oration. . . . What on earth can a ceremony like that mean to anybody?" But by the time she wrote *Jean & Company* Catholicism was of a piece with her artistic outlook and idealization of folk culture. The fictional Jean falls quickly into the routine of the convent, attending Mass every morning with the other girls,

filing into chapel in long double rows. Jean did not understand much of the service, but she loved the statue of the Madonna that looked down on them, the flickering candles on the altar, and the long rays of colored light which filtered in through the stained-glass windows.

Even the misgiving Helen expressed concerning the real-life convent, the requirement that the students maintain silence during meals, is turned to fictional advantage. When Jean, sitting down to her first meal in the refectory, started to speak, Jeannette nudged her and put her finger to her lips. "'It was rather fun,' Jean thought, trying out all these new kinds of food, but how dreadful not to be able to say a word! How would she ever learn to speak French, if she could never say anything?" But Jean is soon delivered from this dilemma. "After luncheon everyone rushed joyously out into the sunshine and then such a chattering and laughing as began, like so many magpies let loose." As the girls gather around Jean, some speaking in French, some in German, "and one or two in strange languages Jean had never heard before," they ask her name. Jeannette intervenes and explains that "Jean" is the same as "Jeanne" in French. "'And Giovanna in Italian,'" exclaims another girl. "'Ich bin Hannah von Austria,'" volunteers a third. "'Voila Janesika from Prague.'" "'Jenny ... another Jean, from Norway.'" [6]

"Jean was now all excitement. 'What a lot of Jeans!' she exclaimed. 'Mother told me that I would find them in every country, but I never dreamed they would be here, all together. We ought to start a club, a Jean-club, this minute.'" Her suggestion, readily taken up, becomes the club "with the nice and business-like name," Jean & Company, Limited. Thus, the framework is provided, the plot launched. Helen is able to move her American girl from country to country, tweaking content from the already-published magazine stories, to allow for the European girl in each chapter to be a convent school classmate, a member of Jean & Company, Limited. And as Jean, in the course of her travels, meets even more girls who share her name, she decides that the club should be called "Jean & Company, *Unlimited*."

Turning the *American Girl* stories into a book was the idea of Helen Ferris, one-time editor (1920 to 1929) of *American Girl* and subsequently (1929 to 1960) editor-in-chief of the Junior Literary

---

[6] The international group of girls was present at the Duncan School in Salzburg rather than the École Ste. Marthe. In one place Helen refers to girls at Schloss Klessheim as coming from six to eight countries, in another she says a dozen nationalities are represented. As she so often did, Helen took details from one situation and applied those to another, in this case from Schloss Klessheim to the convent school. One of her granddaughters said of her, "She wrote from real life, but was not limited by it."

Guild. Helen Ferris and Helen Perry Curtis were friends of long standing, another of these useful associations the latter was so skilled at cultivating. [7] It is not clear how the two first met, but it is not surprising that they did. Both were born in Nebraska (two years and seventy-five miles apart; Ferris in Hastings, Curtis in Crete). Both were daughters of clergymen. Ferris's 1912 graduation from Vassar put her in the same cohort of young women Helen met in Summit in 1908-1909. Following graduation from Vassar, Ferris worked in the personnel department of the Wanamaker department stores in New York and Philadelphia. There she organized and served as the first executive secretary for the Women Employees' Organization, an experience that formed the basis of her first book, *Girls' Clubs: Their Organization and Management*, published in 1918. Sections of the book deal with the activities of wartime volunteers with the YMCA (Ferris served on the War Work Council from 1918-1919) as well as women involved in settlement house work. In finding a connecting structure and unifying thread for turning *American Girl* stories into *Jean & Company, Unlimited*, it is no accident that, working with Helen Ferris, author of *Girls' Clubs*, Helen Perry Curtis found that thread in the notion of a club of girls sharing the same name.

An offshoot of the Literary Guild, the juvenile version offered subscription service to libraries and individuals. Board members— including Eleanor Roosevelt, who served on the board from the Guild's founding in 1929 until her death in 1962—chose books for Guild designation. Selection of a book by the Junior Literary Guild was a distinction valued by authors and publishers. Such designation assured library sales, as many had standing orders for the Guild's "Book of the Month" selections. *Jean & Company* would be selected as the January, 1938 Junior Literary Guild Book of the Month.

Helen was thoroughly enmeshed in the social circle surrounding the Junior Literary Guild. An article in the *Newark Evening Journal* from November 5, 1931, entitled "Child Critics Review Books," described the Guild's practice of having children read manuscripts or galley proofs and provide a short review, earning twenty-five cents per book. Among the "child editors" were the nine-year-old daughter of

---

[7] According to *The Courier-Journal* (Louisville, KY), September 9, 1939, "*Jean and Company, Unlimited* ... was first written as a series of short stories for the *American Girl* magazine. At the suggestion of Miss Helen Ferris ... the stories were combined and published in book form." See also, "Obituary, Helen Ferris Tibbets, Author, Philanthropist, *Patent Trader* (Mount Kisko, NY), October 2, 1969; https://nebraskaauthors.org/authors/helen-josephine-ferris.

Carl Van Doren, author and founder of the Junior Literary Guild; ten-year-old Freddie Ferris, Helen Ferris's nephew; Ernest Gruenberg, son of Sidonie Gruenberg of the Child Study Association; Elbert Fretwell, Jr., whose father was executive director of the Boy Scouts of America; and Jeanne Curtis.

The Junior Literary Guild had a pronounced agenda. At a time when new standards of child rearing and the popularity of radio threatened the centrality of reading, the Guild provided direction in the choice of reading material, along with the assertion that reading was "preparation for citizenship in a democracy."[8] This agenda explains the tone of the last chapter of *Jean & Company.* "Jean Discovers America" begins as a mirror to the first chapter, where Jean, on the eve of departure, "was afraid she was making a terrible mistake. Wouldn't her friends forget her? Wouldn't she have to drop back a grade in school when she came home again? Wouldn't she find foreign girls very queer and very different? Wouldn't she die of homesickness?" Now, two years later and returning home, Jean is again beset by misgivings.

> At home in America again, she would probably have to go
> to stupid dances and the movies, which she hated, learn
> to play bridge, and do everything that American girls and
> boys did. But would she ever hear again the singing boats
> in Venice . . . or be able to sit quietly in a dim cathedral or
> dream romantically in a castle tower? Her friends would not
> understand, of course. She remembered with a little shiver
> how they had all thought that Rosemary was conceited
> when she came home after a summer abroad and could talk
> of nothing but what she had seen in Europe.

But Jean's father provides the resolution: "'You have had the great advantage,' he tells her, 'of traveling and seeing beautiful things and making friends, at the very most impressionable time of your life. You have also learned how to use your eyes and ears as you never used to. Perhaps now you'll know how to use them better in your own country.'" Promising to show her every day something in America as interesting and beautiful as what she had seen in Europe, Jean's father takes her to St. Patrick's Cathedral, to the Cloisters, to a Swedish restaurant, to

---

[8] Anne Morey, "The Junior Literary Guild and the Child Reader as Citizen," *The Lion and the Unicorn* 38:3 (September 2014), 279-302, accessed online muse.jhu.edu/article/565973, 10-3-2019.

the collections of the Metropolitan Museum of Art. But Jean discovers something else.

> The things that she was beginning to enjoy most of all were things that she had not seen anywhere else in the world, like the Radio City building. . . the New York skyline, paintings of snowy New England landscapes, murals of workmen straining at great machines, factory smoke in the sunset light, fields of asters and goldenrod, tall-spired country churches. . . .
>
> All the other countries had brought their treasures, their talents and personalities, their. . . traits and. . . traditions. . . and America had absorbed them all. But out of this great melting pot had grown other things that were magnificently American, young and strong and vital, and beautiful, too. She would never stop loving European things and would look forward eagerly to returning as often as she could, but now she would begin to use her eyes and ears for discovering America.

Helen brought Jeanne and Polly to Europe in 1932 with the goal of supporting the three of them by writing for magazines. In that she was successful. She had a vague idea that she would someday write a book about European folklore, costumes, and customs. In the form of *Jean & Company, Unlimited*, the story of an American girl's encounter with a picturesque—if rapidly vanishing—Europe, Helen did indeed write that book.

Chapter 9
Mapping *Jean & Company, Unlimited*

E ven as she was still writing the *American Girl* stories, and revising them for publication as *Jean & Company, Unlimited*, Helen embarked on two more trips to Europe, in the summers of 1936 and 1937. Billing herself as a mature woman guide, experienced in travel and knowledgeable in European languages, she put herself forward as someone to whom parents could entrust their daughters for their European Grand Tour. Working as a guide enabled Helen to continue her own traveling and writing, and to take Jeanne and Polly back to Europe as well.[1] And by actually going with her daughters to places about which she had peremptorily written an *American Girl* story, Helen could stand behind what she wrote in the preface to *Jean & Company:* "Together [Jean] and her mother visited every country mentioned in this book. . . ."

There looms over these trips a sense of lengthening shadows. The countries through which Helen traveled in 1936 and 1937 included Germany, Austria, Hungary, Poland, Czechoslovakia, and Yugoslavia. The majority of those countries were successor states to the now-vanished Russian and Austro-Hungarian empires. All but one of those countries— Czechoslovakia—was, by the mid-1930s, a dictatorship or, at the least, under authoritarian rule. Helen and her daughters were travelling through a Europe experiencing the final years of an uneasy peace.

In 1936 Helen conducted her trip through the tour company Europe on Wheels. Headquartered in Manhattan's fashionable Murray Hill district, Europe on Wheels had offices in London, Paris, and Berlin as well. The company recruited its participants and tour guides from the Seven Sisters colleges and alumnae. In an era of limited employment opportunities for women, travel agency work made use of the cultural background and language abilities of college-educated women. In

---

[1] Helen's arrangement with Europe on Wheels and Orbis allotted her one free ticket for every five participants she recruited. Linda George, "Jeanne Whitesell: Buxton Alumna and Far Brook Grande Dame," *Bulletin* [Far Brook School], June, 1998. A small, chauffeur-driven, guided tour of Europe in the 1930s did not come cheap. The tour Helen led through Europe on Wheels in 1938 cost $895.00; translating into approximately $15,500 in 2020 US dollars.

Europe, with a single exception, the local guides who took Helen and her groups through the various cities and countries in Europe were all women. Some were American expatriates, others were Europeans, whose fortunes, diminished by the First World War, led them to seek work in the growing travel industry. [2]

Promotional literature from Europe on Wheels noted that its tours provided "a way of getting into the nooks and crannies of foreign countries and seeing people, places, customs that are indigenous; instead of just the 'high spots' [the countries] are famous for." That kind of European travel matched Helen's preferences. "I care less and less for the big cities, and more and more for the quaint and charming places," she once wrote. Tour groups were small. Helen's party in 1936 had ten participants, including herself and Jeanne and Polly. [3]

There are far fewer letters written by Helen during these trips than had been the case in 1932 and 1933, or during her wartime service in France. Helen's mother, the frequent recipient of her letters from abroad, died on March 21,1935, in San Diego, where she had long since made her home. Helen, Tom and Ethel, and Henry and Evelyn joined Doane faculty and alumni in the Lee Chapel on the Doane campus to honor the one-time first lady of the college. Margaret Thompson Sheldon, former dean of women and Brainerd's trusted colleague of so many years, delivered one of two eulogies. Big Helen was laid to rest beside her husband and infant son in Riverside Cemetery. [4]

Fortunately, there are sources from which to reconstruct the travels of those summers. Helen wrote about the 1936 and 1937 trips in "Travel is a Liberal Education," published in *Parents' Magazine* in April, 1938, as well as in three unpublished manuscripts describing those trips. Uncle Harry Twombly went to Europe in 1936, bringing along his great-nephew Tod Perry, son of Tom and Ethel. Harry and Tod went to the Netherlands before joining Helen's tour in Berlin. Uncle Harry's letters are priceless, because no letters from Helen or the girls from 1936 have survived. Harry's account, as was the case when he accompanied John and Helen in 1930, is politically astute. His observations lend weight to an odd but eerily prophetic line in a Europe on Wheels brochure from

---

[2] The only male local guide who accompanied one of Helen's tours, in Chartres in 1938, was a Russian émigré.

[3] *The Survey*, Survey Associates, New York, May 1, 1932, Vol 68, No. 3, Page 164 (page 174 in pdf document). Accessed on archive.org on December 29, 2017.

4 In October, 1930, Big Helen made her final visit to Crete, to attend the dedication of a baptismal font, in honor of herself and Brainerd, at the First Congregational Church. She described the occasion in her memoir, "Memories of Me and Mine:" "Very beautiful words by Dr. Dean about Brainerd, and a regular obituary about me to my living face!"

the summer of 1936: "A look at Europe, now before it is perhaps too late, is in many minds this year. . . ." [5]

The 1936 trip began as a family affair. On July 3, the four Curtises, sailing tourist class, docked in Plymouth, England. This information, one of the few certainties about those early weeks, comes from the passenger manifest of the *S.S. Volendam*. (John's profession is listed as "artist," Helen's as "housewife.") The family's address in London was 14 Regent Street, a hotel in London's fashionable Mayfair district. The next piece of information is the passenger list from—remarkably—the *Hindenburg*, showing that John returned to the United States a week later, leaving Frankfurt-am-Main on July 10. The dirigible, whose fiery crash ten months later at Lakehurst, New Jersey, made the name *Hindenburg* synonymous with aviation disaster, successfully landed on July 13 at Lakehurst with John on board.

In an age of jet travel, a stay of a single week in Europe is nearly the norm, but a trip of such short duration, at a time when an ocean liner took eight or nine days to reach the Continent, was highly unusual. But perhaps the point of the trip for John was the very novelty of the return trip on the *Hindenburg*. The eight days he was able to spend at sea with his wife and daughters, a stay in London, a quick cross-Continent journey to Frankfurt, and then a flight on what was billed as "the fastest and most luxurious way to travel between Europe and the United States," all constituted a trip worth taking. [6]

Knowledge of Helen's next moves depends on circumstantial evidence, pointing to the conclusion that Helen and the girls spent the next two weeks in Scandinavia. There are two photos, showing Helen and Polly in a rowboat, labeled "Lake Lillehammer, Norway, 1936." [7] Additional evidence comes from a letter Jeanne wrote to her father a year later. In 1937, Helen and her tour group docked in Copenhagen, where they enjoyed a shore excursion, "the same one we went on last year." [8] This reference from Jeanne's 1937 letter places Helen and the girls at the least in Denmark in 1936.

---

[5] *Survey Graphic Magazine of Social Interpretation*, April 1936, Vol 25, No. 4, page 275 (page 293 in pdf document). Accessed on archive.org on December 29, 2017.

[6] The *Hindenburg's* speed and luxury came at a price. Passage between Frankfurt and Lakehurst, New Jersey cost $400 in 1936. Compare this with the price charged participants for Helen's 1938 trip: round-trip, tourist-class accommodations on shipboard accounting for $287.50 out of a total cost of $895.00 for two months in Europe. John's ability to take the voyage on the *Hindenburg* indicates either that the decorating business was doing remarkably well, or, more likely, this was another example of Uncle Harry's generosity.

[7] The actual name of the lakes in and around Lillehamer are Lake Miosa and the River Lågen.

[8] Jeanne also mentions looking for the stork's nest "which Jimmie pointed out to us last summer." Jimmie was the six-year-old son of artist Jimmy and Kirsten Scott. Kirsten and Jimmie were in Europe in the summer of 1936. In addition to meeting the Curtises is Denmark, they spent two months with Kirsten's mother in Norway. The Curtises may well have been with Kirsten in Norway as well.

What about Norway and Sweden? In the preface of *Jean & Company*, Helen wrote that "together [Jean] and her mother visited every country mentioned in this book, with the exception of Iceland. Only Jean's father saw that. . . ." John *did* go to Iceland, in 1934, as part of his trip to Russia with Uncle Harry. Every other country in *Jean & Company* can be accounted for. So if Helen asserts that "Jean and her mother" visited Norway and Sweden, they did. And 1936 has to be the year.

That said, Helen took considerable license in fictionalizing the Norwegian and Swedish adventures. For one, she set the stories in winter, anticipating that her American readers would expect snowy scenes of winter sports in Scandinavia. And in writing the Sweden chapter, Helen drew on a book of illustrations by Carl Larsson (1853-1919), a Swedish artist working in the Arts and Crafts tradition. [9] Helen tips her hand when she describes Jean's arrival at the little red wooden cottage, "almost buried in snow, its welcoming lights gleaming out through the small-paned windows."

It was not like a real house at all, she decided, but much more like the picture in her favorite book at home. Even when she was a tiny child, her mother had let her turn the pages in the book of drawings by Carl Larsson. She could still remember how heavy it was. When she was so small that her feet stuck straight out from the huge, winged chair, her mother carefully had laid the big book open on her knees. Her eyes never tired of the enchanting pictures of Swedish children and Swedish houses. . . . Tonight, she felt as if she had moved into the pages of the Larsson book. [10]

In the fictional account, Jean, along with convent school classmates Jenny and Greta, visit Greta's great-grandmother (Lilla Mormor) at her country home in the Delarna region of Sweden. The rural setting gives Helen free rein to indulge in descriptions of folk costumes and customs. Following an afternoon of skiing, the three girls return to the

---

[9] *American Girl* published "Sue Goes to Sweden" in February of 1936, four months before Helen and her daughters visited there. This argues further for Helen having relied on the book of Larsson drawings in writing the story. *American Girl* never published a Norway story. Norway appears only in *Jean & Company*.

[10] *Larssons: Ett Album Bestående af 32 Målningar med Text och Techningar allt af Carl Larsson*. Stockholm: Albert Bonniers Förlag, 1910. (Larsson: An Album Consisting of 32 Paintings with Text and Drawings by Carl Larsson. Albert Bonniers, Publisher). The book is in the possession of Helen's granddaughters Martha and Pat Wells. "The huge winged chair" is one in which Clara Sipprell once photographed Jeanne and Polly.

cottage and change from heavy snow suits to bright peasant dresses. "Greta always kept one to wear when she visited Lilla Mormor. She had lent one to Jenny, and Jean had bought one to take back to America with her." Dinner was a full smörgåsbord: "caviar and anchovies, stuffed eggs, goose breast, cheese, fish, smoked eel," all set on a table decked with "hand-woven table linen, gleaming red glass, and quaint peasant china." Afterwards, the girls sit at the feet of Lilla Mormor in front of the tile stove, where the great-grandmother recounts tales of folk customs and celebrations throughout the seasons.

The visit concludes with the traditional observance of the Feast of St. Lucy, Santa Lucia, celebrated on December 13. Lilla Mormor herself, in a white robe and a crown of candles on her head, wakes the girls while it is still dark, followed by three maids bearing trays of coffee and saffron cakes. The Grace Paull illustration in *Jean & Company* is clearly drawn from Carl Larsson's illustration of the celebration of the Feast of St. Lucy.

The "Norway and the Long Winter Night" chapter again features winter sports, along with Jean and Jenny's attendance at a traditional Hardanger country wedding. Helen again takes the opportunity to describe folk costumes and customs: "At the head of the procession marched the fiddler . . . Behind him came the bride. . . . On her head was a wide, flaring crown. . . . Her short fur coat was open, and underneath Jean could glimpse a crimson beaded bodice. Fluttering ribbons hung from her waist over her richly embroidered white apron."

Jean and Jenny join Jenny's doctor-grandfather in a trip up the western coast of Norway to Hammerfest, sailing for days in a mailboat through rugged fjords, as Jenny's grandfather makes his annual inspection of rural hospitals in the towns and fishing villages. Many years later, Polly recalled sailing the fjords on a mailboat, but there is another source on which Helen could rely as well: the trip John took in 1934 to Iceland, Scandinavia and Russia with Uncle Harry. Harry's descriptions—in another of those green-bound, gold-stamped volumes—of sailing the Norwegian coast north to Hammerfest, are remarkably similar to the narrative in Helen's fictionalized account. Again, Helen shifts the seasons. In Hammerfest Uncle Harry and John witnessed the "midnight sun that never sets." Jean, by contrast, sailing ever northward, experiences the long winter night of the chapter's title, wherein "the sun appeared for only a few moments, an angry, red ball rising halfway above the horizon and then apparently going down in a rage."

From Hammerfest, overlooking "the wildly tossing Arctic Ocean" the girls, guided by scouts, ski to the tip of the North Cape. In the final pages of the chapter, Helen provides one of the most moving passages in *Jean & Company*, one that expresses the author's aspirations for her fictional character and a mother's hopes for Jeanne and Polly as well.

> Surely this was the high point of her trip, Jean thought, this one moment of facing the elements, longing to make of her life something strong and courageous and new. Out of darkness to search for light and find it. To reach into the unknown for knowledge, and then give it as a gift to the world. She tried to tell Jenny what she was feeling, but her lips were stiff with the cold, and a great wind blew the words back into her throat. She wished her father were standing beside her, because he would understand without the need for words.
>
> She was very quiet as they climbed down the dim, zigzag trail to the little ship whose lights were bobbing in the harbor. She wanted to keep in her heart that moment of exaltation. The rest of Norway did not really matter.

From Scandinavia the real-life travelers went next to Germany, where in Berlin not only Uncle Harry and Tod but a plunge into the reality of 1930s Germany awaited them. It was in Berlin that Helen met up with her seven tour participants. The group had tickets to the Berlin Olympic Games, which they attended on their first afternoon. There they witnessed Jesse Owens win his third gold medal of the games, in the 200-meter sprint. "We had good seats," Uncle Harry wrote, "directly opposite Herr Hitler, whom we saw there only once." Uncle Harry noted the success of the American athletes, citing the fact that "the negroes did particularly well," not only Jesse Owens but "[Archie] Williams and [James] LuVallee [and] several others. Our white boys also did well.. . .The Washington crew won the eight-oared rowing race in good style." [11]

From Berlin, the group went to Prague, "City of Towers." There they gazed at the statue of Jan Hus, religious reformer and martyr, and visited the Town Hall tower and clock, the figures of Christ and the Twelve

---

[11] The story of the victory of the University of Washington rowing team at the 1936 Olympics is told by Daniel James Brown in *The Boys in the Boat* (New York: Viking Press, 2013).

Apostles moving across the face in slow procession. The Charles Bridge, lined with statues of the saints. The Alchemists' Lane behind the Hradcany Castle, where mad King Rudolf imprisoned the unfortunate scientists who failed to turn base metal into gold. The tomb of Good King Wenceslaus. The Jewish cemetery, whose poignance and tragedy a few years hence they could not have guessed. All these locales had already been described by Helen in the *American Girl* story, "Sue Goes to Prague," written on the basis of her visit to the city in the summer of 1933, when she met John prior to rejoining the girls in Salzburg for the trip home.

From Prague they went next to Vienna, one-time imperial city now reduced, since the end of the First World War, to the capital of a small struggling country. Again, the itinerary included the highlights: the Art History Museum, with room upon room of Titians, Tintorettos, Raphaels, and Bruegels. The Belvedere Palace, Schönbrunn, and St. Stephen's Cathedral. They took in the magnificent view of the city from the Kahlenberg, high above the city. And Uncle Harry recorded in his diary letter a lesson in contemporary Austrian history from the local guide, "an intelligent man who had sung in the opera before his voice gave out. [He] told me that the Versailles Treaty had deprived Vienna of its means of existence by cutting off her richest lands and revenues and that Austrians would like to join a big Germany, but not on Hitler's terms." The price of that resolve was brought home as they toured the Hofburg Palace, now the seat of government. There the guide showed them the room where, two years earlier, Austria's chancellor was assassinated by a Nazi paramilitary squad. "The guide spoke of the murder with bated breath," Uncle Harry wrote. "The crisis must have been great, and trouble imminent." Only a month before Helen's group arrived in Vienna, Austria's new chancellor was forced to sign an agreement with Hitler expanding German influence in Austria.

From Vienna Helen's group headed to Budapest, traveling by bus across the Hungarian plain. Once again, Uncle Harry surveyed the surroundings with a perceptive eye.

> The land in Hungary is mostly owned by the few and
> worked by the peasants in shares. . . . The peasants live in
> villages in houses separated by little lanes opening into
> back compounds with barns, flowers, and manure heaps,
> some kempt and some pretty bad. There are deep gutters
> on each side of the main street with little bridges for each

house. The houses are a story high, with slanting roofs and little peep holes for the attic windows. How hot those attic rooms must be!

Helen and the tour group stayed at the St. Gellért, the art deco complex on the Buda side of the city, overlooking the Danube and the modern city of Pest. Their third-floor rooms opened onto balconies fronted with iron railings, furnished with geranium and petunia-filled planters. The St. Gellért was renowned for its pools and mineral baths. The outdoor pool, set in landscaped gardens with a restaurant poolside, featured a wave machine—the first in Europe—creating additional excitement for bathers. Helen wrote the St. Gellért and its pools into *Jean & Company*, describing Jean frolicking with her friend Jovanka:

> Jovanka came up spluttering and gasping after her dunking
> in the first big wave, and looked around for Jean, who
> was diving neatly through the following one. Quick as a
> dolphin, Jovanka leaped after her, caught her by the foot,
> and pulled her under. There was a momentary struggle.
> Then Jovanka scrambled up the ladder and fled around
> the marble portico, with Jean in hot pursuit. They avoided
> several leisurely strollers in brief bathing suits, almost fell
> over a portly female sunning herself in a steamer chair,
> and simultaneously dove from the diving board and slid
> down the slide. Arriving in the water at precisely the
> same moment, amid the cheers of the spectators, they
> disappeared from view beneath the waves.

Budapest was, until 1918, one of the twin capitals of the Austro-Hungarian Empire. Helen and her travelers visited the Coronation Church of St. Matthias, high in the Buda hills, where for centuries the kings of Hungary were crowned. They visited the great outdoor park on Margaret Island in the middle of the Danube. But the highlight was the Pearly Bouquet. With its folk costumes, music, and dances, the festival was promoted in tourist brochures as "an attraction not to be missed by foreign tourists who visited Budapest." [12]

---

[12] Alexande Vari, "From 'Paris of the East' to 'Queen of the Danube': International Models in the Promotion of Budapest Tourism, 1885-1940," in Eric G. E. Zuelow, ed., *Touring Beyond the Nation: A Transnational Approach to European Tourism History* (London: Ashgate, 2011), 112-113. Helen titled the Hungary chapter of *Jean & Company* "The Dancing City of Budapest."

The Pearly Bouquet was the creation of Hungarian anthropologist Béla Paulini. First performed in 1931, the festival grew out of Hungary's tortured twentieth-century history: defeat in World War I, the collapse of the Austro-Hungarian Empire, and the punishing Treaty of Trianon. Political upheaval in the aftermath of the war led, in quick succession, to the declaration of a constitutional government, a soviet-style republic, and a counterrevolution resulting in an authoritarian regime under Nicholas Horthy, a former admiral in the now-vanished Austro-Hungarian Navy. In light of this turmoil, it is not surprising that many Hungarians "sought proof of the uniqueness, greatness, and indestructibility of the Magyars in folk culture." [13]

Paulini's motives in founding the Pearly Bouquet were sincere, but Hungary's right-wing government quickly capitalized on the staging of a pageant of folklife in the nation's capital. To conservatives and nationalists, Budapest's prewar reputation as "the Paris of the East" connoted a foreign environment, shaped by Western and Jewish influences. Some referred to the city as "Juda-Pest." The Hungarian government now sought to rebrand the city as "The Queen of the Danube," emphasizing geography, in contrast to earlier claims that Budapest was a "world city," and attempting "to root Budapest in the Hungarian soil." [14]

It is easy to see why Helen was so enthusiastic about the Pearly Bouquet. Its display of peasant costumes and customs hearkened back to the Homelands Exhibits, and appealed to her belief in the superiority of pre-industrial culture. Even Uncle Harry, who noted the poverty of rural Hungary, took the Pearly Bouquet at face value, writing that "the costumes were a bouquet of color, brilliant and wonderfully variegated . . . [The dancers] performed with abandon. It was very charming and unique."

Salzburg was next. Helen had already published an *American Girl* Salzburg story, based on the summer three years earlier, when she and the girls were there. The magazine story, with one addition, formed the Salzburg chapter of *Jean & Company*. Helen adapted an incident that happened to Uncle Harry in 1936, en route to Salzburg, into the revised version, making Jean's mother the protagonist. In real life, it was Uncle Harry who went to a market to buy a bag of peaches, and missed the

---

[13] Carmala Patrias, *Patriots and Proletarians: Politicizing Hungarian Immigrants in Interwar Canada* (Montreal & Kingston, London, Buffalo: McGill-Queen's University Press, 1994), 48.
[14] Vari, 117.

bus. Great-nephew Tod Perry added a postscript to Uncle Harry's diary letter, describing what happened next. "The bus driver was all for going on without him, whereupon he became penniless and very feeble. . . . The other people on the bus were so touched by our lurid description of Uncle Harry's senility that there arose a great shout to wait for the *Grosspapa*, a name he hasn't lost yet." In *Jean & Company* it is Helen's alter ego, Jean's mother, who goes to buy peaches and is left behind; the bus driver is persuaded to stop only after Jean, using every language she can summon up, bursts into tears and is joined in her appeal by the indignant passengers.

In Salzburg the group attended a performance of "Fidelio," conducted by Arturo Toscanini, with Lotte Lehman singing the lead soprano role. (Helen titled the chapter in *Jean & Company* "The Singing City of Salzburg.") They took the funicular up to the fortress, from which they surveyed the landscape; Uncle Harry noting that they could see Elizabeth Duncan's palace "where the children danced." By now, however, Elizabeth was no longer at Schloss Klessheim. Her long-time partner, Max Merz, was a committed supporter of Adolf Hitler. He and Elizabeth moved the school to Munich. In Merz's case it proved to be a short journey from an aesthetic philosophy championing the Greek ideals of classical beauty and physical perfection to an embrace of the Nazi Aryan ideal.

On to Munich—where Helen made no attempt to contact Elizabeth Duncan—and then to Lucerne, Switzerland. Here Helen and her group parted company with Uncle Harry and Tod. The two men went to Geneva, where Harry was deeply moved by the memorial to the Protestant reformers, John Calvin and John Knox. Harry, the son of a Congregational minister, found the monument to be "striking. . .most impressive. We sat and gazed for a long time. A very fitting memorial to a lot of big, determined, and godly men."

Helen, meanwhile, took her group to Paris, including day trips to Versailles and Chartres. Uncle Harry and Tod rejoined them for a final two days in Paris before they boarded the *S.S. Statendam* at Boulogne-sur-Mer, heading for home.

In the summer of 1937 Helen returned to Europe. It was the most daring of her European tours. The itinerary cut a swath across Eastern Europe, from Danzig to the Tatra Mountains on the Czechoslovakian-Polish border. They went to rural Hungary and to Yugoslavia. The itinerary took Helen and her party through some of the most troubled regions of interwar Europe, where territorial arrangements following the First World War created festering disputes. Only two years after Helen's trip, the Second World War would begin on this contested ground.

Helen conducted the 1937 tour through Orbis, the Polish tour agency. The switch was dictated by the itinerary, which, with the exception of the trip's conclusion in Italy, focused entirely on Eastern Europe. The group resembled a Europe on Wheels tour in size and composition. The party included Rosanne French, classmate and close friend of Polly; along with Marquart Powell and Barbara Bower, the latter making her first trip to Europe. Two older women completed the roster: Pauline Fihe, a librarian from Cincinnati; and Bertha Baehr, a friend of Pauline, fellow Cincinnatian, and frequent European traveler. Miss Baehr joined the tour in Copenhagen. It is likely that the two women knew Helen's sister-in-law Evelyn, who grew up in Cincinnati and still had close ties to the city.

The *M/S Piłsudski* left New York on July 20. Helen, true to form, made friends with the ship's captain, leading to an invitation to join the captain for cocktails before dinner. "I didn't like the cocktail one little bit," Jeanne wrote to her father, "though Mummy liked it much better than usual. The captain is awfully nice, and loads of fun."

Six days later they sighted land. "Everyone crowded to the rail to see the barren shore of Scotland, until it disappeared in the mist." A day later the ship reached the Norwegian fjords. Jeanne stayed awake to experience the Land of the Midnight Sun. "I didn't go to bed till

Rosanne French, Marquart Powell, Jeanne and Polly Curtis on the M/S Pilsudski, July 1937.

after three, and even then, I could hardly tear myself away from the porthole. . . . The sky was . . . as light as day, we were so far north. And the sea reflected back the whiteness."

The *Piłsudski* docked in Copenhagen, allowing passengers a shore excursion, including a visit to the castle at Fredricksborg. Jeanne wrote that they vied to identify the landmarks from the city tour the year before. The next day they disembarked in Gdynia, built up since the war into a modern seaport. The city was situated at the tip of the Polish Corridor—the swath of land carved from eastern Germany in order to give newly independent Poland an outlet to the Baltic Sea. The Corridor cut off the historic province of East Prussia from the rest of Germany. The old German port of Danzig, twelve miles from Gdynia, lay inside the Corridor. Designated as a Free City, administered by the League of Nations, Danzig was at the heart of Europe's post-World War I territorial disputes. Ethnic grievances compounded economic ones. Adolf Hitler exploited both the loss of German territory to the Corridor and the loss of control over Danzig as grievances against Poland.

Helen and her charges cleared customs in Gdynia and went by taxi to Danzig. There they stayed at the Danziger Hof, a prewar luxury hotel whose stately dining room seated 400 people. After lunch they embarked on a city tour, following an English-speaking guide through medieval streets so narrow that they could only be explored on foot. For Helen the highlight was the Patrician House, a northern Renaissance-style merchant house with furniture and interiors preserved intact. "Mummy . . . was crazy about it," Jeanne wrote to her father. Jeanne also noted a small but telling example of Danzig's postwar status: the local currency, the Danzig gulden, was accepted alongside the Polish złoty.

The experience in Danzig was but one of many the travelers encountered which demonstrated the impact of the post-World War I territorial settlements and upheaval and prefigured the cataclysm to come. Helen and her group would encounter difficulties at new national borders: crossing from the Corridor to Germany and back to Poland; an episode at the Czech-Polish border where the girls and Pauline Fihe inadvertently left one country and entered the other; and a journey through the Tatra Mountains where they wove back and forth between Poland and the Slovak region of Czechoslovakia. In Yugoslavia they visited three of the republics: Croatia, Bosnia, and Montenegro, which coexisted uneasily in a federation carved out of the ruins of the Austro-Hungarian and Ottoman Empires.

Another phenomenon Helen and her group encountered in Eastern Europe was the return of individuals to lands from which they or their ancestors had fled political or economic oppression. Helen referred to encounters with an American art student in Warsaw, and "crowds of Polish-American students traveling in Poland." A Polish-American seminarian studying in Krakow intervened on Helen's behalf at the German-Polish border, allowing her to re-board the train and rejoin her group after he helped straighten out a dispute with train officials who initially refused to honor the Orbis vouchers. The seminarian, Brother Joachim, confessing to homesickness, joined the group at their Krakow hotel one morning and took them sightseeing while Helen attended to business at the Orbis office. Their local guide through much of Czechoslovakia was Valerie Hezmuka. The daughter of Czech immigrants, Valerie was born in Jersey City and had lived much of her life in Newark. After the war she went to Czechoslovakia to study. Back in the United States, she earned a master's degree at Columbia, and now, again in Czechoslovakia, worked for the American Institute. And Jeanne commented on the presence of several hundred American tourists in Zoppat in Poland, site of a recently launched international festival of Wagnerian opera, where Helen took them to hear a performance of *Lohengrin*.

While postwar changes created opportunities for some to return to lands of origin, for others the decades following the war were a time of social dislocation. Helen, in an article in *Parents'* magazine, wrote that they encountered "members of the old aristocracy of these countries who are now obliged to earn a living" as tour guides. [15] In Budapest and on their excursions through rural Hungary they were accompanied by Madame Lazzari, a former aristocrat. In Yugoslavia, their guide, Wanda, told them her family story: in 1921, her parents, living in a villa outside Zagreb, were warned by a rider on horseback that rioting and pillaging was occurring nearby. Wanda and her sister were away at school, but the parents seized a few belongings and fled. When they returned the next day all that was left of their estate was a smoldering ruin. Wanda subsequently inherited a small house from her father; she now took in boarders and did guide work to support herself and her mother.

The travelers also encountered examples of aggrieved nationalism. In the Hungarian town of Szeged, they attended the drama festival

---

[15] Helen Perry Curtis, "Travel is a Liberal Education," *Parents'*, 13:20 (April 1938): 90.

staged in the plaza before the cathedral. Founded in 1931, the same year as the Pearly Bouquet in Budapest, the festival drew nightly crowds of up to 8,000 people. In a letter to Anita Zahn, Jeanne described the play, *Byzance*: Turks firing down on the stage from towers in all corners of the square, fireworks, "and lots of excitement." The next night they saw *John of the Maize*, an operetta based on tales of Hungary's resistance to Turkish occupation in the sixteenth and seventeenth centuries, complete with Hussars dashing up the neighboring streets to the stage on horseback and a military band playing a victorious march. Both performances played into Hungary's sense of a nation beset by foreign enemies, with salvation to be found in military might. Likewise, the festival surrounding the Feast of St. Stephen in Budapest was crafted to stoke Hungarian nationalist sentiments.

All that lay ahead of them. For now, leaving Danzig, the group crossed the border to the German province of East Prussia, to Marienburg, less than an hour away. There they saw the castle of the Teutonic Knights, a red brick fortress emblematic of the German *Drang nach Osten,* the eastward expansion during the Middle Ages. The castle commanded a location on the River Nogat, whose waters reflected the medieval towers and turrets. The colors of the murals and tapestries in the grand rooms made Jean think of the Orient. The group picnicked in the courtyard of the castle and roamed the complex's expansive grounds. "I really cannot do justice to the place," Jeanne enthused. "I can only praise my stars that I was able to see it."

Next came Poland, newly reconstituted as a nation following the collapse of the Russian, German, and Austro-Hungarian Empires. They went to the capital city of Warsaw, and to Krakow, its former Cloth Market filled with flower stalls and souvenir stands. They toured Wawel Castle, a monument to Poland's medieval power and wealth. But what made an impression on Jeanne was the Jewish ghetto: the men bearded, their hair in ringlets, dressed in knee-length black coats and fur-trimmed hats; the women wearing wigs; the poverty and squalor in which the ghetto's residents were forced to live.

From Krakow, Helen's group departed for Czechoslovakia.[16] It

---

[16] Helen never wrote an *American Girl* story or a *Jean* chapter set in Poland. The trip in 1937 was her first visit to the country, and by that time *Jean & Company* was in press.

was at Bohumín, formerly the German town of Oderberg, where they met the American-born Valerie Hezmuka, their Orbis guide while in Czechoslovakia. Traveling eastward along the Czechoslovak-Polish border, the group came to Cieszyn, formerly German Teschen. There was not much there, Jeanne (erroneously) reported, but they did visit a restored tower, "which Polly and Rosanne energetically climbed while we sat down below and wondered how they did it." Pauline Fihe filmed a group of soldiers outside their barracks with her movie camera. The young men were delighted until they learned that, being movies, they would not be able to get copies of their pictures. Pauline's friend Bertha Baehr obliged, taking photos with her camera and promising that she would somehow get each of them a print. "They were all tickled to death, and had great fun over the whole thing." It was here that, in filming the soldiers, the group inadvertently crossed back into Poland, and had to show their passports to re-enter Czechoslovakia. Pauline and Bertha managed the situation by speaking German, the only language they and the Polish soldiers had in common. What the American visitors did not realize was that the border area was a source of bitter disputes between Czechoslovakia and Poland; disputes which had, in the 1920s, led to armed clashes.

Continuing eastward, the train took them through the Tatra Mountains, a region spanning Poland and Slovakia. They glimpsed "fertile, peasant-tilled valleys . . . hillsides striped with crops of various grains, vegetables, and clover." Most thrilling for Helen and her daughters was the fact that the peasants working in the fields were dressed in "costumes;" brightly colored skirts with contrasting color aprons, embroidered blouses, and bright kerchiefs. The men wore embroidered jackets as well, and "the little girls' costumes were just like their mothers'." Entire families worked the fields; occasionally an entire village appeared to work together cutting and gathering grain in a communal field.

The Tatra Mountains were a winter playground. It was now high summer, but for Helen the goal was to spend time in the countryside. They went first to the resort town of Tatranská Lomnica on the Slovak side, high in the mountains. Arriving in Tatranská, they walked from the station through a "lovely, wild park" to their hotel. Although reputed to be the best in town, the hotel was "definitely mediocre in the matter of modern conveniences, newspaper being used instead of toilet paper, for instance," Jeanne reported. Nevertheless, they were delighted with the airy rooms and excellent food. Walking from the station they noticed a store filled with peasant crafts. Polly and Rosanne clamored to return there after supper, a request Helen was happy to oblige.

From Tatranská the group zig-zagged back to Poland, to Zacopane, thirty miles from Tatranská. "The village below and the view is divine.. . .You never saw such distance [and] such forests, either." They continued to thread their way thought the Tatras, returning to Czechoslovakia and the spa town of Trenčianska Teplice. The Grand Hotel was fully booked, so they stayed instead at a small overflow pension, taking their meals at the hotel.

Jeanne had dismissed the wares found in the shops in Zacopane: "Everything was so obviously touristy." But Teplice more than met expectations for authentic, handcrafted clothing, "real, old costumes."

> While waiting for supper . . . we walked in the village . . . keeping an eye out for costumes and costume cards, when what did we spy but a whole window full of real peasant aprons, blouses, etc. Of course, before you could wink an eye, we were across the street and in the shop, and the result of a half hour's bickering and bargaining was the purchase of an apron for each of us . . . and the makings of a blouse for Polly and me.

Polly and Jeanne in costumes they assembled on their trip through Eastern Europe, 1937.

Grace Paull worked from Curtis family photo albums in doing the illustrations for *Jean & Company, Unlimited.*

The search for folk costumes was another feature of the 1937 trip, a passion shared by Helen and her daughters, and one at the center of *Jean & Company*. When it came to collecting traditional garb, Helen exercised discriminating judgment—based on her experience with the Homelands Exhibits—and passed this on to Jeanne and Polly. Both girls were intent on acquiring authentic items in order to assemble folk costumes from the countries they were visiting. There is significance in Jeanne's use of the words "real, old costumes." Helen provides a clue in the Yugoslavia chapter of *Jean & Company*, set in the busy Zagreb market.

> [Jean's] mother was not half so interested in the cheeses and ducks and strawberries as she was in the costumes that the women wore, and before the morning was over . . . she had bargained for a blouse and cap, a gay skirt, and a brilliantly embroidered apron. It was not easy to persuade the women to part with these treasures. They were not just dresses . . . but were traditional costumes identical from one generation to another, embroidered by each bride on homespun, hand-woven linen, to last a lifetime of feast days and market days. But there were some younger women who now preferred the newer dresses they could buy in the shops, with the money given them by those foolish foreigners who wanted somebody else's clothes. Jean wondered how she would feel if some casual traveler in America tried to buy her clothes. [17]

From the Tatra region the group went to Brno, known in the days of the Austro-Hungarian Empire as Brünn. While Valerie Hezmuka took the others sightseeing, Jeanne and Helen spent time alone, a real-life version of the mother-daughter expeditions Helen portrayed in her fictionalized accounts. "Mummy and I wandered about, saw the fruit and flower market, and ended up by going to the museum. . . because we had been told there was a collection of costumes." Again, they were not disappointed. "A whole room full of costumes on models, with the walls lined with cases of religious and traditional ornamentations, figures, etc. There was a case of beautifully painted eggs which I felt like taking home with me."

---

[17] Jeanne's daughter Susie recalls her mother describing an incident where Helen bargained with a woman for the clothing she was still wearing, literally buying the clothes off the woman's back.

From Brno, a three-hour train trip brought them to Prague. There they bade farewell to Valerie Hezmuka. Taking her place was Mrs. Friedl, also from the American Institute. Sizing up the group, Mrs. Friedl returned that evening with her brother and a friend, both young men in their early twenties, hoping to "plan some sort of a nice evening." Jeanne begged off; but Barbara and Marquart joined the boys for a night of dancing at the hotel, while Helen, Mrs. Friedl, Bertha Baehr, and Pauline Fihe spent the night sitting and talking at the rooftop café, and, Jeanne told her father, having "a wee bitty to drink."

Mrs. Friedl's young friends returned the next day to collect Barbara and Marquart, leaving the others to visit Prague's Ethnographic Museum. Helen had taken her daughters there the year before, "and it was such fun to recognize things again." That evening Helen took Jeanne and Polly to the restaurant where she and John had dined during their visit in 1933. From high on a hillside above Prague, they looked out over the twinkling lights of the city below.

An all-night train from Prague brought them to Budapest, where Madame Lazzari, the noblewoman turned tour guide, met them at the station. Helen's group was booked into the Bristol Hotel, as the St. Gellért was unavailable. But after breakfast on the terrace, overlooking the Danube, they went to the St. Gellért, where they were able to buy tickets for an hour of swimming in the hotel's famous pools. That evening, Madame Lazzari, like her predecessor, returned to the hotel with her son Freddie and his friend Felix, whom Jeanne found to be "very charming." After dinner the young men departed with Barbara and Marquart, leaving Jeanne this time wishing wistfully that she could have gone with them, "but what could a third girl do, except be a stumbling block for the others."

Helen planned the time in Hungary to coincide with the Feast of St. Stephen, including, again, performances of the Pearly Bouquet. But first the party made two extended excursions to rural Hungary. Their first destination was Szeged, Hungary's second largest city. It was here they attended the drama festival, portraying Hungarian exploits of days gone by. Szeged lay at the heart of Hungary's agricultural region. En route, the group ate lunch at the small town of Kecskemét, and Jeanne described the "beautiful clusters of blue, green, and red grapes, such peaches and plums!" There was more of the same at the hotel that night, where they were greeted in the dining room with the sight of a long table laid with white tablecloths, gleaming crystal and china, and runners of leaves and flowers the length of the table. The waiter carried in "an enormous silver platter, raised like a huge goblet, and piled high with all imaginable fruits," melon, grapes, figs, pears, peaches, plums, and apples. The meal consisted of goulash; fish from the River Tisza, stuffed with mushrooms; chicken paprikash; a salad of onion, green pepper and tomato; ears of black and white sweet corn; and poppyseed strudel for dessert.

Szeged's shops proved to be a source of fine Hungarian fabrics, and Jeanne, Polly, and Rosanne acquired material for their costumes. On the return trip to Budapest, they stopped in the town of Kiskunhalas. There, in 1902, a local teacher, working with the Hungarian Royal School of Applied Arts for Girls in Budapest, revived the craft of lace-making, incorporating designs from Hungarian folk art and legend. Halas Lace, as it was known, gained international recognition, winning the gold medal at the 1937 Paris World Exhibition. The workshop was located in a former farmhouse. The young women were dressed in costume, as were the men in the village ("they somehow knew we were coming"). Underlining that last point was the fact that the mayor of the town greeted them, accompanied by a young woman who spoke excellent English. During lunch they were entertained with music and dancing. The younger girls were, to their delight, invited to dance by some of the men. Afterwards, the mayor and interpreter accompanied the group through the town. They visited a private home: the kitchen with its hanging copper pots; the living-dining room and bedroom, furniture piled high with embroidered pillows.[18] A year earlier, traveling through Hungary, Uncle Harry observed of the houses that "some [were] kempt and some pretty bad." Jeanne described the houses in Kiskunhalas as "all immaculately white. . .stenciled with an intricate pattern. . .making it quite gay and nice." Kiskunhalas was clearly marketed for tourists, another example of the irony that, but for modern-day tourism, the survival of a traditional craft would have been impossible.

"Home" to Budapest and the Bristol for a night, and then the second of the two excursions, this one six days in duration, taking Helen's group first to Mezőkövesd. The town, some seventy-five miles north and east of Budapest, came to the attention of American tourists in 1922 when Béla Mátéka, from the Budapest Tourism Office, accompanied a group of Vassar students and faculty on an excursion to the town. Mátéka reported back on the enthusiasm with which the Americans responded

---

[18] Helen, in a manuscript entitled "Adventure in Hungary," attributed the group's special treatment to the presence of Madame Lazarri, whom Helen referred to elliptically as "the Princess O-----," and well-known in all these villages."

to the costumes and crafts, and urged officials to promote Mezőkövesd. Beginning the next summer, American and European tourists were recruited, often by Mátéka himself, from Budapest's hotels, and taken by chartered train on day trips to Mezőkövesd. The fact that Helen included a visit to Mezőkövesd in *Jean & Company*, already in press before she actually visited the village, indicates that she was able to write an accurate description of the town from available tourist literature. As further proof of Mezőkövesd's fame, Helen's group encountered there a group of American students, enrolled in the International Art Institute in nearby Eger, taking part in a five-week study tour of folk art and costumes. "Mummy gave them her name and address."

Jeanne responded enthusiastically to Mezőkövesd, describing the colors of the costumes: magentas, greens, blues, oranges, and reds; worn by men, women, and children alike. The men wore voluminous white trousers, almost like skirts, with hats tipped at a rakish angle; the women were in embroidered skirts, ruffled blouses, and richly embroidered aprons. Small children were dressed as miniature adults.

Mezőkövesd, Hungary; photo taken by Jeanne Curtis. Europe, 1937.

Following an overnight in Lillafüred, the group went on to Debrecen, an hour from the Romanian border. They stopped in Tokaj, and were entertained by gypsy music over lunch at an inn. Afterwards they toured the wine cellars, ten long underground corridors lined on both sides with casks of the famous Tokaji, or Tokay, wine. Helen's aversion to wine was, by now, a thing of the past. "We all, except Polly, Rosanne and I, who occasionally used Mummy's, carried glasses, and the man who took us through gave us sips of the different wines, and everybody was very gay."

In Debrecen they stayed at the Grand Hotel Arany Bika, and the next morning headed for the Hortobagy Plain. No amount of tourist promotion, no presence of an Orbis escort, could disguise the ruggedness, the otherness, of the surroundings. The landscape was utterly flat, with the result that every house, well, or clump of trees stood out in stark relief and appeared to be twice its actual size. The whole thing, Jeanne wrote, "gave me a weird, unreal feeling." She described sheep with long horns twisted into spirals; cattle of an ivory-grey color, also with enormous curved horns; and dogs that looked like a cross between a sheepdog and Russian wolf hound, coats so matted that the fur hung in scrawny ringlets, "quite unpleasant." The Hortobagy plain was known for its horses, and Jeanne, Polly, and Pauline Fihe all braved a ride. The herders rode without saddles, sitting or standing on a strip of leather to which were attached stirrups. They mounted by throwing themselves onto the horses before scooping up a rider, who sat side-saddle, leaning back "on the arm of our gallant, and you felt as if you must slide off every step." They had lunch at an inn, enjoying "the best tomato soup I have ever had," along with foot-long ears of roasted corn, roast goose, and apple and poppyseed strudels. One of the herders invited them to his home, to see how three generations lived together, some members of the family sleeping in the barn. Living and sleeping quarters were in one large room, beds and sofas again piled high with colorfully embroidered pillows.

Back in Budapest, the celebration of the Feast of Saint Stephen was underway. Revered as the founder (circa 1000 A.D.) of the Kingdom of Hungary, Stephen was credited with the nation's conversion to Christianity. Before the First World War, the feast day was a marginal event. However, as Hungary reasserted its national identity—simultaneously fanning the flames of resentment at the fate of Hungarian minorities assigned by treaty to Czechoslovakia, Romania, and Yugoslavia—the day grew in importance. The cult of Saint Stephen served the agenda of conservative nationalists in that it promoted an ideology of "faith, blood, and soil," emphasizing Hungary's Christian national identity. The feast day grew to a week-long event, including pageants, sporting contests, fireworks, and performances of the Pearly Bouquet. At its heart was a religious procession on August 20, when the mummified hand of Saint Stephen, wrapped in ropes of pearls, was carried through the streets to the Coronation Church in the Buda hills.

Helen and her group left the Bristol Hotel early in order to be outside the church before 8:00 a.m. Their seats were in the back row, but this allowed them to stand on their chairs, the better to see and to take pictures—Miss Fihe again filming with her movie camera. From the four corners of the square the procession converged on the church; the music from the church organ amplified over loudspeakers. Police in silver helmets, mounted on dappled-grey horses; military veterans in khaki uniforms, their helmets decorated with clusters of green oak leaves; wounded war veterans, many leaning on canes, others carrying banners. From another corner came representatives of the Hungarian army, marching in goose-step. Hussars, clad in red and green, or powder-blue, wore fur-lined cloaks flung jauntily over one shoulder. Government officials were dressed either in formal wear or stylized medieval costumes. A priest carried a cross, followed by long lines of members of religious orders in their distinctive garb. More priests, in gold brocade robes, and then the casket-bearers with the hand of Saint Stephen. The casket, as Jeanne described it, was made of pure gold, with inset windows on all sides, allowing the crowd to see the relic. Bringing up the rear were various church dignitaries, "all robed in reds, magentas, purples, and Chinese vermilions. A sight I will never forget."

Peasants in folk costume were also in the square. After the procession they dispersed and headed for the turrets and promenades of the Fisherman's Bastion, perched on the edge of the Buda hills overlooking the Danube. Helen, Jeanne, Polly and the rest followed them. "We saw a lot of the young girls we had seen at Mezőkövesd and had a jolly time recognizing each other. The girls called over to the men to point us out to them."

The afternoon featured a performance of the Pearly Bouquet (Helen's group would attend three performances in all). They saw again the dancers from Mezőkövesd, and were delighted with the presentation of a tableau from the Hortobagy Plains. The day concluded with fireworks over the Danube. Everyone crowded into Pauline Fihe and Bertha Baehr's room to watch the bursting rockets reflected in the waters of the Danube.

It is not clear whether Helen understood the political overtones of the festival, and the nationalistic purpose it was designed to serve. She embraced the color and the costumes, as well as the Catholic pageantry, something on which her views had altered over the years. It may also be that, beyond political exploitation, Helen recognized something genuine, even primal, in the pageantry. Seeing again the young people from Mezőkövesd, and their delighted recognition of Jeanne and Polly, also contributed to a sense of something authentic.

After the immersion in folklore, the final days in Budapest offered Helen and her daughters a more contemporary experience. They visited the Kadars, artists known to friends of John back home. Helen, Jeanne, Polly, and Rosanne spent an afternoon at the couple's villa outside Budapest, and Helen purchased etchings for the decorating business. The Kadars invited the girls and Helen for a return visit, hosting them to a traditional Hungarian meal. Another evening, the three girls enjoyed Budapest's nightlife in the company of Madame Lazzari's son and his friend, Freddie and Felix, the two young men Jeanne had regretfully watched go off with Marquart and Barbara. Marquart left the group after the Saint Stephen festival to visit a friend living in France, and Barbara embarked on a romantic escapade, one which would reach a rocky conclusion in Yugoslavia. With Helen trailing discretely behind, Freddie and Felix took the girls to a gypsy café, and then by car to the ruins of the fortress in the Buda hills. Any city is beautiful at night, Jeanne wrote, and that night there was "a full moon which made the river look like a ribbon of mercury." The young people finished the evening at a nightclub, the Parisian Café on Margaret Island (the regime had evidently not entirely succeeded in wiping out Budapest's "Paris of the East" character). "As nightclubs go," Jeanne wrote to her father, "and you know how much I know about them, I daresay it wasn't bad." They saw a fan dance routine, "very artistically done," but "Polly wouldn't be convinced that the women had a stitch on." Jeanne most enjoyed the revolving dance floor, the first time she had been on one. The boys were good dancers, she reported, and the evening just flew by. Before they knew it, it was 2:00 a.m., and later yet when they returned to the Bristol. "But it was all swell fun."

Taking leave of Madame Lazzari and the young escorts, Helen's group, minus Marquart and Barbara, went to Yugoslavia, arriving in Zagreb. Like the other successor states of Central and Eastern Europe, Yugoslavia experienced political and ethnic upheaval in the post-World War I years. In 1929, clashes between Serbs, Croats, and Muslims led to the suspension of the constitution and the proclamation of a royal dictatorship under King Alexander I. In 1934 Alexander was assassinated during another spasm of ethnic violence. The American travelers learned firsthand of Yugoslavia's ethnic conflict from the dramatic story of the burning of the family estate told to them by Wanda, their guide in Zagreb.

Helen based the Yugoslavian *American Girl* story, and corresponding chapter in *Jean & Company*, on her trip there with John, in 1926. The *American Girl* version contained the most overtly political passage of any of the stories or book chapters, as she describes Sue and Jovanka listening as

> the grown-ups talked about this strange land of Jugoslavia
> . . . made up of people of every race and religion—Latin,
> Slav, Oriental, Greek Catholic, Roman Catholic, Moslem.
> Here was a land with great variety of climate, with fertile
> valleys, barren mountains, sunny shores and snow-clad
> peaks, a land in which each man fears his neighbor because
> he was once his enemy or loves him because he is now his
> countryman.

On their first evening in Zagreb, a combination of exhaustion and pouring rain outside kept the travelers inside the hotel. Jeanne read aloud to her mother from Louis Adamic's *The Native's Return*. "And everything we learned from Miss Wanda about the government, torture, dictatorship under Alexander, etc. confirmed most of Adamic's statements."

Taking her group to Yugoslavia was a daring move. With the exception of Zagreb, Yugoslavia fell outside the reach of Orbis. Helen was on her own to make local arrangements: hiring drivers or guides, or leading the group by herself. She enjoyed two advantages. German and French were widely spoken, and Helen could rely on her prior experience and connections from 1926. Much of the 1937 itinerary retraced that of 1926, albeit in reverse order. The *American Girl* story and *Jean & Company* mapped John and Helen's real-life trip: from Venice on a steamer across the Adriatic, then along the Dalmatian coast to Split and Dubrovnik, Sarajevo, and finally Zagreb. In 1937, traveling south from Budapest, Helen took her group first to Zagreb. From there they went to Sarajevo, Dubrovnik, the Montenegrin towns of Kotor and Cetinje, and back to Dubrovnik. From Dubrovnik they made excursions to small towns and islands off the Dalmatian coast: Korchula, Havar, and Lokrum, then on to Split, before heading north to Fiume and Susak. They concluded by taking a steamer across the Adriatic to Venice.

The two weeks in Yugoslavia provided some of the most dazzling sights and scenery of the trip, along with the most unusual experiences. From their rooms in the Hotel Milinov, they looked down on one of the city's many bustling markets, and Polly wrote to Anita Zahn that "all day long in the marketplace outside our window one can hear the peasants shouting their wares. . . . All the stalls have red umbrellas and all the women have white homespun dresses with red embroidery, and baskets on their heads." On a tour of Zagreb, in the company of Wanda, they passed the house of the Croatian artist and sculptor, Ivan Mestrovic, a friend of Clara Sipprell, much to Helen's excitement. Wanda knew the maid, so the group was admitted to the courtyard to admire the statuary. On their own, Jeanne and Helen visited the Ethnographic Museum; and with Polly and Rosanne shopped for fabrics for the girls' costumes. Walking through the market one day, Jeanne and Helen spied a young woman wearing a pair of red shoes that Jeanne instantly coveted. Attempts to question the woman as to where she had purchased them were futile; leery of Jeanne's camera, she turned her back and refused to engage with them. A crowd gathered, and one of the men, speaking halting German, offered to take Jeanne and Helen to the shop. He led them on a half-hour walk through increasingly narrow streets and shabbier neighborhoods, to Helen's growing misgivings; but they finally reached the shop where Jeanne was able to purchase the shoes: "a work of art, a maze of fine leather strips with bright colors woven in."

More adventures awaited them in Sarajevo. They stood before the black marble tablet marking the spot where Gavrilo Princip fired the shots that killed Archduke Franz Ferdinand and Archduchess Sophie, igniting the First World War. The tablet referred to Princip as "the Herald of Liberty." "It makes you stop and think," Jeanne wrote to her father. They drove up into the mountains above the city to look down on the minarets which pierced the skyline. They had no way of knowing that, six decades hence, the vantage point from those mountains would give to the city's main boulevard below the name "Sniper Alley."

Jeanne's letters from Sarajevo remarked on the "oriental" character of the multi-ethnic city, a city divided between Muslims, Orthodox Christians, Roman Catholics, and Jews. As women, they were denied admittance to mosques, allowed only as far as the courtyard; neither could they enter the coffee shops. Helen sought out a shop she and John visited in 1926. The proprietor brought out bolt after bolt of brocade and embroidery, oriental rugs, and countless silver buttons and buckles. Helen made purchases for the business; Jeanne and Polly bought gifts for Aunt Patty and others at home.

While in Sarajevo the group had a bizarre experience. Leaving the Ethnographic Museum, Helen was accosted by a man recruiting an audience for a performance by a whirling dervish. In a practice unique to the Sufi minority of Islam, a dancer, to the sound of chanting, achieves a mystical state, impervious to the piercing of his body by skewers, spikes, and a sword. How much of this Helen understood when she agreed to bring her teen-aged daughters and Rosanne to this performance is unclear, but Jeanne described the evening in graphic terms in her letter to her father, admitting that by the end of the evening they were all feeling "queerer and queerer. . . . It's just as well you weren't there."

From Sarajevo they headed to the Dalmatian coast and Dubrovnik. Helen described Dubrovnik in *Jean & Company* as rising from the blue sea, "a city of gleaming opal. Round it stood tall, green cypresses and spreading palms, and in the distance the amethyst hills paled against a turquoise sky. Only jewel words could describe its sparkle and color." The architecture of Dubrovnik resembled that of Venice; the fact that this region was at one time under the control of the Venetian Republic accounted for the similarities. "Many of the buildings . . . looked as if they might have sailed over from Venice themselves."

Hiring a chauffeur, Helen and the group went south on a day-long excursion to Montenegro, to the towns of Kotor and Cetinje. The latter was the capital of the pre-war Kingdom of Montenegro, now absorbed into Yugoslavia. The tiny houses and churches of Kotor's bewitching ancient city clustered against the barren limestone mountains, slate-blue and grey, devoid of any trace of greenery.

By this time the group was reduced to Helen, her two daughters, Rosanne, and Pauline Fihe. Bertha Baehr left the group in Zagreb; returning home on her own later in the autumn. Barbara's romantic escapades led to her dismissal from the trip. Jeanne kept her father apprised of the unfolding story: Barbara left the group in Budapest to fly to Vienna to see a man she met on the *Pisudski*. She rejoined them in Zagreb. In Dubrovnik, "Barbara, true to practice, hooked a male and went out to lunch with him." The day before the group left Dubrovnik, Barbara sailed from Trieste aboard the *Vulcania*, bound for home. "She was becoming rather a strain. . . . Mummy has probably written you all about it." Barbara was over twenty-one, but this series of events was probably more than Helen, to say nothing of Barbara's family, bargained for in sending her to Europe with "a mature woman guide."

Boarding the steamer in Dubrovnik, Helen, Jeanne, Polly, Rosanne, and Pauline Fihe sailed to the islands of Lokrum, Korchula, and Hvar. They visited Split, the town that so fascinated Helen on her earlier trip with John. She described it in *Jean & Company*: an entire town built within the ruins of the walls of the Emperor Diocletian's palace. The boat sailed on to the port cities of Fiume and Susak, towns which offered a parallel to the fraught status of Danzig and Gdynia at the start of their trip. Crossing the Adriatic, they came to Venice. Jeanne wrote to her father that "everything [was] covered with a soft blue haze, and as we came into the harbor, we watched the sun climb down the pink-walled houses and yellow lateen sails. . . . We vied with each other at picking out familiar landmarks: Santa Maria, San Marco, the Doge's Palace."

After the novelties of the last weeks, Venice offered the embrace of the familiar. They had a joyful reunion with John and Helen's old friends, the artist Gennaro Favai and his wife Maria. Helen and the girls went in search of the apartment where they lived four years earlier. Their former caretakers were still in residence, and they enjoyed a sentimental stroll through the premises. From Venice they went to Bergamo, and another reunion, this time with Rose Previtali. From there it was a short trip to Genoa where, on September 15, they boarded the *S.S. Rex*, bound for New York.

Three months later, Helen experienced the thrill of holding in her hands a copy *Jean & Company, Unlimited*. More than a fictionalized account of her trips with Jeanne and Polly, the book synthesized the experiences of a lifetime: her love of folk costume and culture, her museum work, her travels with her mother as well as her daughters— all brought together into the story of an American girl's first encounter with Europe.

Chapter 10
European Coda

*J*ean & Company, Unlimited* was published in November 1937. Grace Paull, a New York artist and illustrator of juvenile fiction, did the artwork. Paull's lithographs are crisply executed, based on photographs supplied to her by Helen. Jean—when not shown in folk costume—is portrayed as a smartly dressed American girl of the era.

Notices of the book appeared as early as mid-November. These were often simply a mention of the book as an acquisition by a local public library; other times *Jean* received a full review—this at a time when even small-town newspapers had their own book critics. The reviews were favorable. "A lovely Christmas book, one really worth owning," stated the Salt Lake *Tribune*. "A grand book for young people who are interested in the culture and customs of traditional Europe," opined the *Pittsburgh Press*. The Bryan, Texas *Eagle* called it "a travel book that is sure to be popular with older girls," because "readers see the various countries portrayed through the eyes of a gay, friendly, happy-hearted American girl on her first trip abroad. What normal fifteen-year-old girl would not be thrilled to spend a whole year in Europe, especially such a year as Jean had!" [1]

Jean & Company caught the attention of major newspapers as well. The *Boston Transcript* stated that the book "is a perfectly fine answer to questions which young people ask about studying in foreign schools. . . . The author, who has traveled extensively with her daughters, answers all these queries, and more, in a charming and delightful manner." *The New York Times* gave *Jean* a lengthy and positive review. "More fact than fiction, this account of a 15-year-old girl's first trip to Europe is based upon the actual experiences of the author's daughter . . . loosely recast into story form." The *Times* called the book "a bright, quick, bird's-eye view of thirteen countries," one that "probably covers more territory than any other one travel story for young people." While noting that the book's approach "is largely visual and gustatory . . . and the style

---

[1] *Salt Lake Tribune*, December 5, 1937; *Pittsburgh Press*, December 19, 1937; *Eagle* (Bryan, TX), September 19, 1938.

tends to gush with adjectives and superlatives," the *Times* nevertheless concluded that *Jean & Company* "is a tempting invitation to travel which stresses the most essential of travelers' requirements: good-will and a readiness for experience." [2]

The book benefitted from its designation as the Junior Literary Guild's January, 1938 selection of the month. By February of 1938 the initial printing of 10,000 copies had sold out.

In July and August of 1938 Helen led one more Europe on Wheels trip, this time to France and Italy. The political situation made a return to Central and Eastern Europe risky. In March of 1938 Germany had annexed Austria. Hitler was already fixing his sights on Czechoslovakia.

An air of nostalgia, along with a sense of impending change, pervaded the trip. The itinerary largely retraced the journey Helen made with John and Uncle Harry in 1930, and to some extent the 1926 trip with John. The tour began in Paris, and then took participants south: through the chateaux country of the Loire Valley and then to Angouleme, Rocamadour, and Carcassonne; followed by Avignon and Nîmes, the heart of Roman/Gallic France. From there they headed south, via Aix-en-Provence, to the Riviera. The route took them to Chaumont, where Helen was stationed with the YMCA during the First World War. They spent a day in Grasse, where Helen and Polly made a sentimental visit to Tourlaque. After three weeks in France, the group sailed from Cannes to Naples, where, over the following month, they wound their way through Ravello, the Greek ruins at Paestum, and Rome. They spent ten days in the hill towns of Tuscany and in Florence—before going to the Italian Lake District, then from Stresa to Paris, taking the boat train to Boulogne for the shipboard journey home.

Although Helen, on more than one occasion, expressed the wish that "the next trip must be all together" it was clear that life was changing. Jeanne did not go to Europe with Helen and Polly that summer. She was at home, preparing to enter Swarthmore College in the fall. And in letters to her father, Polly wages a persistent campaign to be allowed to return to Buxton School in the fall rather than following her parents' intention to send her to the more structured environment of Kent Place School in Summit.

---

[2] *Boston Transcript,* December 11, 1937; *New York Times*, February 20, 1938.

The group that Helen led in 1938 was a fluid one, with participants joining and departing along the way. Four girls, along with Helen, sailed from New York on board the US-Holland line ship *Nieuw Amsterdam*. In addition to Polly, now sixteen, there was Rosanne French, Polly's friend, returning for her second trip with Helen. Another participant was thirteen-year-old Anne Kaufman, daughter of Broadway producer George S. Kaufman. Anne, Helen wrote, "is a very good little girl, absolutely unaffected and very sweet." A fourth girl was referred to in Polly and Helen's letters only as "Kitten." An older woman, Julia Maier, rounded out the core group. At age sixty, Julia made a good traveling companion for Helen. "We have a table together in the dining room, and the four girls are just next to us. They are having a good time together, a most hilarious one, in fact."

Anne Kaufman, Rosanne French, Polly Curtis, and "Kitten" on board the *Nieuw Amsterdam*. The smartly dressed girls are all between the ages of thirteen and sixteen.

A woman Helen met on shipboard, who recognized her from *Parents'* magazine articles, joined the group for several days in Paris. Seventeen-year-old Julia Hubbard met them by arrangement in Villeneuve-lès-Avignon and remained for the rest of the trip.[3] Other friends from home: Grace Howe, Julia Wattles, and Julia's eighteen-year-old son Gurdon, joined the group in Chartres, and a Miss Langmeier met them in Cannes for the Italian portion of the trip. "So we have a good-sized party after all."

The departure from New York was accompanied by the usual flurry of gifts from family and friends. Grace Paull, the illustrator of *Jean & Company*, sent flowers. The group sailed tourist class, but—thanks again to Helen's ability to make useful friends—they were able to enjoy the amenities in first class: walks on the promenade deck every morning, coffee in "The Ritz," or movies in the theater. "I observed Mr. Edward Biddle in first class and we have seen him several times. He took us all over first class. Lillian Gish is on board but we haven't seen her yet." Even absent that sighting, Polly concluded that first class "looked just like Hollywood."

There were the usual entertainments and diversions. At the fancy-dress ball Polly and Rosanne, wearing the folk costumes they had acquired in Hungary and Czechoslovakia the previous summer, took the prize for "most beautiful costumes." The two girls performed a Hungarian folk dance, to the delight of the audience. Anne Kaufman borrowed a sailor's outfit and rubber boots from a crew member, and wheedled a dead fish out of the kitchen staff, earning an "honorable mention." A Fourth of July celebration featured a "Boost Your State" competition for which Helen wrote "a silly poem about Nebraska in about ten minutes," winning first prize. Helen gave the prize to Kitten so that all four girls came away with something. A group of Brown University students served as dance partners for the girls and accompanied them to the movies. "Pete went with us" one evening, Polly wrote. "I like him an awful lot. *All* of them." Helen, recalling her own first trip to Europe, looked indulgently at this shipboard flirtation,

---

[3] Julia Hubbard arrived in Villeneuve-lès-Avignon in the company of Mr. and Mrs. Lansing Warren. Warren was the *New York Times* bureau chief in Paris, and most likely a friend of Julia's father, a New York City attorney. Warren (like John Curtis) served in France during World War I in an American Field Service ambulance corps. In 1942, both Warrens were arrested and interred by the Germans, held first in Lourdes and later in Baden-Baden, Germany. To stave off boredom, the prisoners organized a "university." Warren taught literature courses to his fellow prisoners, describing books from memory. Following his release in 1944 he filed the story of his internment with the *New York Times*. He returned to Paris in 1945 when the bureau there re-opened. In 1955 the French government awarded him the Croix de Chevalier of the Legion of Honor. *New York Times*, November 17, 1987.

writing to John that "Pete and Polly have had a good time together, playing shuffleboard and exploring the boat."

Six days after departing from New York the ship docked in Plymouth, and Helen's party briefly went ashore. "We all saw Lillian Gish, and Anne had her picture taken with her for the London papers." The next day the ship arrived at Boulogne, and Helen's group took the boat train to Paris, where they were booked at the Hotel Cecilia, where Helen and her mother initially stayed in 1914. Over the next four days, and in two cars driven by Europe on Wheels chauffeurs, they took in the high points of the city. The Bois du Boulogne and the Hotel des Invalides. Sainte-Chapelle, that stained-glass jewel box, where they heard a concert performed by choir boys accompanied by traditional instruments—for the admission price of twenty cents. The Latin Quarter, the Sorbonne, Notre Dame, and the Church of the Sacré-Coeur on Montmartre. They shopped the Galleries Lafayette and the book stalls along the Seine. Evenings were full. The party attended the opera *Mignon* at the Palais Garnier, Paris's grand opera house; and went to the Louvre to see the sculptures illuminated at night. "The Winged Victory was marvelous," Polly wrote to her father. "The hall and staircase were completely dark where she stands, then she had a very bright indirect light thrown on her. It was thrilling. Tell Jeanne that I took a good long look for her."

One evening Helen hosted Georges Plasse, his wife Louise, and step-daughter Malov at dinner at the hotel. Georges was the artist John and Helen met on the boat on the way to Paris in 1926 and visited again in 1930. "We had a marvelous time, with a long table for nine of us, and lots of fun." Afterwards Helen and Polly stayed and talked with their guests at length in the hotel salon. "Malov is dying to come to America. They all are."

En route to Chartres, the group spent several hours at Versailles. There they toured the palace, with the exception of Marie Antoinette's private rooms, which were being readied for the visit of the British monarchs George VI and Queen Elizabeth the following week. For once Helen was glad to miss an encounter with celebrities, even royalty. "They say no one will be able to stir out-of-doors or cross a street or visit a public building without special permits, so perhaps it is better to be here now." They wandered the Grand and the Petit Trianon, and Marie Antoinette's whimsical peasant village, the Hamlet. Lunch was at the Hotel de la Providence, and Helen charmed the chef into giving them a tour of the kitchen, where they marveled at the array of pewter, brass, and copper pots.

The travelers reached Chartres on the eve of Bastille Day, catching a glimpse of the cathedral at twilight. Later they joined the torchlight parade held in anticipation of the national holiday. The following day, after watching a military parade, they returned to the cathedral, where the four girls, along with one of the chauffeurs, climbed the two hundred steps to the top. Bastille Day was capped off with a dazzling display of fireworks.

From Chartres they spent three days in the Loire Valley, visiting the fabled chateaux: Blois, Chaumont, Amboise, Chenonceau, Azay-le-Rideau, and Loches. [4] "We all have special chateaux," Polly wrote. "We each choose the ones we like unless someone else has [chosen it] first, and then we have fun telling everyone where they are going to sleep and who is going to cook, etc. It's great fun."

Retracing the route of earlier trips through the towns of central and southern France, Helen's mood was reflective, often wistful. "I don't know that I like going through this familiar country without both of you," she wrote to John and Jeanne. "It seems as if we ought all to be seeing it together. There are so many recollections tied up with all these places." The quieter settings, and the smaller towns of this trip matched Helen's mood. "Paris was thrilling, of course, but I care less and less for the big cities, and more and more for the quaint and charming places.... Paris is too much made up of extravagant places to eat, touristy hotels and people, with an occasional museum to go fast-racing through. The whole thing is so artificial, compared to the exquisite charm and atmosphere of a place like this."

Contributing to Helen's reflective mood was the presence of so many old friends and acquaintances. Not only Georges Plasse in Paris, or the familiar faces they would meet again in Grasse and in Italy, but friends who joined them along the way. Julia Wattles, who met them in Chartres and traveled with the group through the Loire Valley, was a childhood friend from Crete. Like Helen, Julia had pursued a career: as head of the home economics department at the University of Nebraska. She met her husband, a prominent Omaha banker, when he was serving as food administrator for Nebraska during the First World

---

[4] It is curious that Helen does not mention the visit to Chaumont in her letters. Polly does, but she says nothing about her mother's time there during the war. Instead, she tells her father about the origins of the town's name (Chaud Mont, literally "hot mountain," site of a former volcano) and praises the chateau with its view of the Loire.

War. Widowed since 1932, Julia was traveling with her eighteen-year-old son Gurdon, a welcome companion for the girls. "Julia and I had such a good time, talking over old times and old friends."

Unlike the trips of 1936 and 1937, where the tours stayed in the grand hotels of major cities, this year saw Helen's group often booked into monasteries or convents; some of those now repurposed as guest houses, others—as in Assisi, where they stayed at the convent of Poor Clare Sisters from America—still active religious foundations. Helen described their hostel in Chartres, located in a former monastery, with its rose gardens and ivy-covered tower, as "the most enchanting place you have ever seen."

The presence of the trusted Europe on Wheels chauffeurs allowed Helen time away from her charges. In Rocamadour she begged off a day of sightseeing. "I wanted to catch up on letters, and accounts, and have a little time to myself," she wrote to John. "This afternoon I went over to the little church to see the ivory Madonna again.. . . Then I walked up to the fortress and hung over the wall, and remembered how we heard the nightingales sing there one late afternoon a long time ago." From Cannes, Helen, in the company of Julia Maier, left the girls in the care of Grace Howe and the chauffeurs and slipped away for a day to visit Carl's grave at Roquebrune. It was her third visit to the cemetery where her brother was buried. "I took a great bunch of long-stemmed white gladioli, with red lilies and Blue Nile lilies. The cemetery is a lovely place; high, high above the sea."

From Cannes it was a short distance to Grasse. "We walked down through the market place and the old gate. It was so familiar. I felt so at home," Polly wrote to Jeanne. But Helen noticed the changes. At the Fragonard Parfumerie, she inquired about Daphne and Georgette, daughters of the family who, six years earlier, hosted the Christmas dance recital. "Daphne came down. She is a lovely lady, very chic and charming, eighteen now. Georgette is married and lives in England, and is about to have a baby. [Daphne] thought Polly was Phebe at first because she was so tall." Later, Polly and Helen joined Stella Cobden-Sanderson at her villa for tea, and then went in search of the maids, Fifi and Cecile. They found only Cecile and her father. "Fifi and her husband are working somewhere. They have one little girl, five years old. Tourlaque," Helen wrote, "looked very desolate, with vines and hollyhocks growing in a tangle all over the front door." Still, "the place made me homesick for the peace and beauty and quiet of France again."

In late July the group sailed from Cannes aboard the *Conte di Savoia*, for Italy. Helen recalled their arrival at Cannes six years earlier, "when we landed . . . with six children and thirty-seven pieces of baggage!" They were compensated for missing the King and Queen of England in Paris when they saw the Duke and Duchess of Windsor, the former King Edward VIII and Mrs. Simpson, disembarking at Cannes. "It was very exciting," Polly reported. "They looked very happy. And both were so much nicer looking than their pictures make them out to be." Arriving the next morning in Naples, the travelers glimpsed Mount Vesuvius, before boarding an excursion boat for Capri and the Blue Grotto. Back on the mainland, they met their Italian Europe on Wheels drivers, and headed to Ravello. This was the town John and Helen visited in 1926, and of which they were so enamored that they changed their plans and lingered there. Helen's group was booked at the Hotel Palumbo, formerly a bishop's palace, more recently a monastery. They dined on the terrace of their hotel, overlooking the water, filled with fishing boats, "each with a star-like light. It looked just as if the sky had slipped into the water." Adding to the romance of the evening was the fact that the hotel's electricity went out midway through dinner. "We finished our supper by kerosene lamp light," Polly wrote. "It was just like Tourlaque."

From their base in Ravello, the group made excursions to Pompeii and Paestum, trips which took them along the Amalfi coast. Pompeii, buried in the eruption of Mount Vesuvius in 79 A.D., was undergoing excavation. Italy's fascist government, as part of its project of restoration of the nation to the greatness that was Imperial Rome, was funding the project. "But we didn't get to see much of it," Polly wrote, "as it was frightfully hot and only a few of us wanted to go, including Anne and I." Next was Paestum, the Greek settlement of Poseidonia, founded in 600 B.C. There they saw the magnificent ruins of the three temples, built to honor Athena, Hera, and Poseidon.

Helen noted the visit to Paestum in a letter to Jeanne, but her descriptive powers and romantic sensibility were most evident in her letter to Anita Zahn:

Now we are at Paestum, taking a little rest after visiting the magnificent Greek temples. The guide told us that a group of Greek dancers from Germany had just given a great festival here, and we wondered if it could possibly have been Tante [Elizabeth Duncan] and her group. It is the most perfect setting you have ever seen, these three great ruins silhouetted against the sky. . . . The stone has turned a warm golden shade. . . . But it's frightfully hot. The place just quivers with heat. After a little rest we are going down for a swim on the beach. They say the sand is golden, too. Perhaps we'll dig up a buried Venus from the sea, or a beautiful marble column, or a lovely fountain that the Saracens tried to carry away. . . . Only a few weeks ago a fisherman brought up a bronze head of Neptune.

Arriving in Rome, the group stayed in the private apartment of an Italian noblewoman, another example of European aristocracy turning to the travel industry for economic survival. They visited St. Peter's Basilica, and took refuge from the heat in the gardens of the Villa Borghese. For Polly a highlight was the opera *Mephistopheles*, performed in the open-air at the Baths of Caracalla, with an orchestra of 300.

After three days in Rome the group headed to the Tuscan hill towns. Lunch was at Orvieto, followed by a tour of the cathedral. Next came Assisi, where they stayed in the convent maintained by American nuns. They visited the tiny San Damiano church and the basilica, the burial site of St. Francis, its walls decorated with frescoes by Giotto. Then Perugia, with its Etruscan ruins, and on to Rimini where, in contrast to Assisi, they were booked at a luxury hotel. Conforming to the setting, the girls donned silk dresses for dinner, and an orchestra provided music for dancing. "Some of us danced with some young cavaliers that the hotel man introduced. One was a baron, and the son of the German consul in Turin, which interested Mummy." This was more than a case of seeking out a connection with an important person; Helen's brother Carl had, after all, served as American consul in Turin. From Rimini they made an excursion to the tiny Republic of San Marino, "on top of the world ... with the most marvelous clouds all around." Braving an impending thunderstorm, they explored the narrow streets of the town, returning to Rimini in a torrent of rain.

The rain proved to be a welcome respite from the August heat. Wherever they went in Italy, Helen made time for the girls to go swimming, either at hotels (none of which, of course, were air-conditioned) or in nearby lakes or the sea. The "hilarious time" that Helen noted the girls enjoying on shipboard continued throughout the trip. "The four of them seem to be having a superb time, giggling over everything." Polly provided her father with details of one escapade, involving Anne Kaufman. Returning to Ravello from Paestum, intending to spend the evening writing letters, Polly placed the tray with its inkwell on the white bedspread, and then sat on the bed, spilling the ink. "Anne and I had the giggles." Anne fetched a glass of hot water, and the girls dipped the stained coverlet over and over until they had almost removed the stain. "The last glass of water that Anne brought she was laughing so hard she had to put it down in a hurry so she wouldn't spill it, and the box that she put it on tipped over and the glass spilled and the water soaked all the way through. It was all very funny." Polly also related an episode from Assisi. At the Convent of the Poor Clares, each bedroom bore the name of a saint on a sign above the door. Helen, without her glasses, hastily read the name "St. Clare" on Polly's door as "St. Glacé"—St. Ice Cream. "Good Saint Clare," Polly wrote to her father, "will she ever live it down?" Polly enclosed a drawing entitled "The Martyrdom of St. Ice Cream," showing herself flat on her back on the bed, the name "St. Glacé" above the door, and the room's furnishings sketched out: candle, water bowl and pitcher on the nightstand; crucifix and picture of the saint on the wall; a small arched window showing cypress trees and church tower in the distance.

This is a picture of the "Martyrdom of St. Ice Cream." My bed at the convent in Assisi was as hard as rock. I could not make a dent in it. The tile floor was cold as ice, and the mosquitoes in spite of screens were as big as hawks. The water was freezing, the pictures stern and the pillows, logs. Amen.

Despite the silliness, Helen praised Polly's growing maturity. She noted that Polly's focus in shopping had shifted from buying things for herself to buying for others, especially her father and sister. "She has stuck to her budget nobly." Polly was proving to be a big help to her mother with the tour group. "She practically packs all the girls' bags now, as they are getting so full of gifts." And Helen proudly relayed a compliment that Polly received from their chauffeur in France: "He thought she was one of the gayest, most gallant, most democratic girls he had ever met."

Helen wrote that she hated to leave the lovely coolness of Rimini for another big city, "but Florence is always thrilling." There they stayed in a villa near the Boboli Gardens. The first night they dined by candlelight around a dark oak refectory table, served by a maid, and a butler in white gloves. "It was so nice and homelike," Polly wrote; adding wryly, "especially the white gloves?" From Florence they went to Siena. Just as Helen had planned the 1937 trip so as to be in Budapest for the Feast of St. Stephen, this trip landed them in Siena in time for the Palio, the horserace conducted twice a year, on July 2 and August 16, in the shell-shaped Piazza del Campo. The medieval pageantry surrounding the centuries' old competition between Siena's often contentious *contrade*, or neighborhoods, made up for the lack of the folk festivals and pageants Helen's tours had encountered on earlier trips.

As the two months in Europe drew to a close, Helen's thoughts repeatedly turned toward home. "I thought of you constantly in Florence," she wrote to John, "and kept wishing you were with us." Polly caught her mother's mood, giving her father the countdown: Siena to Stresa, "and then a twelve-hour train trip to Paris, then two nights in Paris, then HOME. Just think! When you get this, we will be on the boat for the good old U.S. Whoopeedoo!!!.... I'm already trying to decide what to wear off the boat." And Helen wrote to Jeanne from Assisi that "it will be so good to be back with you and Daddy. . . . I can hardly wait." But the same letter underlines the sense of impending change. "When we all get home, we'll give the finishing touches to whatever you need for college."

Yet, the most significant change was not apparent to Helen, or she chose not to see it. "My dear," she wrote to John from Rimini, "this is a most enchanting place. We must all come here together sometime." And despite the sadness invoked by the decrepit state of Tourlaque, she repeated Stella Cobden-Sanderson's suggestion that she and Polly take the villa in Grasse from October to February; John and Jeanne joining them over the holidays.

None of this would happen. Helen and her group sailed from Boulogne on August 20, once again aboard the *Statendam*, arriving in New York on August 28. A month and a continent away, Germany, Italy, England, and France agreed at Munich to the dismemberment of Czechoslovakia. Germany took the Sudetenland. Hungary took a swath of Slovakia. Poland seized Teschen—the town of Cieszyn, where a year earlier Jeanne, Polly, Bertha Baehr, and Pauline Fihe with her movie camera innocently crossed the border and filmed the young Polish soldiers. Eleven months later Adolf Hitler invaded the Polish Corridor. The Second World War had begun.

Chapter 11
After Europe

The outbreak of war in Europe, and newsreel images of Dutch and Belgian refugees fleeing into France, led Helen to embark on a new venture. She established the Refugee Relief Workroom in Summit to collect and send clothing and supplies to France. Within a month French defenses collapsed, and the British evacuated 300,000 men, including French troops, from the port at Dunkirk. In early autumn the Germans imposed a naval blockade around the coastline of France.

Helen quickly adapted, redirecting supplies to Great Britain. With England on a total-war footing, civilian goods were in short supply, a situation that worsened with the Battle of Britain. From July 1940 through the autumn, the Luftwaffe pounded the industrial cities of Great Britain. London endured the Blitz, fifty-seven consecutive nights of bombing, rendering thousands homeless and in need of basic necessities.

The Refugee Relief Workroom started in a vacant A&P grocery store on Springfield Avenue. It quickly outgrew the space, and was relocated across the street. The *Summit Herald* paid tribute to Helen's work, describing her as "a lady of quick action . . . [and] no small amount of determination and courage. No project is ever conceived by her . . . that is not carried through." Volunteers joined in with donations of clothing, blankets, shoes, and cash. Local businesses covered the cost of utilities; laundries and shoe repair shops cleaned and repaired donated goods. A young Summit woman working in Manhattan put together a sample case showing children's outfits that could be made from remnants, and on her lunch hour made the rounds of the garment district, persuading manufacturers to donate surplus goods. Volunteers who did not sew were put to work packing, labeling, and doing clerical work.

In the first six months, representing the efforts of over 1,000 volunteers from Summit and neighboring Chatham and Short Hills, the Workroom shipped 300 cases of clothing, blankets, and layettes, along with twenty-five barrels of shoes, to England. Those cases represented 35,000 garments and blankets. Supplies included 1,000 bars of soap, and toys and games for children's Christmas gifts.

Helen's efforts garnered attention in newspapers and magazines as far away as Ontario, Canada. *Commonweal* published a story on the Workroom; *Reader's Digest* reprinted the article, thus reaching a mass audience. [1] Summit was held up as a model of regional success, with forty-five cooperating groups in towns within a ninety-mile radius. The story noted the ways in which the war relief project overcame long-standing social class divisions in Summit. Armenian, Syrian, and Turkish workers from the silk mills—a population still served by Neighborhood House—volunteered at the Workroom at the end of their shifts. An Armenian laundry owner told the reporter: "I come (sic) to this country 28 years ago without a cent. This town has give me (sic) all I have. I sent two girls to college. Now is my chance to do something for America."

Fundraising events fueled the success of the Workroom. In October of 1940 Helen organized an evening of musical entertainment, raising $2,000. The Summit Playhouse, where John and Helen were still active, staged benefit performances. It was a return to the theater's origins: Summit's Playhouse Association was founded in 1918 as a World War I relief organization. In 1943, Helen organized a program around the theme of "Christmas in Many Lands," returning to a topic about which, in happier times, she had written for *Parents'* magazine, and revised into the "Christmas in Switzerland" chapter in *Jean & Company*.

John shared Helen's commitment to war relief work. In May of 1942 he took a leading role in organizing a gala for United China Relief. The Chinese Nationalist forces were led by General Chiang Kai-Shek, whose American-educated wife, in 1907, attended boarding school in Summit. With 400 people in attendance, the China Relief event raised over $5,000. John designed the decorations for the gala, and served as the evening's auctioneer.

While their parents were occupied with war relief efforts, Jeanne and Polly were moving into the next stages of their lives. Echoing the ways in which the First World War impacted John and Helen, the Second World War altered the course of their daughters' lives as well.

In 1938 Jeanne entered Swarthmore College, majoring in political science. Jeanne excelled in college. Years earlier, the headmistress of the

---

[1] *Commonweal* (July 18, 1941): 297; *Reader's Digest* (August 1941): 75-77; *The Windsor Star* (Windsor, Ontario, Canada), December 11, 1941.

Cours Maintenon told Helen that Jeanne had a "fine mind," and Jeanne's letters to her father during the summer of 1937 gave evidence of an intelligence beyond that of the typical sixteen-year-old. The description of Jeanne in the Swarthmore yearbook captured something essential:

> *Jeanne Hathaway Curtis* is never superficial. That she listens to serial radio skits, goes through all-night agonies writing papers, knits the most beautiful sweaters, or is an ardent patron of the slot machine, give you little clue to her personality. Underneath is Jeanne, the sincere idealist and perfectionist, who mixes easily with Jeanne who loves to have a good time. On top of the world one moment, at the bottom the next, she works tirelessly at whatever she has begun.

Jeanne graduated from Swarthmore in the spring of 1942, into a country at war. During her first year after college, Jeanne worked at the Henry Street Settlement on New York City's Lower East Side. Settlement work was consistent with Jeanne's idealism. Swarthmore's Quaker atmosphere had imbued her with a commitment to issues of racial equality. Jeanne developed an interest in African-American musical traditions; among the books on her shelf was James Weldon Johnson's 1925 *Book of American Negro Spirituals*.

In fall of 1943, looking to enter war work, Jeanne enrolled at The Pennsylvania School of Horticulture for Women in Ambler, Pennsylvania, thirty miles north of Philadelphia. Jane Bowne Haines, Ambler's founder, was born in 1869 into an old Quaker family. She graduated from Bryn Mawr, and taught history at the college before going to work at the Library of Congress. In 1905, Haines went to England and Germany to study schools of gardening. Five years later, she and several friends purchased a seventy-acre farm near Ambler on Pennsylvania's Main Line. Haines implemented a "hands-on, learning-by-doing" philosophy, in which students cared for the orchard, lawns, shrubbery, vegetable and kitchen gardens, did bee keeping, and raised poultry. They learned to use farm tools, and received instruction in carpentry and agricultural bookkeeping. Students took care of the horses, and mucked out the stables. During both world wars, the school trained women to grow and preserve food for the war effort. Philadelphia's social elite—a number of whom came from the country estates on the Main Line —regarded

Ambler as a "proper finishing school" for their daughters, "a school for country life." Along with farm studies, Ambler offered activities typical of college life: glee club, drama club, and formal dances. Graduation exercises were reminiscent of those at the Seven Sisters colleges, complete with May Day festivities and graduates in long white formal dresses carrying bouquets. [2]

In 1924 Louise Carter Bush-Brown was appointed director of the school, a position she held until 1952. A member of the school's second graduating class, Bush-Brown oversaw the expansion of the campus. With her husband, a faculty member at Ambler, she co-authored *America's Garden Book*, a number-one best seller. The couple founded *The Farmer's Digest*, a publication sharing the research of Ambler faculty and students with the wider public.

Jeanne did as well at Ambler as she had done at Swarthmore. She earned As in nearly every course, from Soil Chemistry to Beekeeping, Poultry to Farm Crops, Business Methods to Animal Husbandry. She was secretary and treasurer of the Dramatic Club, and a member of the Dairy Club and Riding Club. Jeanne worked her way through Ambler on an assistantship. Next to her senior photo in the 1945 yearbook is the listing "Student Position, *Farmer's Digest* '44, '45." Jeanne later said of the two years at Ambler that they were the happiest of her life.

Mrs. Bush-Brown became a friend and confidante of Jeanne. The two corresponded after Jeanne graduated. Jeanne affectionately addressed her as "Mrs. B-B." It was Mrs. Bush-Brown, along with Ambler's assistant director, Miss Anna Heick, to whom Jeanne confided, before telling her parents, of meeting Bruce Whitesell, her future husband. Jeanne's letters to the women, along with her wedding announcement and the birth announcement of her first child, John, were preserved by Louise Bush-Brown in Jeanne's student file at Ambler.

Jeanne was offered an opportunity to remain at Ambler as an instructor or to continue with the *Farmer's Digest*. But she had already applied to the American Red Cross. The Second World War ended in Europe in May 1945, and in the Pacific in September, but military bases at home and oversees still needed the services of the Red Cross. In October 1945, Jeanne was assigned to the base at Fort Indiantown Gap, Pennsylvania, a key demobilization site for troops returning from Europe. In February 1946 she was sent to Camp Atterbury, in Edinburgh, Indiana.

---

[2] Ambler merged with Temple University in 1958.

Six weeks after arriving at Camp Atterbury Jeanne wrote to "Mrs. B-B," describing the landscape of rural southern Indiana. "Can you understand what it means to . . . live surrounded by farm country . . . and not have a chance to get out and put in a whack at the work myself? You can imagine me falling out of bus windows to look at the farms I've passed." She wrote of visiting a farm to see a horse adopted by a soldier at the base. Although the skirt of her Red Cross uniform prevented her from riding, she walked the horse around the yard, and spent an hour grooming it. She told Mrs. Bush-Brown that she overheard the farmer remark, "There's a girl that really knows how to work around animals. I'll bet she'd be good on a farm."

But the same letter brought news that Jeanne's life would go in a very different direction. "I have found My Man, at least it looks that way to me." Cautioning Mrs. Bush-Brown that this was confidential information, Jeanne described meeting Edward Bruce Whitesell. Jeanne was hospitalized upon arrival at Camp Atterbury, having come down with German measles en route. Bruce was the doctor who admitted her, and

> he's been coming back every day since, for what reasons, at first, I couldn't imagine, but more latterly because he loves me very much, and I'm falling more and more in love with him. We just seem to fit together in every way, enjoy the same things for the same reasons. . . . It's as if we had known each other for years, and still found everything new and exciting. And I know my family would love him unquestioningly.

Bruce came from East Orange, New Jersey, and was a graduate of Princeton, Class of 1941. He entered the Army Medical Corps in 1943, and received his commission following graduation from Columbia University College of Physicians and Surgeons. Bruce completed an internship in surgery at Bellevue Hospital in New York, and residency at Cornell Medical School. He was then assigned to military bases at Carlisle Barracks, Pennsylvania and Camp Robinson, Arkansas. In November of 1945 Bruce arrived at Camp Atterbury, which, Jeanne wrote, "he hated till, well, to quote him: 'It's been wonderful since you've been here, Jeanne.' And that works both ways."

Jeanne and Bruce Whitesell.

Bruce and Jeanne were married on May 11, 1946, three and a half months after they met. Henry and Evelyn Perry, again living in Cincinnati, gave the couple their wedding at their home, echoing John and Helen's wedding given by Uncle Harry and Aunt Patty. [3]

John and Polly came to Cincinnati for the wedding. Helen did not. Helen was injured in an accident in Summit six weeks earlier, when the car in which she was a passenger collided with another vehicle. Helen spent time in the hospital recovering from her injuries, and was unable to travel to Jeanne's wedding.

Jeanne and Bruce returned to New York later that summer, following Bruce's discharge from the army. Bruce took a position at the Bronx Veterans Hospital where he spent the next several years before establishing a practice in general surgery at Summit's Overlook Hospital.

Upon her return from Europe in 1938, Polly attended Kent Place School. Her repeated pleas to her father in letters home that summer ("Please Daddy, let me go to Buxton . . . oh, please Daddy, let me go!") had fallen on deaf ears. Helen and John held firm in their resolve to place Polly in a more structured environment in order to force her to buckle down to schoolwork and earn grades sufficient for college admission.

---

[3] Helen returned the favor five years later, in September of 1951, when Henry and Evelyn's daughter, Evelyn Keys Perry, "little Evie" of the 1932 trip, was married in Summit. Helen hosted the wedding breakfast and reception at 8 Franklin Place.

Kent Place in 1938 was in many ways unchanged from the time of Helen's first acquaintance with the school thirty years earlier. The Seven Sisters-inspired rituals of the school were still in place, including the Daisy Chain. But the war made its presence felt. Every Saturday morning boarders at the school sewed for the Refugee Relief Workroom. The school's newspaper tallied up the contributions: baby kimonos, children's sweaters, knitted caps and socks. The girls made toy Scottie dogs which, sold at a craft fair, raised funds for the Workroom. "Mrs. Curtis," the paper noted, "is glad to have the work." Kent Place School's annual horse show and carnival in 1941 was turned into a benefit for British War Relief.

Although Polly entered Kent Place as a junior, she took three years to finish high school, graduating in June of 1941. In her final year, she entered an essay on Katherine Mansfield in a contest sponsored by the *Atlantic Monthly*, winning honorable mention. Polly applied for and was admitted to Vassar. Of the fifty-nine graduates of the Kent Place Class of 1941, thirty were admitted to Seven Sisters colleges.

Polly loved Vassar. She formed a lively circle of friends, foremost among them Blanche Ulmer. Vassar was close enough to New York City that Polly, along with Blanche (far from home in Jacksonville, Florida) regularly took the train to the city, where John made a day of it for the two girls: meeting them for lunch, taking them to a matinee, then dinner and an evening performance before seeing them to the train. John, Blanche said later, knew how to make "a little hick from Jacksonville" feel like such a lady. During her first summer vacation, in 1942, Polly worked with the Volunteer Land Corps on a farm outside Mount Equinox in Vermont.

Polly's major was Child Study. While on the face of it the name recalls the progressive approach to childrearing promoted by Sidonie Gruenberg and embraced by Helen, the program was at the center of a controversial curricular innovation: the School of Euthenics. The term was coined by Ellen Swallow Richards, a Vassar alumna and later instructor at MIT. Swallow's book, published in 1910, defined the word in its title: *Euthenics: The Science of Controllable Environment.* Scientific knowledge and democratic idealism would create an environment leading to the betterment of individual lives and society as a whole. Euthenics carried with it the optimism of the Progressive Era. It was linked to the social reform agenda which inspired many of the first and second generation of college women.

But by the time Vassar adopted the program in 1924, times had changed. The post-World War I decade saw a turning inward, an ebbing of the reform impulse, a premium placed on private life. This new mood merged with an enduring bias against college education for woman, critics believing that it rendered them unfit for, or undesirous of, a career as wife and mother.

The introduction of euthenics was greeted with dismay, even anger, on the part of many faculty members. Margaret Washburn, professor of psychology, charged that the new curriculum was "driving women back into the home, [to] the slavery of which education has helped us to escape." But with the generous bequest from Vassar alumna and trustee, Minnie Cumnock Blodgett, Vassar proceeded with the program, and a new building in which to house it. Child Study, and Polly's coursework, combined psychology and sociology courses with supervised work in the nursery school connected to Blodgett Hall. [4]

Polly wrote her senior thesis, "Let the Child Play: A Comparative Study of Dramatic Play Patterns of Children in Four Nursery Schools," based on observation conducted at the Blodgett Hall nursery school as well as nursery schools in Greenwich Village and Harlem. She included—using secondary literature—the preschool at Arthurdale, West Virginia, the New Deal community established in 1933 to provide housing and retraining for unemployed coal miners. Arthurdale was championed by Eleanor Roosevelt, who visited there frequently. The inclusion of Arthurdale, along with the Harlem nursery school, carries echoes of settlement house work and links Polly's project to earlier Progressive Era concerns with social reform. Moreover, her professor's praise of Polly's project indicates that Vassar's faculty found ways to subvert the conservative elements of the euthenics program.

Polly's class entered Vassar as the Class of 1945, but it has gone down in the annals of college history as "The Class with the Dash," the "Class of 1945-44." The class was fast-tracked to graduation so that its members would be free for war work. Polly took two English literature courses at Columbia during the summer of 1944 in order to graduate in December. That summer Polly got engaged to Elliott Foss Brown, a young Summit man serving with the Marines in the Pacific. But at some point, Polly called off the engagement. Jeanne noted as much in a letter

---

[4] Helen Lefkowitz Horowitz, *Alma Mater: Design and Experience in the Women's Colleges from Their Nineteenth-Century Beginnings to the 1930s* (Boston: Beacon Press, 1984), 295-299; "The Disappointing First Thrust of Euthenics," Vassar Encyclopedia, http://vcencyclopedia.vassar.edu/interviews-reflections/two-chapters/the-disappointing-first-thrust-of-euthenics.html; Helen Drusilla Lockwood, *The Meaning of Euthenics: An Essay on Action as a Tool of Knowledge* (Poughkeepsie: Vassar College, 1929), 5-12.

to Mrs. Bush-Brown at Ambler: "[Polly] is still somewhat heartsore from her broken engagement experience, and there is little worthwhile social life for her at home, but there is a Harvard med student of whom she saw a lot at the shore last summer and also for several weeks during the winter . . . who knows, maybe we'll both end up with doctors yet."

Following graduation from Vassar, Polly took a job at a nursery school in East Orange, where she supervised student nurses doing their pediatric practicum. Polly lived at home in Summit, commuting daily the ten miles to East Orange.

But things at home had changed dramatically. In December 1945 Helen and John separated, after twenty-five years of marriage. Jeanne, in a letter to Mrs. Bush-Brown that October, hinted as much, writing that "the general family situation is pretty tense (the worst is happening— tragic)." Helen took an apartment on W. 95th Street in New York City, and accepted a salaried position as director of European post-war relief efforts with the newly-formed Church World Service. In her new position Helen oversaw the collection and warehousing of clothing, soliciting remnants from mills and factories, making new garments, drafting publicity materials and patterns volunteers could use to make clothing for donation. Helen maintained contact with Church World Service workers on the ground in Europe, and served as a liaison with relief organizations at home.

John remained at 8 Franklin Place, running the decorating business from the converted barn behind the house. Polly lived with her father while working in East Orange, but spent weekends with her mother in New York, and regularly joined Helen one night a week for an evening at the theater.

What happened? Jeanne's letter to Mrs. Bush-Brown offers a brutal assessment.

> At home we understand that it just was not meant to be
> from the start, that both Mummy and Daddy did a pretty
> commendable job of bringing up two grand/daughters to
> the age where they could face life maturely and make their
> own way in the world; that they did this with an incredible
> minimum of outward friction; when they had from the start

almost nothing in common to build on, and were perhaps two of the loneliest and most suffering souls imaginable in their own house, lacking love and having only us to dream for.

Jeanne's sympathies lay with her father. Of her mother she wrote, "I feel she is pretty unhappy and lonely, actually, and feels, probably justly, that much of the family trouble has been her fault." Jeanne conceded that her mother "couldn't help being the way she was, any more than Daddy could." But her father "is really a new man. He has the advantage over Mummy of facing the whole thing much more honestly and realistically—there is no attempt at self-justification because he sincerely feels he needs none." For years, "he tried to be what Mummy wanted or imagined he was, and finally discovered that he could be no other than honestly himself."

How much of this is true? This letter to Mrs. Bush-Brown is the same one in which Jeanne wrote happily of finding "My Man," rejoicing that "we just seem to fit together in every way." Jeanne and Bruce's marriage would end, thirty years later, in divorce. Endings do not necessarily negate beginnings.

Jeanne's claim that her parents had "almost nothing in common" is not true. Helen and John shared their work. They shared a love of Europe, of travel. They shared the experience of World War I: John as an ambulance driver in France and his time in the navy; Helen with the YMCA. They knew each other for eight years before they married, during which time they shared a love of theater, something they continued as members of the Summit Playhouse. And they shared the commitment to World War II relief work.

Nevertheless, there were clues. There were the long absences: the year that Helen took Jeanne and Polly to Europe in 1932-1933, and the three summerlong trips of the later 1930s. Helen traveled elsewhere without John. She went to Mexico in 1935 with a woman friend and client, returning home upon news of her mother's death. Helen and Uncle Harry went to Venezuela in 1939. Helen returned, only to leave again, taking Jeanne and Polly out west, without John. Joining the three Curtises on that trip were Helen's sister-in-law Evelyn, and Evelyn's sons Henry and Howard. The trip took them to Nebraska—where Helen paid a sentimental visit to Crete—and then to San Francisco for the World's Fair. There they joined Carl's widow Mai-Mai and her children, living, since Carl's death, in San Diego. It had fallen to Brother Tom to intercede with the State Department one final time, petitioning to bring the family, including Mai-Mai's nephew Horace, never legally adopted by Carl, to the United States.[5] In San Diego Mai-Mai worked as a store clerk. The extended Perry family continued to support Mai-Mai; Big Helen hired the children for chores to give them pocket money.

Despite Helen on occasion pointing out that she and John were frequently separated for business or family reasons with no unhappy consequences ("home and household ... have been rather the sweeter for the brief respite") these absences may have taken a toll. On the other hand, periods of separation were not unknown in Helen's family. Her grandfather Thomas Doane spent months at a time in Crete, with Louisa often remaining in Charlestown. Helen's father Brainerd was away for weeks at a time on fundraising trips. And John *did* join Helen and the girls in Europe in 1932 and 1933, and at the start of the 1936 trip.[6]

Money may have been an issue. In a letter to Jeanne, Polly wrote that "[Daddy] has always been reckless and foolish about money, but that was unimportant; he brought so much happiness." Uncle Harry provided significant financial support to John and Helen during their marriage. It was he who purchased the house at 8 Franklin Place, and set John and Helen up in the business. And it was Helen who hustled to keep the business afloat, and to provide the level of income that allowed for the life to which she aspired since she first encountered it in Summit thirty years earlier. From freelance writing to taking Jeanne and Polly to Europe in 1932 to publishing two books and working as a tour guide, it was Helen who, in the words of that syndicated newspaper article, kept the pot on the boil.

Not that John was unsuccessful. He secured commissions throughout New England, proof of a reputation beyond Summit. Like Helen, he had an entrepreneurial streak, giving lectures at the Metropolitan Museum in New York and at venues in suburban New York and New Jersey. But finances may have been a source of strain.

---

[5] The official "Report of the Death of an American Citizen Abroad", dated a month after Carl's death, indicated that his passport had been "amended for use by the widow and her two children alone." Tom wrote on July 1, 1928, to State Department officer Mr. Wilbur Carr: "You will undoubtedly remember my brother, Charles B. Perry, who was in the consular service some ten years. . . . You may possibly remember that I called on you a couple of times, in the course of straightening out some of my brother's personal financial affairs, and much appreciated your cooperation." This was the same Mr. Carr who wrote to Big Helen in 1915, telling her of Carl's imminent dismissal from the State Department.

[6] Helen did write "Jean's father" into several chapters of her book. The character was working as an engineering expert in Russia, thus able to occasionally join Jean and the mother. This was far from John's actual profession; a job in Russia was once, in fact, offered to Helen's engineer brother Henry. In fairness, Helen could hardly have sent the husband/father to the Soviet Union as an interior decorator.

Ultimately, the explanation may lie in Helen's reluctance to marry in the first place. One reason for her reluctance may have been the difference in age. At the time of her marriage Helen was 32, John 26. The age difference reflected a gap in professional status. When Helen accepted John's proposal, she had been the director of the State Museum in Trenton for three years. John, by contrast, graduated from Columbia and immediately went to France as an ambulance driver, followed by a year in the Navy. At the time he and Helen married, John was just beginning his professional life.

Helen faced the dilemma, not of *balancing* career with marriage, but of career *versus* marriage and motherhood. In the 1920s, public and private-sector employers had policies against hiring married women. In marrying, Helen sacrificed a career she loved. Did she carry some residual resentment?

Helen's mother's diary from those years is revealing. As early as 1917, Big Helen wrote that she liked John, but "Helen does not, sufficiently, to suit him. I am very sorry for him!" In the memoir written in 1933 for her family, Big Helen recalled that "John Curtis was ubiquitous, and I had my doubts about this." As late as two weeks before John and Helen got engaged, Big Helen wrote that her daughter returned home at 1:00 a.m., telling her that "J.C. will not take no for an answer," and Helen was "very blue and forlorn abt. J.C." A few days later Big Helen wrote that she "had long talk with Helen abt. J.C. and her other beaux." Helen was still seeing Donald Rice and John Wimmer ("two other men were in the race. . .") right up to the time she agreed to marry John. Helen may in the end have succumbed to family pressure. Aunt Patty and cousin Edward both weighed in, in favor of John. And there is that extraordinary letter from Aunt Patty: "My dear John Curtis: Congratulations. . . . I don't mind telling you that I think my niece has been pretty hard on you. . . ."

Polly, in a letter to Jeanne, provided the most telling clue. "Mummy told me once that the man you marry must be someone, not whom you *want* to love more than anything or anyone else in the world, but whom you can't help loving more than anyone else in the world."

In the summer of 1946, Polly, at the suggestion of longtime friend Elizabeth Uptegrove, went to teach at the Army Air Corps base on Oahu, Hawaii. The move promised adventure. For Polly it was also an escape from a stressful situation, dividing her time between her parents. "I had to get away", she wrote to Jeanne from Hawaii. "I had a wonderful time living with Daddy this past year but I had to get some new perspective. I needed a vacation from them, and from myself. I had to get away to find out how much they mean to me." She added: "I've always been much closer to Mummy in letters than with her, and she's written me some wonderful ones these last couple of weeks."

At a Christmas party on base, Polly met Russell Wells. Born at Fort Dix, New Jersey, Russ came from a military family. He experienced frequent moves; twice to the Canal Zone, where he attended high school. He went to the Canal Zone Junior College, graduating in 1941. Following Pearl Harbor, Russ joined the Army Air Corps.

In early March, 1947, Polly wrote to Jeanne and her father describing events of the previous weeks, beginning with the Christmas party. "Everything happened so gradually and naturally." Not so gradually! By New Year's, "I began to realize how Russ felt." Russ proposed to Polly at the end of February. "He's sweet and gentle . . . and I love him so much. I never knew I could love anyone the way I love him."

Elizabeth Uptegrove also got engaged to a young officer she met at the Christmas party. The objections of her family to the whirlwind courtship led Elizabeth to call off her engagement. Not so Polly. The end of March found John writing to Russ.

Your letter has given me the greatest comfort and assurance. My heart and mind have naturally been full of concern. . . . [But] what she has written about you: your gentleness, your consideration for her happiness, the many little things that are really the big things, all stack up most favorably. . . . I shall be so glad to know you and look forward terrifically to meeting and talking with you. Thank you again for your good letter. You have my blessing. I have complete confidence in you. My love to you. John.

Polly and Russ were married on April 20, 1947, at Christ Church in Kealakekua, Hawaii. John flew to Hawaii to walk Polly down the aisle. Polly wore her mother's wedding dress: the heirloom gown first worn by a great-great aunt in 1830. Polly also wore the lace wedding veil brought by John from Ireland, intended for Helen. Elizabeth Uptegrove, in daffodil yellow silk, was Polly's only attendant. A simple reception was held at the home of the pastor; friends gathered at Russ and Polly's new cottage to cut the wedding cake and dance to Hawaiian music. Helen did not attend Polly's wedding. "Mums most sweetly said she'd come later; she'd wait until we could have a nice calm visit."

Three weeks later Elizabeth Uptegrove wrote to Jeanne: "Never have a seen a happier pair! I mean it! Polly simply floats and Russ beams. And I sit back and stare!!" Polly "has done wonders" with the little cottage on base; "she has made it into a charming first home as only she could . . . all the rooms (all four of them!) spell Polly."

Helen kept her promise to visit, arriving in Hawaii in mid-June for a two week stay. On July 1, Polly and Russ put Helen on a plane to Honolulu for the first leg of the trip home. Returning to the cottage, they found a telegram from Jeanne. John was found dead in his room at the Columbia University Club in New York City. The cause of death was "Submersion. Visceral Congestion," indicating that John suffered a heart attack and then drowned while in the bathtub. He was fifty-three years old. The obituary in the *Summit Herald* cited only "natural causes." Polly and Russ were unable to reach Helen until the next day to notify her of John's death. It fell to Jeanne to identify her father's body.

Polly and Russell Wells.

Polly's letter to Jeanne reflected her shock and grief. "I just can't believe it. . . . He was so young and had so much to live for. He had so many nice things planned. . . . I'm so happy he came for the wedding. He loved the island, and wanted to come back." Polly told Jeanne that John had given her "glowing reports . . . of all the good jobs he had for the summer." He would have loved being a grandfather, Polly mourned; "I wanted to give him a grandchild as a way to thank him for what he's done for us."

Helen gave up her job with Church World Service and the apartment in New York, returning to 8 Franklin Place. She took over the decorating business, and ran it for the next thirty years.

By the early 1950s Jeanne and Bruce were living in Summit. They bought a house at 203 Summit Avenue, in the neighborhood where Uncle Harry and Aunt Patty had long resided. Jeanne and Bruce's oldest son, John, was born in 1949, followed by Tom in 1951, Margery (known always as Susie) in 1953, and David in 1965. In addition to his surgical practice at Overlook Hospital, Bruce worked for many years as the in-house physician at the Western Electric plant in Springfield, New Jersey. Jeanne enrolled in graduate school, pursuing a master's degree in social work at the New School for Social Research in New York. She completed coursework for a PhD. Bruce was supportive, but Jeanne lacked the confidence to present her thesis for defense, and never completed the degree.

Polly, meanwhile, lived the life of a military wife. Martha was born in 1948 in Hawaii. Russ's next assignment was Orlando Air Force Base, Florida, as an intelligence officer. By 1950 the family were at Mitchell Field Air Force Base on Long Island. Patricia was born in September of that year; Peter in March of 1952. Russ's next assignment was Sidi Slimane Air Force Base in French Morocco. Polly followed him, two months later, in October of 1953, flying to Morocco with three small children. The family lived off-base, on the beach in nearby Rabat. "There are as many children as Levittown, so [the girls] have lots of playmates. This beach is nearly all occupied by Americans, which makes it nice—probably narrow-minded of me— but over here it is better that way." Indeed. Morocco was experiencing the stirrings of decolonization movements, which, in 1956, resulted in its independence from France. While the Wells family was in Rabat, there were shootings and bombings, aimed mostly at the French, but Americans were not readily distinguishable from their European counterparts. The American military ruled the Medina, the Old City, off-limits, and naval and air force personnel were directed to wear uniform when off-base in order to distinguish them from the French.

Nor were external threats the only peril. In April of 1954, Russ and Polly were hospitalized for three months with infectious hepatitis. Neighbors stepped in until Helen, at age sixty-six and making her first transatlantic flight, arrived to take care of Martha, Patricia, and Peter.

The bout of hepatitis was not the end of the Wells family's troubles. After Helen returned home in mid-July, Russ contracted a mysterious virus and was re-hospitalized for three weeks, leaving Polly, suffering from a milder form of the illness, to cope on her own. Russ wanted the Air Force to fly his family home, but Polly resisted.

> All three kids went into shrieking hysterics of varying
> degrees: Martha was the only really genuine one because
> she loves school and her new friends here; Pishy because
> Marf was, and Peter because Pishy was. It was a very
> persuasive chorus. . . . I'm working against [returning
> home] for most reasons—mainly because I married him "for
> better for worse"—though this is slightly overdoing it. . . .
> Russ gave me strict orders not to write you our troubles—
> but knowing you to be a loving, un-hysterical, intelligent
> human being: *my MOTHER*, I figure I can write you
> anything I want—if not you, "whom" else?

After the two years in Morocco, Russ was assigned in September, 1955 to the Willow Run Air Force Base in Ypsilanti, Michigan, where their fourth child, a boy named Robbin, was born in March of 1957. Russ's next assignment was Offut Air Force Base and Fort Omaha, Nebraska. While in Nebraska Polly was able to fulfill a long-held desire to fly with her husband when, after much searching and looking involving the whole family, Russ bought a 1946 Ercoupe, a small two-seater plane. Polly and the children each enjoyed frequent opportunities to go up in the plane with Russ. In 1958 the family moved to Littleton, Colorado, where Russ worked at the Denver Federal Center and Lowry Air Force Base. Russ and Polly's last child, Christopher, was born in Colorado in 1959.

For Helen, the decades of the 1950s and 1960s brought both inevitable loss and unexpected tragedy. Aunt Patty Twombly had died in 1942, following a brief illness. In 1955 Uncle Harry, now ninety-two, suffered a fatal heart attack in the home on Hobart Avenue, where he had lived since 1908. Both Twomblys were eulogized by the Summit community in a manner befitting their decades of civic and philanthropic service.

In 1950, Helen's brother Henry ("Me and Henry") died after falling from a window on the fourteenth floor of his company's offices on 42nd Street in New York. Henry, just sixty years old, suffered from high blood pressure and had a history of fainting spells. He had just opened the window, whose sill was a mere twelve inches from the floor, when he apparently fainted and fell to his death. In 1957, Helen's brother Tom, along with Ethel, was struck by a car as they walked home together from a Christmas concert. The couple had lived for the last twenty-five years in Moorestown, New Jersey, where Tom was a materials engineer. Hospitalized for months, in rooms across the hall from each other, the two shared messages and visits from friends. Tom died as a result of his injuries in March of 1958. Ethel followed her husband in death in August of 1959.

Cousin Edward Twombly died in June 1969, from injuries sustained in a fall at home. Upon returning from France and the First World War, Edward followed his father into the legal profession. At the time of his death he was senior partner in his father's firm. Edward served on Summit's Common Council from 1921 to 1929. In 1930 he was elected to a two-year term as Summit's mayor. Edward's death brought back memories of the year in Summit when Helen and Edward scandalized Aunt Patty with clothes-basket races on the polished wood floors of the house on Hobart Avenue, or climbing into a second-story window after catching the last train from Hoboken.

On December 31, 1962, Polly's husband retired from the Air Force at the rank of major. Russ and Polly had long dreamed of settling on Martha's Vineyard. Their son Peter recalled that "every summer we would drive to Chappaquiddick from Colorado. The car was packed to the roof with kids, cats and a dog. For mom, it was coming home to her favorite childhood haunts."

In spring of 1963, at the end of the school year, the family moved into a rented house in Edgartown on Martha's Vineyard. Russ took a job with a private company, National Executive Airlines. On January 9, 1964, the plane he was flying as co-pilot developed engine trouble on takeoff and crashed. Both Russ and the pilot were killed. There were no passengers on board.

Polly's first letter to her mother following Russ's funeral is raw with grief. "Oh, Mummy," she wrote, "Of all the people in the world you are the closest to me, and I hope you know that I know your love is all around me."

"I go to the cemetery every evening," Polly continued.

I go for love, and I go for peace, and I go to breathe in strength and because I can see a lot of sky. If it's dark I can see all the stars. . . . I go to the beach a lot. The sea has always been a good companion to me. I love it . . . as Russ loved to fly. It's big and beautiful and roaring and endless, but it still helps to be near it, and I can sort out my thoughts and feelings and I'm less lonely when I'm alone with it.

At the same time, Polly resolved to go forward. "I have so much on my side. I have the children. Thank God I have the children.. . . Dear Lord, everyone is so good. There is so much love pouring in, we can't help but be all right."

Polly stuck it out on Martha's Vineyard for four years after Russ's death. She bought a house in Edgartown, which she rented out to "summer folk" every season, moving with the children to often primitive cottages at Manaca Hill or Cape Pogue. In 1967, feeling the need to be closer to her mother and sister, Polly moved back to New Jersey. She bought a 200-year-old farmhouse in Chatham Township. She took a job teaching nursery school, and learned to sew drapes and slipcovers for her mother's decorating business. She put all five of her children through college. Polly was active in civic affairs. She was a founder of the Historical Society of Chatham Township. She was cited for her work with the Park Commission (recalling Aunt Patty Twombly's dedication to parks and recreation). Her closest friend remained Blanche Ulmer Pavlis. The two managed to visit each other once or twice every year. Polly's daughters always knew when their mother was on the phone with Blanche. The two shared a friendship and frame of reference that stretched back to their days at Vassar.

They knew each other for seventy years, and were best friends from the day they met. [7]

Helen lived on in the house at 8 Franklin Place, sharing it with a series of boarders and companions. Also sharing the house was an orange cat named Murphy, a stray found on the Doane campus by Helen's granddaughter Patricia, a student at the college. Pat brought Murphy back to New Jersey, where he was welcomed by his fellow Crete native. Helen remained active in civic affairs. She maintained a wide circle of friends. She was a member of the Summit Garden Club, and continued her decades-long membership in the Playhouse and the Arboretum. Although always a gracious hostess, her culinary skills were limited— remarkable for someone who collected European cookware and dishes, and wrote articles for women's magazines describing European cuisine. She fell back on simple things "dressed up:" Campbell's tomato bisque soup served with a dollop of whipped cream and topped with peanuts. She frequently forgot a pan on the stove, getting involved with a visitor or phone conversation, and would simply fling the scorched mess, pan and all, into the woods behind her house. Helen prided herself on her fudge. She got into a friendly argument with a friend of Jeanne's husband over who made the best fudge; at some point a contest was arranged to resolve the dispute. Someone even produced a marble-top table to give the competition a professional cachet.

Helen continued to travel. In 1965 she took Jeanne's daughter Susie to Guatemala, where Evelyn, Henry's widow, owned a second home. The trip was an opportunity to share with Susie the discovery of native textiles and crafts, and to pass on to another generation the love of folk culture. Helen's love of handiwork continued: she knitted blanket after blanket for her grandchildren, their children, and those of her friends. Her grandchildren (they called her "Gan,") adored her. Never a coddling grandmother, she could be stern. But the grandchildren knew they were well-loved. She played Scrabble with them, allowing

---

[7] Blanche's life is worthy of a book. While visiting her brother, an attaché at the US Embassy in Greece, Blanche met Captain Anthony George Pavlis of the Royal Hellenic Navy. The two married in 1953. King Paul of Greece was best man at the wedding. At age fifty-six, Blanche applied to the Peace Corps. She was rejected because she was an older, married woman. She solved half of that when Tony, twelve years her senior, agreed to a divorce. Blanche served with the Peace Corps in Kenya. Polly visited her there, and the two went on safari. Blanche and Tony remarried at the end of her tour of duty. Polly and Blanche made a pact that they would honor their friendship by not attending each other's funerals. Blanche died in 2011.

them to have a dictionary in their laps so they could develop a good vocabulary. She still had a talent for connecting with famous people. "Most impressed with your going to cocktails with Bette Davis," Polly wrote to her mother. Helen was vacationing in Maine with brother Tom's daughter Frances, whose cottage abutted that of the actress; Frances had evidently inherited her aunt's special knack.

And she still ran the decorating business. Helen had a loyal group of clients, extending now to the children and grandchildren of longtime customers. Helen's granddaughter Martha, who joined her in the business, remembers buying trips into New York, where store owners hurried to open the door ("Welcome, Mrs. Curtis, welcome!") bowing as if she were visiting royalty. But she retained her Nebraska-bred egalitarianism. Once, calling at the home of a wealthy client in Short Hills, accompanied by Morris, her upholsterer, the client directed Morris to the servants' entrance. Helen went around to the back of the house with him. The client never again enforced the distinction.

In her later years Helen attended Summit's Unitarian Church, completing a journey begun as the daughter of a Congregational minister. She served as honorary trustee of Doane College. She returned to Crete numerous times over the decades. She last went to Doane in 1972, for Patricia's graduation and the dedication of the Merrill Hall Memorial Tower celebrating the college's centennial. A citation read on the occasion summarized Helen's education at Doane and Columbia, her museum work, her time in France with the YMCA, her wartime relief efforts. "For twenty years she traveled widely and frequently in Europe, where she studied handicrafts, decorative arts, costume and folkways. These experiences were the subject of freelance writing and two books." The tribute concluded: "Helen Perry Curtis combines in an extraordinary way sophistication with humility, artistry with naturalness, wisdom with youthfulness, and curiosity with patience."

A letter written by Helen's nephew, Howard Perry, provides a glimpse into Helen's life in its ninth decade. Howard, who as a nine-year-old boy shared those months in Grasse, came to Summit in February, 1971, with his teenaged son Jeb, for a three-day weekend. Driving into town, "we spotted the blue-clad, white-haired figure cruising along on foot, and stopped to offer her a ride. I am completely sure that, had we not been friends, she would have disdainfully refused to give up the rest of her walk, being after all only 83 and in good spirits."

Howard and Jeb's visit coincided with the celebration of Jeanne, Bruce, and Helen's February birthdays, with "more presents then I have seen under most Christmas trees." The festivities moved from 8 Franklin Place to "the immense halls" of the Whitesell home, and then to Polly's house in Chatham. "The champagne kept the evening humming, we were all buried in cake and ice cream, and Jeb and I could only squeeze in about 15 minutes of basketball-in-the-rain-between-parked-cars; and it was so dark we never found whose cars got the dents." Next day saw a marathon game of Scrabble. "The battle raged, with no quarter given or received;" the team of Howard and Jeb eking out a narrow victory. But the next day, "following a fantastic meal prepared single-handedly by [Helen] with no apparent strain," the Scrabble board again appeared. "This is a woman who does not like to lose!" Howard and Jeb got off to a seventy-point lead, but

> we watched that huge lead melt away under the relentless
> attack of the steely-eyed grandmother from Nebraska. She
> would not be denied, using incredible cross-combinations
> of words both known and unknown—until checked in the
> dictionary, where they invariably were to be found.

"I am always overcome," Howard concluded, "by the fantastic fun of 8 Franklin Place. Wall and door decorations painted long ago by the girls and Uncle John, still looking fresh and new, wild antiques, treasures, furniture, books, drawings. Always something new and exciting in that house. And with that great Aunt."

One thing was largely absent from Helen's life in its final four decades: travel to Europe. After all those European trips, eight in all between 1914 and 1938, Helen returned only twice: the brief stopover in Paris in 1954, on her way to Morocco when Polly and Russ were hospitalized; and 1970, for a trip through Greece and Italy. Helen took that trip in the company of longtime friend and neighbor, Grace Norton Rosé, along with Grace's daughter Joan and Joan's husband Upton. The younger people came along to assist Helen, age eighty-two, and Grace, at age eighty-five even older and decidedly more infirm.

Helen's final trip to Europe, 1970—still charming the ship's captain.

Why did Helen not return to Europe earlier? Perhaps the thought of the post-war devastation, or knowledge of what the war had wrought in places she loved, was too much to bear. It was, after all, little more than a decade after Helen enrolled Jeanne and Polly in the École Ste. Marthe in Grasse and the Cours Maintenon in Cannes that both schools were hiding Jewish children from deportation.[8] Schloss Klessheim, site of the Elizabeth Duncan School in Salzburg, where Jeanne and Polly danced, and about which Helen had written "in such a setting one could live only in beauty," was appropriated by Adolf Hitler for use as a meeting and guest house. The Teutonic Knights castle at Marienburg, on whose expansive grounds Helen and her tour group picnicked in 1937, became a favorite destination for Hitler Youth rallies. In 1945, Danzig and the surrounding region, where Jeanne noted the intersection of German and Polish culture, was ethnically cleansed; all traces of German culture ruthlessly expunged. Marienburg became the Polish city of Malbork; Danzig was renamed Gdansk. And Helen must have realized that the culture of folk costume and custom which had drawn her to Hungary, Czechoslovakia, and Yugoslavia had vanished forever in the war and Sovietization of those countries, now behind the Iron Curtain. Indeed, the Communist government in Hungary banned

---

[8] Fred Coleman, *The Marcel Network: How One French Couple Saved 527 Children from the Holocaust* (Washington DC: Potomac Books, 2013).

the Pearly Bouquet, the folkdance festival which had so enchanted Helen and her daughters. The festival's founder, the scholarly Béla Paulini, committed suicide.

It was not only world-historical events that transformed once-loved places, leaving those to be found only—and perhaps best—in the realm of memory. Helen made this poignant discovery during the 1970 trip to Italy, a country she first visited in 1914 and 1915 with her mother; returned to in 1926 and 1930 with John, and in 1933, 1937 and 1938 with her daughters. Over thirty years later, writing to Jeanne and Polly in September of 1970, Helen described Florence as "now a busy bustling, crowded, noisy city. . . . Pedestrians and cars and shrill motor cycles dodge around like beetles in all the main squares and narrow alleys, but nobody even turned a hair!—or even bothered to look around."

Other places evoked wistfulness and nostalgia. Of Pisa and San Gimignano, Helen wrote that "these places bring back happy memories of visits with my mother in 1915, and later trips with Daddy and Uncle Harry and one of the summers that I had a party of girls. Do you remember, Polly? I think it was the summer that Jeanne stayed home with Daddy." The summer of 1938, Jeanne preparing for Swarthmore, the penultimate summer of peace. "It made me sad not to be able to go to Bergamo and see the Previtalis. I don't even know if they are still alive." Rose Morrow Previtali, the American-born friend turned rural *padrona* and Mussolini enthusiast, an acquaintance of 1915, visited by Helen and John in 1926 and 1930, and with Jeanne and Polly in 1937. When did Helen lose touch with Rose? A friendship severed by war? Or by time and distance? Rose, in fact, died in Bergamo in the summer of 1963. "As I write this, I am remembering the little *pensione* where you girls and I stayed for a dollar and a quarter a day, including four meals, in that year that we came to Italy for the summer." The summer of 1933, the year Helen took the girls to Europe while John stayed home and kept the decorating business afloat and Helen wrote her way across the Continent, writing the stories that became *Jean & Company, Unlimited*. "Florence was different then."

A week later, with that summer of 1933 still in mind, Helen wrote to Jeanne from Venice:

> This afternoon I have been over on the Zattere, hunting for the little Palazzo that we had, Polly and you and I, for six

weeks, but I couldn't find it. Do you remember anything about it? I remember a little piazza near the water, with fishing boats tied up all along it, decorated with paintings of the Virgin, angels, etc., with lovely gold sails. Now the fishing boats no longer tie up there, they all have motors, and the golden sails are gone.

Even the still-recognizable sights brought memories tinged with sadness.

Today we rode up and down the Grand Canal in a Vaporetto to see the wonderful palaces on both sides. I remember when you [girls] picnicked way out beyond the Lido on the rocks . . . and the fishermen gave you shells and sea-horses. And do you remember how we gondola-ed in rented gondolas, and picnicked out in the lagoon to see the fishing boats go out at sunset? I miss Ricardo and Favai, and our other good friends here. We had some good times, didn't we?

But time, Helen discovered, also heals. Twenty-five years after her separation from John and his sudden death eighteen months later she could write: "We had luncheon today . . . at the old Pensione Fiallo, where Daddy and I stopped several times. It is an old palace, with a lovely garden. . . . I loved remembering the times that Daddy and I were there together."

In the end Helen remained, as always, the optimist; alert to the present and able to find something uplifting even in the midst of profound change and loss. Her descriptions of Europe's landscapes were as vivid as ever. "This is hill country," she wrote of Florence, "with towers and dark, pointed cypresses on each hilltop, and silvery olive trees and vineyards climbing up the sides." She described their hotel in Venice, the Metropole Venezia, with its "crystal chandeliers, Oriental rugs, and the furniture all painted in the Venetian manner, fruit and flowers and lots of gold rococo. . . . We have great rooms on the Grand Canal, and spend most of our time hanging out the windows."

And she recognized too that, while her Europe might be gone, for others the adventure was just beginning. "I am so impressed by the Youth Hostels and Student Hotels that we see, often in an old castle, or near some interesting historic spot. And lots of camping too. Young people can certainly get around now!"

Five years after Helen wrote those words, I went to Europe for the first time, figuratively armed with my copy of *Jean & Company, Unlimited*, its descriptions imprinted on my mind, to see for the first time the places already familiar to me from its pages. Over the next five decades, a span of time longer than that of Helen's trips, I returned repeatedly: for research or, increasingly, just to *see* it, just to *be* in Europe, in places about which I taught, places I had always longed to go, and to which I never tired of returning.

But the day came when I recognized that the Europe I knew, the familiar faces and places which defined Europe for me, were passing away. The sale of the *pension* in Vienna where I stayed on several occasions; the sale of the restaurant where, year after year, the owner and the waiter recognized me the moment I set foot in the door, no matter the time that elapsed in between; the conversion of the dormitory where I lived to luxury apartments; all these signaled for me the end of an era, the end of my Europe.

In the course of writing this book I came across Eleanor Perényi's gorgeous memoir, *More Was Lost*. Perényi's Europe began in 1937 on a trip in the company of *her* mother. She was in Budapest the same summer that Helen last brought Jeanne and Polly there. The nineteen-year-old Eleanor's story could, in a flight of fancy, have been Jeanne or Polly's, had Helen managed, with her usual flair, to wrangle an invitation to dinner at the American Legation in Budapest. Instead it was Eleanor who, in that setting, met Zsiga, a Hungarian nobleman whose family estate lay in Ruthenia, territory disputed in that interwar era by Hungary, Poland, Ukraine, and Czechoslovakia. "This too," Eleanor wrote, "was still [merely] of academic interest."

Love followed, and marriage; the few short years together at Szöllös, and then expulsion and exile in the ethnic cleansing that accompanied the Second World War. Describing the flight from Szöllös, Perényi wrote: "When you leave a place you are never going to see again you are supposed to have a sort of premonition." She did not.

> I left as if I expected to be back the following week,
> straightening one of the little cherubs on each side of the
> clock. . . leaving the lid of the rosewood piano open . . . a
> hasty glance around the garden over which I had worked so
> hard. . . . I didn't pay any farewell calls. I didn't go to take a

last look at my trees in the orchard. I walked out with only one bag, got into the carriage to be driven to the station by Sandor as usual, and never looked back. [9]

Helen never had a premonition either. Writing to John from Rimini in August of 1938, she told him that "we must all come here together...."

I did have a premonition. On what has been the last day I ever spent in Vienna, I took a ride around the Ringstrasse on one of Vienna's signature red and white trams, the Number 1 *Strassenbahn* Line that ran clockwise round and round the Ring. It no longer does, I have learned, and that too is part of the story. So on that last trip around the Ring, an elderly lady carrying a dachshund boarded the tram. The woman took the seat directly in front of mine, and the dog, peering over its owner's shoulder, was an invitation to conversation. We passed the next minutes talking about her dog, my cats, and going home tomorrow. Then the woman pulled the signal cord, gathered up her dog, and alighted in front of the Hofburg. She bent to re-leash the dog, straightened up, and, turning back to the tram seeking out my window, with a lovely smile waved goodbye. Something clutched at my heart. "I'm not coming back here."

In my last decade of teaching, my students read Tony Judt's magisterial *Postwar: A History of Europe Since 1945*. Published in 2005, Judt's narrative is expansive and optimistic. Despite setbacks and reversals, the story of Western Europe, at least, was one of prosperity and peace, and of a European Union ever widening and deepening. Judt's decision to write the book came at the moment when the non-violent revolutions of 1989 paved the way for the re-integration of Eastern Europe into the mainstream of the Continent, a return to the "common European home."

Judt's Europe was my Europe: tolerant and progressive, open and accessible. It was appropriate that I first read huge chunks of *Postwar*— the proverbial chapter ahead of the students —while on a spring break trip to Europe. I read Judt's book on a train speeding back to Brussels, Europe's capital. Lifting my eyes from the pages, I could gaze out on the beloved landscape of my Europe.

---

[9] Eleanor Perényi, *More Was Lost: A Memoir* (Boston: Little Brown and Co., 1946; reissued, with introduction by J.D. McClatchy, New York: New York Review of Books, 2016), 267-268.

Now the relevant text is Ivan Krastev's elegiac *After Europe*. The dark politics of authoritarianism and xenophobia have re-emerged, threatening the hopes for a strong and unified Europe. The continent stands, as it did in the late 1930s, on the brink of an uncertain future. Krastev is hopeful that the shock of Brexit and the threats posed by populist regimes will reawaken Europeans to the importance of the values of democracy, reason, and tolerance; and that Europe will, as it has in the past, rise to the challenge.

I share in that hope.

But someone else will have to tell that story.

Myopic it is to think that a continent whose culture and history is measured in millennia should be defined by the decades of one's own experience. But thus it is. Helen's Europe was bookended by the last weeks of peace before the First World War, and the final days before the Munich Agreement ushered in the Second. In between, she saw Europe at its worst: from a trench on the Meuse-Argonne front. But she returned again and again, in the comparatively peaceful days of the 1920s and 1930s, when her love of costume and color led her to mistake a culture even then verging on anachronism for a timeless Europe. And when the second cataclysm came, her Europe was finished.

"So it is," Perényi wrote, "that one passes insensibly from one part of life to another, from the past into the future. You are never given so much as a glimpse of what you will become, and perhaps it is just as well.. . . For a long time, the memory of the past sustains you, and when it no longer does you are already a different person."

Thus there comes the time, as it did for Eleanor, and for Helen, when it is enough to sit on the terrace, gazing out over one's garden, "pondering all that history takes from us, and that memory restores." [10]

---

[10] Perényi, 269; J.D. McClatchy, Introduction, *More Was Lost*, xii-xiii.

Epilogue

From the moment I stepped off the plane in Newark that day in July, 2015 and met Helen's granddaughters Susie and Pat at the top of the concourse, our connection was instantaneous. We seemed to have known each other all our lives. Later, joined by Martha, we gathered around lunch laid out in the back yard of their Revolutionary War-era New Jersey farmhouse. The flow of conversation quickly established a shared love of books, gardens, pets, travel, and history. In the course of this, I casually mentioned my hometown, Ypsilanti, Michigan. Stunned silence, followed by gasps. Martha and Pat, they told me, along with their parents and younger brothers, had lived in Ypsilanti in the 1950s when their father Russell was assigned to the Air Force base at Willow Run. My family's home in those same years overlooked the Willow Run airport, separated only by a field and a highway soon to be upgraded to Interstate-94. Martha, Pat, and their parents were living just a short distance from us. Not long before the afternoon when Mom pulled a book off the shelf at Grandpa's house, "Here, you'll like this. . . ."

That afternoon Martha and Pat brought down box after box from the attic and closets, from under beds and from bookshelves. Letters, photos, travel diaries, magazine articles: a wealth of material documenting a life more fascinating, more historically significant than I had imagined. Walking through the house and looking at family portraits on the walls, I heard for the first time the names of artists Clara Sipprell and Jimmy Scott (who, we discovered, was born and raised in Racine, Wisconsin, where I have now lived for many years). I also grasped, that first afternoon, something of the long line of Doane and Perry ancestors, and the sturdy New England underpinnings of the pioneer Nebraska community and college where Helen grew up. I knew that Helen's life demanded a proper biography.

Over the course of this and subsequent visits to New Jersey I came to learn about the lives of Helen and John, Jeanne and Polly. I went with Susie and Pat to the Newark Museum, where Helen worked from 1915 to 1916. There we sorted through hundreds of documents relating to the Homelands Exhibit, reading documents dated one hundred years to the day of our visit. Susie and I spent another day at the New York Public Library's Performing Arts Division, reading through four cartons of the Anita Zahn papers. We had just opened the first folder in the box labeled "Correspondence" when Susie recognized her mother Jeanne's handwriting on a letter to Anita. We spent time at the Summit Historical Society, reading about the prominent civic roles of Uncle Harry and Aunt Patty Twombly, and about Helen's life in Summit. In October of 2016 I drove, along with my good friend Mary, twelve hours from Wisconsin to Nebraska, spending several days at what is now Doane University and at the State Historical Society in Lincoln, working my way through the Thomas Doane and David Brainerd Perry papers. Doane archivist Janet Jeffries, whose reply to my email in January of 2015 led to so much, carefully unpacked the folk costumes which Helen, Jeanne and Polly collected in the course of their trips across Europe, and which Martha and Pat donated to the museum in Crete following Helen's death.

I continued to visit Helen's granddaughters as the research and writing of this book progressed. It was on one of those visits that we found a box of letters written by Polly. The letters begin with Polly's move to Hawaii in 1946, meeting Russ, their whirlwind courtship and marriage, and continue through the various Air Force postings. Twenty-five of the letters were written from Ypsilanti between 1955 and 1957, the years Russ was stationed at the Willow Run Air Force Base.

I read Polly's letters with a shock of recognition. It was not only the references to places deeply woven into my childhood: street names, parks, lakes, family trips to Greenfield Village and The Henry Ford Museum. The letters are ones my mother could have written: descriptions of the life of a young, well-educated wife and mother, at home in Ypsilanti, with a growing family. (And Polly, like my mother, evidently resisted buying a new typewriter ribbon until even the red stripe on the top was exhausted!) Polly wrote those long letters to her mother in time stolen from attacking the mountain of ironing that never seemed to shrink, and the need to have dinner on the table for five every night when Russ got home from work.

A delightful discovery in Polly's letters was the fact that she and Russ looked at houses in the subdivision where my parents, that same year, bought their first home. "There are a lot of development houses but they have puny rooms and puny lots and no dining room," Polly complained. I can't dispute that description. "It would be OK," Polly continued, "if you didn't have any furniture, and got bunk beds for every member of the family and stood up to eat, but we would never fit into one with our family and accoutrements." For many a young Ypsilanti family in 1955, including mine, those "new little brick ranches" marked a step up from a rented flat. But for Russ and Polly, whose furniture was en route from Morocco where the family enjoyed spacious quarters, expectations were different. In late September they moved to a house on a rural road just outside of town, a house recently vacated by another Air Force officer and his family. This would be home for the Wells family for the next two years. The family grew by one while in Ypsilanti, with the birth of Robbin in March, 1957. Helen made one of her two visits to Ypsilanti at that time to help Polly with the new baby, just as she had done when Martha was born in Hawaii and Patricia and Peter at Mitchell Field Air Force Base on Long Island.

Polly set about making the house into a home, knowing all the while that their stay would be of short duration. She wrote of painting rooms and sewing curtains, and enclosed drawings detailing the placement of furniture in each of the rooms. She wrote happily of the playhouse that she and Russ assembled in the back yard:

> barn red with white trim and green door and window boxes, and the inside will be yellow with white trim and a deck grey floor.... Russ and I sat out in the playhouse last night with the electric lantern and made a folding table which can fold flat against the wall. Russ gets a huge kick out of the playhouse. He made a small weather vane for the roof; looks very cute.

Polly's letters are witty, often sarcastic. Describing the house at 1704 LeForge Road she wrote: "We live on a dirt road (in a house—hah!)" In a letter to her Vassar friend, Blanche, Polly described Pish's exhuberant manner of expression: "'Daddy, I just love you so much I can't stand you!' I told Russ those were sometimes my exact sentiments." Towards her children Polly directed clear-eyed attention. She writes about them with such honesty and insight that, meeting Martha and Pat for the first time as women in their late sixties, the descriptions from six decades earlier rang true.

With hindsight it is impossible not to see the poignancy in these letters. From the outset Polly was looking forward to Russ's retirement from the Air Force and the dream of moving back east, for good. "Got a bee-Utiful 10 cu ft GE refrigerator-freezer 2-door and a GE stove. . . . Our first purchase for our New England dream house." Subsequent letters count down the years and number of postings remaining until Russ's retirement, and speculate on what he will do afterwards. "Six years aren't long when you think we've been here a year less 3 days—but they seem a lot longer when you think its 2/3 of the time we've been married and all the things we've done in nine years. Keep your ears open if you hear of any fascinating houses someone is giving away. We might even buy it now and spend our vacations working on it. . . ."

And she wrote movingly to Blanche about one thing she had not yet experienced with Russ—flying. "It's a part of his existence which is entirely separate from me and to which I can never belong." She was dying to go up in a plane with him, she told Blanche, but it was against regulations for him to take her. "He talks about flying when I can draw him out on it—the beauties of night flying. I don't worry when he is flying—I have complete faith in him."

Ypsilanti was a way station for Polly, two years out of ninety-four. My mother, by contrast, was born in Ypsilanti and eventually lived there a total of thirty-seven years, nearly half her life. Yet in some ways Ypsilanti was always a way station for her as well. Her ambitions were bigger than the town, just as Big Helen once observed of Crete that "there was nothing [there] for Helen." Mom began college as a journalism major, with dreams of going to New York to write for *Time* magazine. She thought about law school, but was gently—perhaps realistically—dissuaded by my grandfather ("that idea of yours of changing to the law course is a big assignment . . . but am not prepared to say if your chances of employment would be limited.") Mom returned home after college, first teaching high school, and then, after years in junior high and with Dad's job transfer to Ohio, finishing as she began: as a high school Latin teacher.

Mom instilled in all her children a love of books. She saw us off to college, and took it as a mark of success that we made independent lives for ourselves. She went to Europe three times with Dad: to

London, to Paris, and to Vienna, her first trips back since her own post-college graduation *Jean & Company*-inspired Grand Tour. She retired after a full career as a teacher, having influenced countless students in ways that—as is the case with all good teachers—will never be known. And she lived to see her granddaughter Sally major in journalism and pursue the dream of New York and a career as a magazine writer and editor.

Mom died in 2004 after a brave fight with pancreatic cancer. She did not live to see my successful search for Helen Perry Curtis and the origins of the book which meant so much to us both. On the eve of my first trip to New Jersey, as Susie, Pat, Martha and I exchanged a final flurry of emails, Pat wrote: "Gan would have loved this!" "My mom would have loved this too," I replied. "I wish she were here to see it." "They both know," Martha chimed in. "And they are probably saying: 'What took those girls so long?'"

Helen Perry Curtis died on June 3, 1980, in her home at 8 Franklin Place where she lived for nearly sixty years. She was ninety-two years old. Surrounded by books, the ones she most relished towards the end were the green-bound, gold-stamped volumes recounting the European trips of the 1930s. In Helen's final months Polly hired three Jamaican immigrant women to tend to Helen. Rooted in traditional culture, they were at ease caring at home for a dying woman. Whenever Polly worried about how much her mother was sleeping, or about her lack of responsiveness when awake, the women assured Polly that this was part of the process of detaching from life. "She's just traveling," they told Polly. "She's traveling."

Jeanne died on December 6, 1999, at age seventy-eight. At the end she too was surrounded by her books, her family, and her friends. For someone who had spent a significant part of her teenage years travelling through Europe, Jeanne's last decades were spent close to home. She lived the last eight years of her life in an apartment in Millburn, a few miles from Summit. Jeanne volunteered for over twenty years at Far Brook School in Short Hills, the successor to Buxton School, which both she and Polly had attended and from which Jeanne had graduated nearly sixty years earlier. There she was known as the "Kitchen Lady," presiding daily over the noon lunch. A special joy for Jeanne was the invitation from the school's director to teach an occasional Latin class. In the last weeks of her life, even after failing health required her to give up much of her volunteer work, Jeanne was at the school helping to roll pennies collected by the Far Brook students for New Jersey families affected by Hurricane Floyd. At her death her family requested that memorial gifts be designated for the school, specifically for the purchase of Caldecott and Newberry Medal children's books.

Polly outlived her mother and sister by many years. It was my great good fortune, on the last day of my first visit to New Jersey, to meet her.

On a glorious summer afternoon Susie, Martha, Pat and I piled into the car and drove the short distance down the road to the nursing home. "Wait here," said Martha, as we entered the reception area. "I'll go get Mom." Minutes later Martha came back up the corridor pushing a wheel chair in which sat an erect, smiling, white-haired lady with beautiful blue eyes. "I found her." I thought. "It's Jean!"

We sat outside on the sun-drenched patio. "Mom," said Pat, "you remember we told you about Laura. She's interested in the book Gan wrote about your trips to Europe with Jeanne, and wants to ask you some questions." "Oh," said Polly, "I don't remember much. It was a long time ago." But the stories poured forth. The name of the ship on which they sailed to Cannes in 1932. How she and Jeanne and their cousins explored the boat from top to bottom. The neighbor's dog who visited daily at Tourlaque. How Polly and Jeanne freely roamed Venice, getting rides from a young gondolier while their mother stayed at her desk and wrote. The trips of the later years. Norway. Yugoslavia. Salzburg, and the Elizabeth Duncan School at Schloss Klessheim, where the girls slept in a dormitory room, the dark blue ceiling decked with silver moons and stars. Just like *Jean*. Just like in the book. And with her daughters and her niece standing behind her I took a photo of Polly holding the copy of *Jean & Company, Unlimited* that my mother had handed me so many years before.

Nine months after our visit, Polly died in her sleep, ten days short of her ninety-fourth birthday. Her ashes were interred alongside Russ's on her beloved Martha's Vineyard.

Full circle: Polly Curtis Wells holding the copy
of *Jean & Company, Unlimited,* that my mother
handed me so long ago. Behind Polly: Susie Fauteux,
Martha and Pat Wells.

When Martha and Pat emailed to tell me of their mother's death, my feelings were those of sadness, mixed with an overwhelming sense of gratitude for the circumstances that allowed me to meet her at all. And at the moment of taking in Polly's death, Jean became somehow, suddenly, more insistently real. Everything that went into her creation: two daughters merged into one, multiple trips taken by mothers and daughters over a span of three decades, Helen's fascination with folk culture, her museum work and her writing: all that resolved itself once and for all time into the story of Jean and her mother's Grand Tour of Europe.

So we are left where we started—with a book. *Jean & Company. Unlimited.* A book about which Helen had written:

Now that it is finished, it is not a proper book at all, written
respectably at a desk with dictionary, atlas, and grammar close at
hand. . . . It is the simple chronicle of Jean's journey, written down
here, there, and everywhere, gathered into a single packet, and
placed with affection between two covers—a journey come to life!

A book, a journey, in which Jean is forever a young girl, standing beside her mother in the bow of the ocean liner, turning her face "toward the palm-shaded shore which was Cannes," and exclaiming with joy: "'O Mother, here comes our adventure!'"

Acknowledgements

Words cannot express my gratitude to Susie Fauteux and Martha and Pat Wells, Helen Perry Curtis's granddaughters. Susie enthusiastically responded to an out-of-the-blue letter inquiring about her grandmother. Over the next years she assisted in the writing of this book: transcribing scores of letters written in Helen's nearly indecipherable script, providing reams of Xeroxed materials, and serving as an always-enthusiastic reader of drafts of chapters. Martha and Pat opened their home, along with those boxes in the attic, on my numerous visits to New Jersey. Pat helped me navigate the more obscure corners of Ancestry.com and the HathiTrust Digital Library, and shared the various family histories she has written as Christmas gifts for the Curtis/Wells/Whitesell families. For their hospitality, for all the "spa meals" shared in their beautiful back yard or around their dining room table, my deepest thanks go to Martha and Pat. All three women unselfishly shared with me the story of their grandmother. I am grateful for the three special friends I have made in Martha, Pat, and Susie.

I owe an enormous debt of gratitude to my niece Sally Errico, my biggest cheerleader. Sally believed in this project from the start. ("I absolutely think you have a book.") Sally read early drafts of the manuscript, and connected me with Anne Trubek and Martha Bayne of Belt Publishing/Parafine Press.

My good friend Mary Matton served as reader, honest critic, exacting proofreader, transcriber, and tech guru: scanning photos, de-bugging the computer, and dealing with the mysteries of Dropbox. Mary drove twelve hours with me from Wisconsin to Nebraska for the Crete/Doane research trip ("Who knew Iowa was *this big*!?")

Janet Jeffries, Doane University Historian and Liaison for the Doane Family Association, was the critical link in my search for Helen. It was Janet's history of Crete that I discovered during that fateful Google search; Janet who gave me Susie's address. Janet made the resources of Doane University's archives available during my visit, and offered helpful corrections on the history of Crete and the college in the book's early chapters.

Dr. William Peniston, Librarian/Archivist of the Newark Museum of Art, graciously gave access to the Homelands Exhibit materials and provided additional information on Louise Connolly. The staff of the New York Public Library, Performing Arts Division, made available the papers of Anita Zahn. Dr. William Rhoads, professor emeritus at SUNY New Paltz, and Leslie Melvin of Bard College shared valuable information on Jimmy Scott, based on their ongoing research project on the Elverhoj Artist Colony. Christopher Paulson and Mary Nelson of the Racine Heritage Museum provided material on the Danish heritage of Racine, Wisconsin, the birthplace of Jimmy Scott. Jack May was a veritable encyclopedia of information on the trains and transit systems in New York and New Jersey in the first decades of the Twentieth Century. Patricia Meola from the Summit Historical Society provided information on the Twomblys. Thanks go to Suzanne Glatt, director of development at Far Brook School, for information on Jeanne and Polly's time at Buxton, Far Brook's predecessor institution, and Jeanne Curtis Whitesell's years on the staff at Far Brook. Sarah Stapperfenne, development manager at Kent Place School, provided a digitized copy of a scrapbook covering the years of Polly's attendance.

Numerous friends and colleagues listened as I described this work-in-progress, offering insight and encouragement. My sincere thanks to Dr. Sylvia Beyer, Dr. Larry Duetsch, Dr. Carla Hay, Richard Karwatka, Dr. Vera Kolb, Kim Lindas, Dr. Jonathan Olsen, Gina Radandt, Dr. Ed Schmitt, and Marc Smiley. Special thanks to Dr. Siegfried Christoph, whose probing questions forced me to think more carefully about how to frame and tell Helen's story. Dr. Kenny French helped identify the "Alphabet Towns." Dr. Mary Lenard encouraged me to present an early version of my research at the 2016 meeting of the Children's Literature Association. Colleagues and fellow book-clubbers Christine MacDonald and Erica Eddy offered encouragement. Erica connected me with her mother, Ann Eddy, who attended Doane College, and who was a gracious hostess during my visit to Nebraska.

An affectionate *in memoriam* acknowledgement of my mentor and friend Dr. Ruth Roebke-Berens, in whose company I made my first trip to Europe, to Vienna and Budapest.

My thanks go to Anne Trubek, of Belt Publishing/Parafine Press for agreeing to take on this project, allowing Helen's story to reach the audience it deserves. Martha Bayne provided careful editorial assistance, affirmation, and encouragement. Meredith Pangrace's interior layout, as well as her striking and elegant cover design, make this the attractive book that it is.

CPSIA information can be obtained
at www.ICGtesting.com
Printed in the USA
BVHW070442110921
616347BV00003B/19